Weekly Calendar Planning Activity (WCPA):

A Performance Test of Executive Function

Joan Toglia, PhD, OTR, FAOTA

The American
Occupational Therapy
Association, Inc.

AOTA Centennial Vision
We envision that occupational therapy is a powerful, widely recognized, science-driven, and evidence-based profession with a globally connected and diverse workforce meeting society's occupational needs.

Mission Statement
The American Occupational Therapy Association advances the quality, availability, use, and support of occupational therapy through standard-setting, advocacy, education, and research on behalf of its members and the public.

AOTA Staff
Frederick P. Somers, *Executive Director*
Christopher M. Bluhm, *Chief Operating Officer*

Chris Davis, *Director, AOTA Press*
Caroline Polk, *Digital Manager and* AJOT *Managing Editor*
Ashley Hofmann, *Development/Acquisitions Editor*
Barbara Dickson, *Production Editor*
Joe King-Shaw, *AOTA Press Business and Customer Service Administrator*

Rebecca Rutberg, *Director, Marketing*
Amanda Goldman, *Marketing Manager*
Jennifer Folden, *Marketing Specialist*

American Occupational Therapy Association, Inc.
4720 Montgomery Lane
Bethesda, MD 20814
Phone: 301-652-AOTA (2682)
TDD: 800-377-8555
Fax: 301-652-7711
www.aota.org
To order: 1-877-404-AOTA or store.aota.org

ISBN: 978-1-56900-369-5

Library of Congress Control Number: 2015935129

Cover design by Debra Naylor, Washington, DC
Composition by Maryland Composition, White Plains, MD
Printed by Automated Graphic Systems, Inc., White Plains, MD

Contents

Acknowledgments

I would like to thank all of my occupational therapy colleagues who have contributed to the initial research and development of the WCPA and who have provided valuable feedback along the way, including Christine Berg, Nikki Weiner, Racheli Kizony, Noomi Katz, and Orit Lahav, as well as numerous others who are currently using the WCPA in research projects, including Erin Foster, Heather Forst, Gunnel Janeslätt, Suzanne White, and Sharon Zlotnick.

A very special thanks to Steve Lichtman and all of the Mercy College occupational therapy graduate students and their participants who contributed normative data on the WCPA over the past 5 years.

Sincere appreciation and special acknowledgement is extended to Jacqueline O'Rourke and Claire Dunn, OT graduate students who provided extra valuable support and assistance for this project and for preparation of this manual.

Finally, I would like to thank my husband for all of his patience, love, and support during this project and many others.

About the Author

Joan Toglia, PhD, OTR/L, FAOTA, has more than 30 years of experience in occupational therapy and is recognized internationally as a leader in the rehabilitation of persons with cognitive–perceptual deficits. She has presented more than 250 workshops and lectures around the world on cognitive rehabilitation, with a focus on cognitive strategies, metacognitive skills, and executive function across different ages and diagnostic groups.

Dr. Toglia has a BS in occupational therapy from New York University, an MA in cognition and learning, and a PhD in measurement and evaluation from Teachers College and Columbia University, School of Arts & Sciences. She is currently Dean of the School of Health & Natural Sciences at Mercy College, Dobbs Ferry, New York, and Professional Associate in the Rehabilitation Medicine Department at New York Presbyterian–Weill Cornell Medical Center in New York.

List of Figures, Tables, Exhibits, and Appendixes

Figures

Tables

Exhibits

Appendixes

CHAPTER 1 Overview

The Weekly Calendar Planning Activity (WCPA) is a performance-based assessment of executive function (EF). It is appropriate for use with adolescents and adults who experience subtle difficulties in executive functioning. The task involves following and organizing a list of either 17 or 18 appointments or errands into a weekly schedule while keeping track of rules, avoiding conflicts, monitoring passage of time, and inhibiting distractions. Performance of multiple-step activities such as the WCPA requires coordination and integration among EF subcomponents. The WCPA provides the opportunity to observe how a person manages a cognitively challenging functional task. It provides information on accuracy of performance as well as on task efficiency, error types, and strategy use that can be compared with normative data for people ranging in age from 16 to 94 years.

Observations made during the WCPA provide in-depth information about performance on a complex, cognitive instrumental activity of daily living (IADL) as well as about EF abilities. The WCPA is easily portable and can be used in a wide variety of settings to screen for performance deficits in higher-level cognitive activities and to provide information relevant to occupational therapy treatment.

Executive Function

Executive function encompasses a set of interrelated cognitive abilities that are critical to the control, coordination, and regulation of thoughts, emotions, and goal-directed actions (Zelazo & Carlson, 2012). The main subcomponents of EF include initiation, inhibition, working memory, cognitive flexibility, and self-monitoring. Together, these subcomponents contribute to the cognitive control and self-regulation needed for planning, organization, multitasking, and problem solving, particularly in novel situations (Lyons & Zelazo, 2011; Prencipe et al., 2011). In routine, predictable, or familiar activities, procedures are automatic, and there are fewer demands for executive or top-down control. Executive functioning, therefore, is particularly important in learning and coping with new, complex, or challenging activities.

A person with intact executive functioning can recognize obstacles; plan ahead; inhibit distractions; keep track of relevant information; shift back and forth between task components; monitor ongoing performance; and take an organized, strategic approach to achieving goals (Meltzer, 2010; Zelazo & Müller, 2011). EF allows a person to adapt to new or unexpected conditions, modify performance, and cope with complexity and everyday challenges (Hofmann, Schmeichel, & Baddeley, 2012; Meltzer, 2010).

Populations That Experience Subtle Executive Dysfunction

Impairments in EF can occur across a wide range of ages and diagnostic groups. For example, subtle executive functioning deficits have been identified in youths and adults with concussion (Howell, Osternig, Van Donkelaar, Mayr, & Chou, 2013), seizure disorders (Campiglia et al., 2014), attention deficit hyperactivity disorder (ADHD; Bueno, da Silva, Alves, Louza, & Pompeia, 2014), nonverbal learning disabilities (Semrud-Clikeman, Fine, & Bledsoe, 2014), high-functioning autism (Semrud-Clikeman et al., 2014), depression (Dybedal, Tanum, Sundet, Gaarden, & Bjolseth, 2013; Osorio, de Lozar, Ramos, & Aguera, 2009), substance abuse (Crean et al., 2011; Houston et al., 2014), obsessive–compulsive disorder (Lewin et al., 2014), bipolar disorder (Laes & Sponheim, 2006), and schizophrenia (Orellana & Slachevsky, 2013; Puig et al., 2012). Early life stress, impoverished environments, social deprivation, and adverse life experiences such as abuse are among the factors that contribute to poorer EF development in children and youths (Hsu, Novick, & Jaeggi, 2014).

Neurological disorders including stroke (Poulin, Korner-Bitensky, Dawson, & Bherer, 2012), traumatic brain injury (Cicerone, Levin, Malec, Stuss, & Whyte, 2006), multiple sclerosis (Voelbel et al., 2011), mild cognitive impairment (Clément, Gauthier, & Belleville, 2012), and Parkinson's disease (Foster & Hershey, 2011) are frequently associated with executive dysfunction. Subtle impairments in EF have also been identified in many chronic illnesses not traditionally associated with cognitive dysfunction, including cardiac disease (Foster et al., 2011), chronic kidney disease (Yaffe et al., 2014), amyotrophic lateral sclerosis (Achi & Rudnicki, 2012), systemic lupus erythematosus, and systemic sclerosis (Yilmaz et al., 2012). In addition, subtle impairments in EF have been recognized as a frequent sequela of chemotherapy treatment among cancer survivors (Ganz et al., 2013) as well as after prolonged critical illness (Pandharipande et al., 2013).

This list of populations is not exhaustive because EF impairment is present in almost every condition that affects information processing, learning, and brain functions, even in the absence of frontal lobe injury (Wolf & Baum, 2011). Occupational therapists working in a wide range of practice areas encounter people with subtle executive functioning difficulties that may not be readily apparent and may easily go unnoticed.

Executive Function and Its Relationship to Occupational Performance and Participation

Executive dysfunction can significantly interfere with learning and everyday functioning in school, home, work, and social settings. Numerous studies have found that executive functioning is the cognitive domain most closely linked to IADLs and participation (Cramm, Krupa, Missiuna, Lysaght, & Parker, 2013). In older adults, executive functioning is an independent correlate of functional status (Royall, Palmer, Chiodo, & Polk, 2004, 2005). In addition, lower executive functioning predicts risk of falls (Buracchio et al., 2011) and future cognitive decline (Boyle, Paul, Moser, & Cohen, 2004; Muir, Gopaul, & Montero Odasso, 2012).

Across ages and diagnostic conditions, subtle difficulties in EF have been associated with social participation (Hommel, Miguel, Naegele, Gonnet, & Jaillard, 2009; Yeates et al., 2004), treatment compliance (Insel, Morrow, Brewer, & Figueredo, 2006; Stilley, Bender, Dunbar-Jacob, Sereika, & Ryan, 2010), productivity and employment (Eriksson, Tham, & Borg, 2006; Ownsworth & Shum, 2008), and quality of life (Glanz et al., 2010; Mitchell, Kemp, Benito-Leon, & Reuber, 2010; Reid-Arndt, Yee, Perry, & Hsieh, 2009; Ritsner, 2007; Von Ah, Russell, Storniolo, & Carpenter, 2009). EF independently predicts participation in complex activities (Foster & Hershey, 2011; Marshall et al., 2011), and in younger populations EF is associated with successful academic performance (Best, Miller, & Naglieri, 2011).

The literature has suggested that EF has a broad and pervasive effect on occupational performance and engagement across multiple populations (Cramm et al., 2013), highlighting the critical importance of assessing EF within the context of complex activities that are relevant to everyday life.

Assessment of Executive Function and Instrumental Activities of Daily Living, and Benefits of the WCPA

Typically, EF is assessed with neuropsychological tests that use abstract tasks to identify impairments in separate components of EF. Although this information is valuable in providing an indicator of strengths and weaknesses in specific domains of EF, performance on neuropsychological tests is not predictive of real-world complex task performance that requires an interplay among multiple aspects of EF (Chan, Shum, Toulopoulou, & Chen, 2007; Chaytor, Schmitter-Edgecombe, & Burr, 2006). Ecologically valid assessment tools are needed to supplement standardized measures of EF impairment so that the skills needed in everyday functioning are fully captured and a more complete profile of executive functioning is obtained (Burgess et al., 2006).

Most standardized functional assessments used in rehabilitation are designed to examine routine, everyday activities or basic activities of daily living (ADLs). People with EF impairments typically perform well in the context of familiar, predictable, and routine activities (Morrison et al., 2013). Difficulties in performance may be observed only during complex activities or higher-level cognitive IADL activities that require novelty, challenge, or the ability to simultaneously keep several variables in mind while planning and organizing information. In rehabilitation, functioning in higher-level activities or IADLs is often measured by means of self-report or report by proxy rather than by direct observation of performance. Direct observation of performance may yield different results, so it is important to have higher-level, cognitively challenging activities that can be used in assessment (Vaughan & Giovanello, 2010).

Existing IADL performance-based assessments in occupational therapy are often not sufficiently complex or challenging for higher functioning people and lack normative data for comparison. In addition, performance-based IADL assessments typically focus on competency in performing a specific task or on the level of cues and assistance needed for success rather than analyzing how the person goes about performing the activity. One exception is the Assessment of Motor and Process Skills (AMPS; Fisher & Bray Jones, 2010a, 2010b), which is norm-referenced, includes complex tasks, and rates quality of performance. However, intensive workshop training and certification are required for use, making it inaccessible for many clinicians.

Performance-based measures of executive functioning include the Executive Function Performance Test (EFPT; Baum et al., 2008) and the Multiple Errands Test (MET; Shallice & Burgess, 1991). The EFPT involves observation of executive function components while simultaneously using a graded cue sequence to determine the degree of support needed to successfully complete four basic IADL tasks: simple cooking, telephone use, taking medication, and paying bills. Although this information is valuable, tests that include more challenging activities and provide an in-depth analysis of performance also are needed in clinical practice.

The MET is a complex activity that involves following a list of 12 errands and adhering to rules within a real-world environment such as a shopping mall or hospital. Several different scoring systems and versions of the MET have been described (Alderman, Burgess, Knight, & Henman, 2003; Dawson et al., 2009; Morrison et al., 2013). The MET captures mild executive functioning deficits but is time-consuming, site-specific (tasks are dependent on the location), and not always feasible in a clinical setting.

The WCPA has several advantages. It

- Is suitable for people with subtle EF difficulties;
- Has wide clinical applications;
- Has alternate forms for retesting;
- Provides objective scores;
- Has normative data available for comparison (for ages 16 or older);
- Is easily portable and can be used consistently in any setting;
- Provides in-depth information on the process and quality of performance;
- Provides unique information on task efficiency, strategy use, and self-monitoring skills; and
- Yields results that are directly relevant to treatment.

The WCPA uses an activity (i.e., completing a weekly calendar) that is generic and functionally important in everyday life across a wide range of ages. Following a list and entering information into a schedule is a key component of school, work, social activities, and health and household management. In addition to the specific task of completing a weekly schedule, the WCPA provides a broader analysis of how a person manages and copes with a complex and cognitively challenging activity. Task complexity is increased by providing constraints and rules that challenge the person to think flexibly and keep track of multiple pieces of information while planning, organizing, and resolving problems or conflicts that may arise.

The WCPA is unique in that it provides measures of accuracy and normative comparison, as well as focusing on analysis of the process or how the activity is completed. Examination of error types, efficiency, strategy use, and self-monitoring skills allows in-depth assessment and a broader indication of executive functioning abilities and performance skills that goes beyond specific tasks such as the weekly calendar. The WCPA can be used to screen for deficits in higher-level functioning, understand the underlying nature of performance problems, and provide information relevant to occupational therapy treatment.

For Whom Is the WCPA Appropriate?

The WCPA is appropriate for those people who are independent in routine or basic ADLs but who may have difficulties in nonroutine or complex activities.

The person should be oriented, able to sustain attention for at least 10 minutes, and able to comprehend written sentences without difficulty. Different versions of the WCPA have been developed to accommodate youths to older adults (ages 12–94).

The WCPA has wide clinical application and was designed to be useful across a variety of populations that exhibit subtle difficulties in EF or higher-level cognitive IADL activities. The WCPA has been studied with at-risk youths (Weiner, Toglia, & Berg, 2012), typical adolescents (Toglia & Berg, 2013), and young adults with ADHD (Lahav & Katz, 2015). Studies are currently being conducted with people with substance abuse, seizure disorders, stroke, traumatic brain injury, and Parkinson's disease.

Because the WCPA is a newly developed assessment tool, additional research is needed, but the format, portability, and different versions of the WCPA make it suitable for the wide range of populations identified as having subtle EF deficits.

Administration of the WCPA

The WCPA appears to be a simple functional task, but it involves multiple aspects of executive functioning. Analysis of performance is complex because there is dynamic interaction among EF abilities, the demands of the activity, performance skills, and personal context, including familiarity, experience, culture, personality characteristics, ability to cope with challenges, and the person's beliefs or perceptions of the task and performance (Toglia, 2011).

Administration requires a full understanding of the dynamic interactions among cognitive abilities, activity demands, and context as well as skills in observation of occupational performance, activity analysis, and interviewing. The WCPA was therefore designed to be administered and interpreted by occupational therapists, who have a unique focus on analysis of occupational performance and performance-based assessment and whose educational training includes cognition, activity analysis, and interviewing skills (American Occupational Therapy Association [AOTA], 2013, 2014). Examiners should carefully review all sections of this manual before administering the WCPA.

Identifying Performance Deficits: Objective Scores and Normative Comparison

The WCPA assesses EF performance deficits and identifies people who have difficulty using a list and entering information into a weekly calendar. Because use of lists and schedules is an inherent aspect of many everyday tasks, identification of difficulties in these areas provides important targets for occupational therapy intervention.

Key WCPA scores include number of appointments entered, accuracy, time for completion, efficiency, rules followed, and total number of strategies used. Preliminary normative data and percentiles for these scores are provided in this manual for ages 16 to 94 and allow comparison of the client's performance with that of a healthy population in the same age group. This comparison provides an indication of the degree to which performance such as accuracy, efficiency, or strategy use is different from that of a typically functioning person. A recently developed version of the WCPA for students ages 12 to 16 is included in this manual, but normative data are not yet available for this age group.

The WCPA can provide an objective baseline from which to measure outcomes or change over time. A minimum of two different but comparable alternate forms or appointment lists were developed for each WCPA age group so that they could be used before and after treatment to limit practice effects.

Performance Analysis and Treatment Implications

The WCPA extends beyond the calendar task and provides more general information on underlying performance deficits that are likely to influence functioning across multiple-step activities or multitasking situations. The WCPA provides a rich opportunity to observe and analyze the quality of performance within the context of a complex cognitive IADL, including efficiency, error types, strategy use, and self-monitoring skills. A combination of quantitative scores, observations, and responses to interview questions provides insight into difficulties that may be contributing to performance deficits. This in-depth analysis of performance skills provides information that is highly relevant to treatment. Treatment implications are discussed in Chapter 4, "Interpretation," and through case illustrations.

Efficiency of Performance

The WCPA provides information on performance accuracy and efficiency. *Performance accuracy* reflects task competency and is measured by the number of correct appointment entries. *Efficiency* is the ability to complete the task with both minimal time and errors and is measured by a time/accuracy weighted ratio.

Both accuracy and time required for task completion need to be examined because there is often a trade-off between them. Performance can be accurate but inefficient, as reflected by taking excessive time for completion. In addition to providing a measure of time needed for task completion, the WCPA provides a method to objectively score performance efficiency and compare it with normative data.

Efficiency scores are examined in combination with observations and other WCPA scores. For example, during the WCPA, the examiner may observe that the person performs unnecessary steps, overfocuses on irrelevant information, or becomes stuck on problems that arise. All of these behaviors contribute to performance inefficiencies or increased time and are important to note because they may be part of an overall performance pattern. Inefficient performance can be a significant hindrance in everyday life and work, so it is important to identify and use treatment to address problems that contribute to inefficiencies.

Types of Errors

The WCPA provides the opportunity to analyze the type and patterns of errors that the person makes. For example, errors may include omissions, repetitions, inclusion of extraneous information, or detail-related errors. These errors represent the outcome of deficiencies in performance skills, including the failure to attend, pace, adjust, accommodate, or organize performance. The analysis of error patterns in a complex IADL is important because the same types of errors often affect performance across different activities. Intervention aims to reduce performance errors in everyday activities, so understanding the frequency and types of performance errors that occur is critical.

Strategy Use

The ability to use strategies to keep track of things to do, follow a list, organize a schedule, recognize conflicts, and monitor errors is an essential skill for everyday life, and analysis of such strategies is a key component of the WCPA. The examiner observes and rates the person's use of strategies during WCPA performance. In addition, an after-task interview is used to probe strategies used during the activity as well as to examine the ability to generate alternative strategies. Restricted use of effective strategies has been reported across age and diagnostic groups and is linked to limitations in executive functioning and occupational performance (Toglia, Rodger, & Polatajko, 2012).

Cognitive strategies help people process information more efficiently and help them cope and manage challenges successfully. Healthy control participants typically use multiple strategies when faced with cognitively challenging activities. Because strategies help people monitor and control performance errors, analysis of strategy use along with error types provides an indication of strategies that might be useful during intervention.

Self-Monitoring

Self-recognition of performance errors and self-checking strategies are recorded during WCPA performance. The After-Task Interview and Rating Scale is used to probe the person's perceptions of his or her performance and asks the person both to identify aspects of the activity that were challenging and to self-rate his or her performance. This provides information on the person's self-awareness, including the ability to recognize errors or task challenges and realistically appraise his or her own performance. This information has implications for treatment because limited recognition of performance deficits could suggest that techniques designed to help a person self-recognize and monitor performance errors are needed as a first step toward improving performance effectiveness.

Test–Teach–Retest Format

The WCPA also includes the option of a dynamic test–teach–retest format as described in Chapter 6, "Dynamic Assessment." This format has been widely used in the dynamic assessment literature and is designed to examine responsiveness to mediation or the extent to which a person is able to modify or change performance with guidance from another person. This method goes beyond observation and analysis of quality of performance and is hypothesized to provide the most direct information related to intervention planning.

In addition to providing information on strategy use, it also provides information on the ability to learn and carry over strategies to an alternate task. The WCPA's dynamic format has not yet been empirically studied, but it is included in this manual because it may be clinically useful in certain circumstances, particularly if the sole purpose is intervention planning.

Description of the WCPA

The WCPA involves entering 17 or 18 appointments and errands into a weekly calendar. The adult versions of the calendar have 17 appointments, and the youth versions have 18 appointments. Some of the appointments are fixed or have 1 designated day and time, and other appointments are variable or have choices in day and time. Planning is required to avoid time conflicts.

The WCPA includes three levels of difficulty. It was initially designed for adults, but the appointment lists have been modified for different age groups. Level II is the most frequently used level and has been researched more extensively than the other two levels. It has been shown to discriminate between younger and older adults well and is the version that is recommended for use in most cases. Only Level II has forms tailored for use with both adolescents and adults.

Level III is an option for exceptionally high-functioning adults, and Level I is for adults who are lower-functioning. The WCPA (Levels I and II) requires approximately 20 to 25 minutes to administer; however, Level III can require increased time (30–40 minutes). Each level has alternate forms or variations of the appointment list. These different but comparable appointment lists were developed to reduce practice effects that might occur when the WCPA is administered more than once to the same person.

Care was taken so that appointments remained equivalent in length and complexity across alternate forms. Each appointment list has its own corresponding Calendar Scoring Worksheet. The appointment lists and scoring worksheets for the different levels are included in Appendixes A–D.

Level I

Level I (adults/older adults) is a simplified format that involves copying an organized list of appointments into a weekly calendar. Fixed appointments or errands are generally presented first, in order from Monday through Friday. Flexible appointments are presented last. The list is presented in a checklist format to cue the person to check items off the list. In Level I, preplanning is not required. If the person enters appointments into the calendar in the order in which they appear on the list, the person will not run into any conflicts. Normative data have not been formally collected for Level I. It is assumed that typical adults will not have any difficulty with this format. Level I has two alternate forms (Version A and Version B). Level I appointment lists and accompanying scoring worksheets are found in Appendix A.

Level II

Level II involves entering a list of appointments (that are not in order) into the weekly calendar. Preplanning or rearrangement of the list is required to avoid conflicts and time overlaps between appointments or errands. Unlike the list in Level I, the list in Level II is unformatted, so there are no check boxes to cue the person to check off each item. An efficient method of approaching this task requires preplanning and recognizing that some appointments are fixed and others are flexible. Entering fixed appointments first is one of the most effective strategies. Level II has several alternate appointment lists and versions:

- *Middle School/High School:* Two alternate appointment lists were designed for middle and high school students ages 12–18 (see Appendix B).
- *Youth:* Two alternate appointment lists were modified slightly from the adult version so that they would be appropriate for youths and young adults ages 16 to 21. This format was tested with healthy adolescents and young adults (n = 49) and at-risk youths (Toglia & Berg, 2013;

Weiner et al., 2012). The youth appointment lists and scoring worksheets are in Appendix C.

- *Adult/Older Adult:* This format uses two alternate appointment lists (Version A and Version B). Version A is the original WCPA version, and normative data for this form were collected for healthy adults ($N = 386$) ages 18 to 94. The Level II Adult/Older Adult appointment lists and scoring worksheets are in Appendix A.

Level II has two possible modifications:

- *WCPA–Short, Versions A and B:* The WCPA–10 uses the same adult/older adult appointment lists as Version A and B (just described), but the appointment lists were reduced from 17 appointments to 10. This version was created for therapists in inpatient settings who may have lower-functioning clients or who may be limited in time. The WCPA–10 requires only 10 to 15 minutes to administer. The appointments that had a low error rate, or were easiest, were eliminated, and appointments with conflicts were retained. On the basis of normative studies with the 17-item appointment lists, it was assumed that healthy adults would not have difficulties with a 10-item list. The WCPA–10 appointment lists and scoring worksheets are in Appendix A.
- *WCPA–S: College Student:* The original appointment list and instructions were modified by Lahav and Katz (2015) for use with college students in Israel, ages 20 to 34 (see Appendix D). The 17-item list was translated into Hebrew for use in Israel and tested with both college students without ADHD and students with ADHD. This version differs from the other versions in that the calendar does not have Saturday and Sunday reversed and a time limit of 30 minutes is imposed. The student has to indicate when 20 minutes and 10 minutes are remaining. In addition, there are only three rules to follow (instead of the five rules used in other versions). This version has been tested only in Israel. Further information can be obtained from Orit Lahav, PhD, at lahav.orit@gmail.com.

Level III

Level III (adults/older adults only) is a complex format that presents the appointments in paragraph format rather than in the Level II list format and adds extraneous information. Although the number of appointments is the same, the paragraph format can be overwhelming because more information is presented at once, which places greater demands on the ability to choose and focus on what is important while ignoring distracting information. Increased interference or distractions can impede performance because less important information captures attention and relevant information can get lost.

Similar to the adult/older adult version for Level II, Level III has two alternate versions (Version A and Version B). Appointment lists and scoring worksheets for Level III are in Appendix A. Normative data have been collected for Version A on 175 healthy adults ages 18 to 84.

General Similarities Across Levels

Although the appointment list and difficulty levels can differ, the same client instruction sheet, rules, and weekly schedule are used across different versions. The calendar is divided into 15-minute appointment slots from 7:00 a.m. to 6:00 p.m. The evening appointment slots from 6:00 p.m. to 9:00 p.m. are divided into half-hour appointment slots (rather than 15-minute slots), which requires the person to recognize and adapt to this change.

Coping with problems

In addition, the calendar contains two problems. Saturday and Sunday are reversed, and it ends at 9:00 p.m. even though an appointment may extend past 9:00 p.m. These errors are not pointed out and are included to provide the opportunity to observe how the client copes and deals with unexpected problems. All observations should be noted. In all versions, the amount of time required for planning and activity completion is recorded. The combination of accuracy and total time required to complete the activity provides a measure of performance efficiency.

Rules

The client has 5 rules to follow.

1. Once you have entered an appointment into the calendar, you cannot it cross out.
2. Tell me when it is (specified time).

Table 1.1. Summary of WCPA Versions and Forms

Age Group	Level	Versions	Free Day	Appendix
Adults/older adults (ages 18–94)	I	A	Wednesday	A
		B	Tuesday	A
Adults/older adults (ages 18–94)	II	A	Wednesday	A
		B	Tuesday	A
Adults/older adults (ages 18–94)	II	10-item short Version A	Wednesday	A
		10-item short Version B	Tuesday	A
Adults/older adults (ages 18–94)	III	A	Wednesday	A
		B	Tuesday	A
Middle/high school (ages 12–18)	II	A	Wednesday	B
		B	Tuesday	B
Youth (ages 16–21)	II	A	Thursday	C
		B	Wednesday	C
College students (ages 20–34)	II	WCPA-S (tested in Israel)	Tuesday	D

Note. Because normative data were collected for ages 18 to 21 for both the youth and adult versions, either version can be used with this age group.

3. Leave (specified day) free. (Do not schedule any appointments or errands on this day.)
4. Do not answer questions from the examiner during this activity.
5. Tell the examiner when you are finished.

Some rules place demands on *inhibition,* or the ability to restrain actions or immediate responses and ignore distractions. For example, clients are provided with a pen (not a pencil) and told not to cross out appointments after they have been entered into the weekly calendar and to avoid scheduling appointments on a particular day. Adherence to these rules requires careful planning and review of the list before entering appointments. Another rule involves ignoring irrelevant questions asked by the examiner during the activity. This rule provides the opportunity to observe the client's ability to manage interruptions and resist or inhibit distractions.

The last two rules require *prospective memory,* or the ability to remember to perform future intentions. For example, the client is asked to indicate when it is a specific time and inform the examiner when he or she is finished. In general, the rules place greater demands on *working memory* (ability to temporarily hold and manipulate information during a task) and multitasking because they increase the amount of information the client needs to keep track of while simultaneously engaging in the activity.

Table 1.1 summarizes the versions available for different age groups. Alternate forms can be used for retesting.

Summary

This chapter provided an overview of executive functioning and introduced the WCPA, including its uses, purpose, and description. The WCPA involves entering 17 or 18 appointments into a weekly calendar while adhering to rules, managing conflicts, and ignoring distractions. The WCPA can be used across different populations with adolescents or adults who may have mild EF impairments or difficulties in higher-level cognitive IADL tasks. Different versions and alternate forms of the WCPA have been developed to accommodate different ages or settings and allow for retest.

The WCPA provides information on underlying performance deficits that are likely to influence executive functioning across multiple-step activities or multitasking situations. The WCPA can be used for several purposes, such as to assess the ability to use a list and enter information into a schedule, screen deficits in EF performance and cognitive IADLs, identify underlying errors contributing to performance deficits, evaluate outcome or the efficacy of intervention, and guide development of an intervention plan, in addition to use as a research tool.

CHAPTER 2 Administration

Before administering the Weekly Calendar Planning Activity, the examiner should be familiar with all administration procedures and accompanying forms. It is recommended that the examiner administer the WCPA to at least 2–3 healthy people before administering it to a client, to practice scoring appointments, observing and rating strategy use, and administering the After-Task Interview and Rating Scale.

Selecting the Appointment List and Obtaining Materials

When preparing to administer the WCPA, the first step is to select the appointment list according to age (youth or adults), level, and version and the accompanying scoring worksheet, as outlined in Table 1.1 and presented in Appendixes A–D. The second step is to gather the forms and materials needed for the examiner and participant. (*Note.* All forms listed also are available on the flash drive.)

Materials Needed for Participant

- Weekly Calendar Activity Instruction Sheet (Appendix E.1)
- Appointments and Errands to Be Scheduled list (Levels I or II) or paragraph (Level III; Appendixes A–D)
- Blank Weekly Calendar (Appendix E.2) and the weekly calendar samples, which have several times (Appendix E.3) and appointments (Appendix E.4) filled in
- Pen (*Note.* Do not put out any pencils)
- Two different color highlighters (Levels II and III)
- One or two pieces of blank scrap paper (Levels II and III)
- A watch or a clock in clear sight (or placed on the table).

Materials Needed by Examiner

- Stopwatch
- Examiner Directions for All Levels
- Optional Adult Background Form (Appendix E.5)
- WCPA Recording Form (Appendix E.6)
- After-Task Interview and Rating Scale (Appendix E.7)
- Optional Observation Form (Appendix E.8).

Scoring Forms (Used After Administration)

- Calendar Scoring Worksheet (Appendixes A–D, depending on which WCPA format is used, to score appointment accuracy immediately after the activity)
- Optional: Forms to summarize results (Appendix F).

Administration Procedure

Present the client with the instructions, blank weekly calendar, appointment list or paragraph, 2 pieces of blank paper, calendar sample page, pens, and 2 different colored highlighters, placing them on the table as shown in Figure 2.1. Blank paper and highlighters are not needed for Level I. The specific appointment list and calendar scoring worksheet must be selected from Appendixes A–D. Other client materials are in Appendix E.

Placement

The appointment list or paragraph and the blank weekly calendar are placed directly in front of the client (appointment list on the left and the blank calendar on the right; see Figure 2.1). The client instructions and rules are placed on the upper left of the appointment list (the page can be folded in half). Highlighters are placed on top of extra blank paper in the middle of the table. The sample weekly calendar, showing how

Figure 2.1. Set-up and placement of materials.

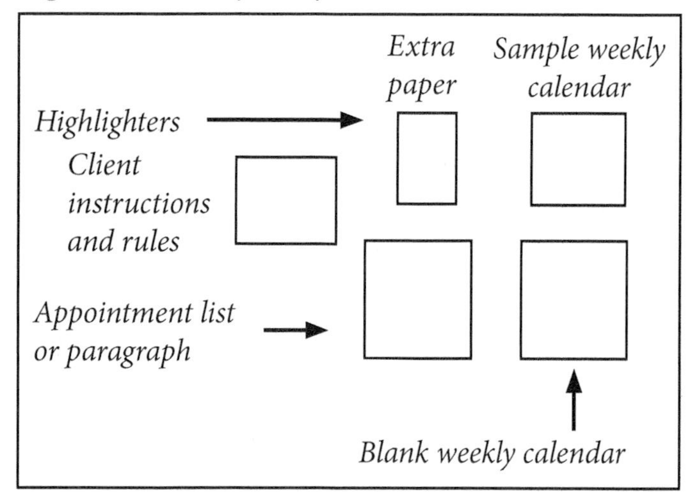

to indicate the time of errands and appointments, is placed on the upper right, also as shown in Figure 2.1.

The examiner can choose from two sample calendars. The first sample shows how to indicate the time (Appendix E.3) and was used in the normative studies. Some clinical populations have had difficulty understanding this sample, so a second sample was created that illustrates the time and appointment entry (Appendix E.4).

The examiner should place the instruction sheet in front of the client and point to each detail on the page while explaining them. The examiner can use the Examiner Directions for All Levels as a guide to further explain the written instructions placed before the client. The examiner should be familiar with and fully understand the instructions, but the instructions can be paraphrased if needed.

General Preparation

A sample of the client instruction sheet is presented in Exhibit 2.1. When presenting the client instruction sheet to the client, the examiner should note the current time and choose a time estimated to be approximately 7 minutes after the client begins the task. This time is incorporated into the instructions; the examinee is told to keep track of time and tell the examiner when it is the time indicated. For example, if the person starts the assessment at 10:20 a.m., he or she would be asked to tell the examiner when it is 10:27, and this time would be written on the client instruction sheet.

Exhibit 2.1. Sample Weekly Calendar Activity Client Instruction Sheet

Directions

1. Enter the appointments in any order in the weekly schedule.
2. Enter the entire or complete appointment or errand.
3. Mark the exact time needed on the weekly schedule (when it is indicated).
4. It is more important to be accurate than to be quick.
5. Remember to follow the rules below.

Rules to Remember

- Once you have entered an appointment into the calendar, you cannot cross it out.
- Tell me when it is ____________.
- Leave ______________________________ free (do not schedule any appointments or errands on this day).
- Do not answer questions from the examiner during this activity.
- Tell the examiner when you are finished.

Depending on the specific appointment list or version used, the day that is designated as free varies. The examiner should indicate which day of the week should be left free on that line of the instruction sheet before giving it to the client. The designated free day for each version is indicated in Table 1.1 and at the top of each appointment scoring worksheet. The full instructions for the client are presented on the following pages.

Examiner Directions for All Levels

The following directions are presented orally with the Weekly Calendar Activity Instruction Sheet (Appendix E.1).

This activity involves putting appointments and errands into this weekly schedule [*point*]. Here is a list of appointments that need to be scheduled during the week [*point*]. [*Place the Weekly Calendar Activity Instruction Sheet in front of client and point to each item on the abbreviated direction sheet as it is explained.*] You can enter the appointments in any order you would like, but you should always enter the entire appointment. For example, if the appointment is a meeting with Mary, you would enter "meeting with Mary" or "Meeting—Mary." You would not just enter "meeting." You should also be careful to mark the time needed.

[*Show a sample and demonstrate if necessary.*] In other words, if the appointment starts at 9:30 a.m. and is 30 minutes, you would indicate this by drawing a line here and here (*point*).

You may need to be careful because some of the appointments could conflict with others, and you will have to make some decisions. There are extra paper and pens for you to use if you would like [*point*].

There are several rules that you will need to follow [*point to the rules on the instruction sheet as you say them*]. Once you have entered an appointment on this weekly calendar [*point to weekly calendar*], you should not cross out the appointment on this sheet [*emphasize and point to the weekly calendar*]. Do not schedule any appointments or errands on ________ [*indicate specified day: Tuesday, Wednesday, or Thursday*]. In addition, you should keep track of the time and tell me when it is ______ [*choose time 7 minutes later and write it on examinee instruction sheet—make sure the person has a watch or that there is a clock in the room, and point it out or place a watch on the table*].

The next rule is not to answer questions from me during the activity. I will try to ask you questions that have nothing to do with the activity (such as "What is your favorite color?"). Do not answer these questions. Just ignore them. If I have reason to ask you a question that I want you to answer, for instance, if I want to be sure you are okay, I will say "time out," and we will stop the task for a minute and you can answer me. Finally, the last rule is to remember to tell me when you are finished with the activity.

Try to be as efficient as possible. I will be timing you, but it is more important for you to be accurate than to go quickly. We will keep the directions and rules here [*point*] so that you can look at them at any time. Let's quickly review the directions and rules [*point to the instruction sheet and ask participant to state the rules out loud*]. Once you begin the activity, I cannot answer any additional questions. I can only restate the directions. Before we begin, do you have any questions? [*Answer all questions.*] OK. Let's begin. [*Begin timing.*]

Examiner guidelines: Ask the following questions after 2, 5, and 10 minutes (or when the person is almost finished, if it looks like he or she will finish before 10 minutes are up). An exception to this is the 10-item Short-Versions A and B. For the WCPA–10, the questions are asked after 2, 5, and 7 minutes.

1. Do you know what the weather is supposed to be tomorrow?
2. Do you have any pets?
3. What day is your birthday?

General Administration Guidelines for Use and Completion of the WCPA Recording Form

The WCPA examiner forms include an optional Adult Background Form (Appendix E.5); the Recording Form (Appendix E.6) that is used to record time, adherence to the rules, strategy use, and observations during performance; an After-Task Interview and Rating Scale (Appendix E.7); a Calendar Scoring Worksheet (specific to each appointment list; Appendixes A–D); and an optional Observation Form (Appendix E.8) and optional summary worksheets or report templates that summarize results on one page (Appendix F). This section focuses on the Recording Form (Appendix E.6), which is completed as the person is doing the activity.

Adult Background Form

An example of background information obtained during normative data collection appears in Appendix E.5. The background information gathered may differ depending on the client's age, but the client's familiarity with and routine use of a weekly calendar, including the type of calendar the person uses, should be investigated.

WCPA Recording Form

The WCPA Recording Form (Appendix E.6) is used across different levels and versions. The examiner indicates the level (I, II, or III) and the version that is being used.

Begin timing after you say, "Let's begin." Record the time on the Recording Form at two points:

- *Planning time:* Record the time when the client enters the first appointment on the weekly calendar. Planning time is entered in both minutes and seconds. If planning time is less than 1 minute, only seconds are recorded. An optional scoring method, used in the Hebrew version (Ben Ari, Lahav, & Kizony, 2012), is to record two planning times, from "Let's begin" to

- The time the client enters the first appointment and
- The time the client enters the second appointment.

The reason for the latter method is that many healthy people immediately enter the first appointment because it is fixed (without choices). After entering the first appointment, they often realize that some of the appointments are variable, so they adjust their approach and pause, plan, and reread the entire list. Thus, recording the two different planning times may provide a more accurate measure of time spent planning.

- *Total time:* Record the time when client states that he or she is finished or puts down the pen. This includes both planning time and time to complete the entire task. This is recorded in both minutes and seconds.

During administration, the examiner observes and records adherence to all five rules on the Recording Form. The rule score ranges from 0 to 5. Adherence to each rule is recorded as described next.

Rule 1: Questions answered

During the activity, the examiner asks the client 3 irrelevant questions, which the client has been instructed not to answer. This requires inhibition, or the ability to ignore extraneous information. The questions should be asked after 2, 5, and 10 minutes (or when the client is almost finished, if it looks like he or she will finish before 10 minutes is up). An exception to this is the 10-item Short Versions A and B. For these versions, the questions are asked after 2, 5, and 7 minutes.

These questions were used during the initial normative data collection:

1. Do you know what the weather is supposed to be tomorrow?
2. Do you have any pets?
3. What day is your birthday?

The examiner also can choose substitute questions. Examples of questions that can be substituted if the examiner feels other questions might be more appropriate or during retesting include

- *Instead of Question 1:* Where do you live? What is your favorite TV show (or movie)? Where do you shop for groceries? What is your favorite holiday? What is your favorite color?
- *Instead of Question 2:* Do you have any siblings (or children or grandchildren)? Do you own any cars? Do you have a tablet or cell phone (computer)?
- *Instead of Question 3:* What year were you born? What day is today? What is tomorrow's date?

For each of the questions, the examiner should record yes (Y) or no (N) to indicate whether the client responded to the question. If the client answers any of the 3 questions, Rule 1 is considered broken.

Rule 2: States time within 5 minutes of targeted time

If the time is stated by the client more than 5 minutes after the targeted time has passed, Rule 2 is considered broken. On the recording sheet, the examiner indicates whether the time was completely forgotten or remembered too late.

Rule 3: States when finished

The examiner indicates whether the client remembers to state that he or she has finished the task by placing a check mark next to either "yes" or "no" on the Recording Form.

Rule 4: Appointments scheduled on free day

The client is instructed not to schedule any appointments on a specified day. For most versions, the free day is Wednesday, but some alternate versions use Tuesday or Thursday. The Calendar Scoring Worksheet specifies the day that should remain free. If an appointment is entered into the calendar on the specified free day, the rule is considered broken. The appointment is also recorded as a location error on the calendar scoring worksheet. An exception to this is "taking meds" for Level III because some people enter this into the calendar even though it is unnecessary; therefore, it is not considered an error.

Rule 5: Number of appointments crossed out

The client is instructed not to cross out appointments on the calendar. The number of times the client crossed out appointments is recorded. If the client crosses out at least one appointment, Rule 5 is considered broken. Exhibit 2.2 shows a sample of a completed rule section from the Recording Form.

Alternative scoring method for rule following

Another option for scoring the rules is to consider each separate question as a separate rule, resulting in a total of 7 rules rather than 5. If the client answered all 3 questions, 3 rules would be considered broken rather than 1, which could potentially increase the sensitivity of this score. An additional option is to count the number of times the client crossed out appointments as separate rule breaks. However, initial studies indicated that the standard rule method score was effective in differentiating between performance of younger and older adults.

Observations

The general frequency with which the client refers back to the instruction sheet is indicated on the Recording Form by placing a check mark next to the appropriate choice:

Refers to Instruction Sheet: __ Never __ 1–2 times __ 3–5 times __ > 5 times

Calendar error management refers to how the client handles the calendar errors (Sat./Sun. reversal), evening time error (appointments that extend past calendar time), or the change in the evening time format starting at 6:00 p.m. (from 15-minute to half-hour time slots). These observations are not included in the scoring, but the examiner should note the way in which the client handles these difficulties because they provide important qualitative information about how the client copes with the unexpected.

If the client recognizes problems and asks what he or she should do, the examiner should encourage the client to decide himself or herself and not provide guidance. Some people do not notice the errors or they ignore them. Others easily adapt. Some people in clinical populations can become fixated on the errors, which can interfere with task completion. The examiner should indicate if any of the errors affected performance by placing a check mark next to the appropriate statement on the Recording Form:

__ Did not affect performance __ Interfered with performance

Additional Guidelines

- *Response to questions:* If the client asks the examiner questions during the activity, the examiner can restate the directions or point to the instruction sheet at any time but cannot answer

Exhibit 2.2. Sample Rule Section of Recording Form

Rules
1. Questions answered (Y = *yes*; N = *no*) 1. Y 2. Y 3. N
2. States time at 7 min (± 5 minutes) __ States time too late ✓ Forgets time completely __
3. States when finished: ✓ yes __ no
4. Appointments scheduled on free day (**Tues.**/Wed./Thurs.): ✓ yes __ no
5. No. of appointments crossed out 1

Total no. of rules followed = 1/5

The client followed only 1 of 5 rules (stated when finished).

Rules
1. Questions answered (Y = *yes*; N = *no*) 1. N 2. N 3. N
2. States time at 7 min (±5 minutes) __ States time too late ✓ Forgets time completely __
3. States when finished: ✓ yes __ no
4. Appointments scheduled on free day (Tues./**Wed.**/Thurs.): __ yes ✓ no
5. No. of appointments crossed out 4

Total no. of rules followed = 3/5

The client followed 3 of 5 rules (did not respond to questions, stated when finished, did not schedule appointments on Wed).

questions. If the client asks, "Can I cross out or erase?" the examiner should refer the client to the instruction sheet, and restate the instructions. The examiner can add, "I am not able to answer this question. I can only restate the directions," "Try to do the best that you can," or "You can decide the best way to handle this."

- *Correcting errors:* If the client makes a mistake and asks whether he or she can fix it (e.g., writing over an appointment, drawing an arrow), the examiner can state, "You decide what to do" or "You decide the best way to handle this."
- *Task completion:* If the client stops writing and appears to be finished but does not say anything, the examiner can ask, "Are you done?"
- *Time required:* The average length of time to complete the WCPA for Level II is between 14 and 17 minutes. Thirty minutes represents approximately 2 standard deviations away from the mean. Therefore, the examiner can stop the test after 30 minutes if the client has not completed the task and there are time constraints. However, the efficiency score cannot be calculated if the test is stopped.
- *Clarification:* After the activity, the examiner should ask the client questions for clarification if needed and write any notes or observations on the back of the calendar. For example, if the examiner cannot read the client's handwriting or does not understand abbreviations that were used, he or she should ask for clarification at the end of the task.

Strategy Use and Observations During Administration

The examiner should carefully observe how the client goes about completing the WCPA, including how the client begins, how he or she initiates and proceeds through the activity, and how he or she copes with conflicts or problems that arise. The examiner should note strategy use, efficiency, self-monitoring abilities, and self-recognition of errors. Self-recognition of errors is indicated by nonverbal signs, verbalization, or attempts at correcting an error and is recorded on the Calendar Scoring Worksheet as described in Chapter 3, "Guidelines for Scoring Appointments."

Strategies Observed

Strategies that are spontaneously initiated and used during performance are documented on the WCPA Recording Form. The examiner should record both the type and the frequency of strategies used. The Recording Form has a list of frequently used strategies, each of which is described in Table 2.1. The strategies are grouped by their general purpose, such as attention to key features, keeping track, and so forth. The categories are not mutually exclusive but are intended to help the examiner organize his or her observations of strategy use.

On the Recording Form, the examiner indicates strategies that are observed with a check mark in the appropriate column. To simplify administration, the examiner can choose to record whether a strategy was used (yes or no) without differentiating frequency. During normative studies, examiners were asked to place an asterisk next to the most frequently used strategies, but frequency was not consistently recorded. The current revised form differentiates whether a strategy is not used, is used occasionally or partially, is used frequently or consistently, or is used but is inefficient or counterproductive.

Occasional or partial strategy use is defined by infrequent use of a particular strategy (once or twice), lack of persistence or consistency, limited use for a small part of the task, or quick abandonment of a strategy. Frequent or consistent strategy use is indicated by regular, steady, and appropriate use throughout the task.

Ineffective or inefficient strategy use typically involves unnecessary steps, increased time or effort, or increased disorganization and confusion. An example is copying the list of appointments in the same order on another piece of paper before entering them into the calendar, which requires increased time and is unnecessary. If a strategy is considered inefficient, the examiner can place a check mark in both the inefficient column and the frequency column. If an observed strategy is not listed, the examiner would specify the strategy under "other" and record the frequency of strategy use.

In the original version of the WCPA, highlighting and talking aloud were each considered a strategy.

Table 2.1. Types of Observed Strategies

Strategy Purposes and Examples	Strategy Description
Attends to key features	
Underlines, circles, or highlights key words or features	Underlines, circles, or highlights the most important words or details in sentences (or crosses out irrelevant information).
Uses finger	Uses finger to keep track of place or focus while reading or to hide other rows while reading.
Keeps track	
Verbal rehearsal: Repeats key words of instructions or appointment list out loud	Rehearses or repeats key words or directions to self, for example, repeating "Check the time" to remember to tell examiner when 7 minutes have passed.
Crosses off, checks off, or highlights appointments entered	Uses an external method to keep track of appointments that have been entered into the calendar. This may include crossing out an appointment on the list once it has been entered, checking it off, or highlighting it.
Simplifies or organizes	
Rearranges materials	Rearranges or adjusts materials before beginning, for example, places instruction sheet or watch in key location as a cue.
Categorizes or organizes appointments before entering them (color codes, highlights, uses symbols, labels)	Uses highlighter, color coding, arrows, open boxes and checks, or other labeling system to group different types of appointments together in written form before entering them, for example, highlighting all of the possible Monday appointments or noting an "M" next to them or coding fixed appointments with a star and circling flexible appointments.
Enters fixed appointments first, then flexible appointments	Separates fixed and flexible appointments or enters the fixed appointments into the calendar first.
Written plan	Makes a rough draft first or plans out calendar in writing before entering appointments by making lists.
Talks out loud about his or her strategy, method, or plan	Talks aloud or whispers to self. States what he or she is doing or will do next. Verbalizations are related to planning rather than repetition of instructions or key words.
Crosses off specified free day (Tues., Wed., or Thurs.)	Physically puts a line through the day so that no appointments can be entered or provides another external cue.
Monitors performance	
Self-checks	Spontaneously reviews work and double checks appointments entered into the calendar against the appointment list. For example, the person may count the number of appointments in the list and the number entered.
Pauses and rereads	After entering a couple of appointments, recognizes conflicts and stops to reread and review list before continuing.

Observations of performance of normal and clinical populations indicated that there are differences in how or why people highlight or talk aloud. For example, highlighting can be used to identify or make key words salient as well as to create a color coding or organizational scheme. Therefore, highlighting was subdivided according to the reason why or how highlighting was used.

Similar observations were made of the talking-aloud strategy. Some people simply repeated or rehearsed key words or directions, and others verbalized their plan and strategy. Studies have suggested that these differences in content could influence performance (Tarricone, 2011). Therefore, the talk-aloud strategy was subdivided into verbal rehearsal and verbalizations related to planning.

On the WCPA Recording Form (Appendix E.6), the examiner should note any other observed strategies. Examples of less common strategies include covering part of the list with scrap paper; making encouraging comments to himself or herself; humming out loud to maintain focus or block out distractions while working, reevaluating approach, and modifying strategies; and putting flexible appointments into the least busy time segments, for example, early in the morning to avoid conflicts.

Strategies Reported (Not Observed)

Because not all strategies can be observed, the After-Task Interview and Rating Scale is used to probe strategy use and identify self-reported internal strategies. Some examples of reported strategies include

- I looked at all the appointments or choices and separated them or categorized them in my mind.
- I talked to myself.
- I paced myself.
- I reread the list several times before I started.
- I reviewed everything first to get a sense of the task before I began.
- I thought of myself doing the errands.
- I repeated the appointment and time to myself several times.
- I prioritized appointments or errands by importance, for example, scheduling doctor appointments first.

Comments Section

On the Recording Form, the examiner should note any positive or negative comments the client makes about his or her performance or the task and record them. The examiner should also note the efficiency of strategy use or any additional observations. Any additional comments or observations can be added on the back of the Recording Form.

Strategy Scoring: Observed Strategies

The examiner should tally the number of observed strategies used occasionally or partially and the number used frequently or consistently, being sure to include in the tally any other strategies noted. Differentiating between the frequency of strategy use (occasional or frequent) is not required for scoring, but it provides additional information that may contribute to understanding the effectiveness of strategy use. Another option is for the examiner to simply observe whether a strategy was used or not used, as was done in normative studies. The limitation with this latter approach is that strategy use can be ineffective if used inconsistently or incompletely, and the total strategy score does not reflect this. The number of inefficient or ineffective strategies used may also be totaled separately.

In addition to strategies observed, the examiner should record any additional strategies that are reported in the After-Task Interview and Rating Scale (open-ended questions). The final total strategy score is the total number of observed strategies plus the total number of reported strategies.

In the example shown in Exhibit 2.3, the total strategy score is 7. Six strategies were observed (4 frequently, 2 occasionally), and 1 strategy was reported.

After-Task Interview and Rating Scale

The After-Task Interview and Rating Scale is conducted immediately after completion of the weekly calendar to assess the client's perceptions regarding the activity and his or her performance (Appendix E.7). The first question is optional and identifies whether the client routinely uses a weekly calendar. Familiarity with a task can influence performance. (Additional questions can be used to further probe calendar use if the examiner chooses.) The calendar-use question is followed by 4 open-ended questions and 4 self-rated statements. The latter are rated by the client on a 4-point scale (1 = *agree*, 2 = *somewhat agree*, 3 = *somewhat disagree*, and 4 = *disagree*). The final 2 optional questions ask the client to estimate the time needed to complete the task (time awareness) and to estimate the number of appointments he or she entered accurately.

Open-Ended Questions

The open-ended questions included in the After-Task Interview and Rating Scale are designed to explore the person's perceptions about task difficulty and strategy

Exhibit 2.3. Sample of Recording and Scoring Strategy Use

Strategies Observed	**Not Observed**	**Occasionally/ Partially Used**	**Frequently/ Consistently Used**	**Inefficient/ Counterproductive**
Underlines, circles, or highlights key words or features	✓			
Uses finger		✓		
Verbal rehearsal: Repeats key words or instructions out loud			✓	
Crosses off, checks off, or highlights appointments entered			✓	
Rearranges materials	✓			
Categorizes or organizes appointments before entering them (coding system, color codes, highlights, labels)	✓			
Enters fixed appointments first, then flexible appointments	✓			
Uses written plan: Makes a rough draft first or plans out calendar in writing before entering appointments	✓			
Talks out loud about strategy, method, or plan			✓	
Crosses off specified free day	✓			
Self-checks			✓	
Pauses and rereads				
Other: *Used paper to cover or screen out information*		✓		
Other:				
Total observed strategies		2	4	
Strategies reported (not observed—reported in After-Task Interview and Rating Scale) Specify and indicate total number of strategies: *Decided to put flexible appointments early as noticed that early appointments would not conflict.*		1		
Total number of strategies used: Total observed strategies (occasional + frequent) + total strategies reported		7		

use. Alternate words and phrases as well as sample follow-up questions are provided in parentheses so that the examiner can choose how the question is asked. The interview should be conducted as a discussion, and responses should be carefully probed in a nonthreatening manner. Responses should be recorded verbatim whenever possible.

Exhibit 2.4 provides examples of probes. If the client does not acknowledge strategy use but the examiner observed strategy use during performance (e.g., crosses off each item), the examiner should state his or her observations and encourage the client to identify specific methods he or she may have used. For example, "I noticed that you crossed off each item. Tell me more about that. Did you use any other special methods to help yourself complete this activity?" or "Did you have a plan?" If additional strategies are reported, the examiner should check off reported strategies on the Recording Form (Appendix E.6) and specify the strategy as indicated above.

Exhibit 2.4. After-Task Interview and Rating Scale: Open-Ended Questions, Response Examples, and Probing for More Information

Examiner Questions (With Probes)	Examinee Responses
Example 1	
Tell me how you went about doing this task. Did you use any strategies or special methods?	I organized the scrap paper with all 7 days of the week and then filled in the appointments for those sections before placing them into the calendar.
Did you have a plan? Did you enter the appointments in any particular order?	I worked down the list from top to bottom.
How did you manage to keep track of everything?	I didn't have a particular method, and I missed some.
Did you encounter any challenges (or difficulties) while doing this task?	At times it was overwhelming.
What made it overwhelming?	I kept noticing more conflicts as I was going along.
Would you do anything differently next time?	I wouldn't have missed those appointments.
What would you do differently? Tell me how you might go about it differently next time.	I would check my work before I say I'm done.
Example 2	
Tell me how you went about doing this task.	I just put the appointments on the calendar.
Did you use any strategies or special methods?	I didn't do anything special.
How did you manage to organize everything or decide which appointment to put down next?	I started at the top of the list and then worked down the list.
Did you run into any conflicts?	A little bit, but I fit all of the appointments in.
Did you encounter any challenges (or difficulties) while doing this task?	No.
What parts of this activity were most challenging? What parts were easiest?	It was pretty easy. It was just a matter of going down the list.
Would you do anything differently next time?	No. That's how I do things.
Are there any other approaches or special methods that could be used?	Not that I can think of.
Example 3	
Tell me how you went about doing this task. Did you use any strategies or special methods?	I had to write down each appointment in a list corresponding to its day. Choosing times before putting them on the calendar made it easier to transfer.
How did you manage to keep track of everything or organize everything?	It helped to get the most rigid appointments in first.
I noticed that you crossed off Wednesday; I noticed that you were talking out loud to yourself.	Yes, I couldn't put appointments on Wednesday so I crossed it off so I wouldn't have to think about it.
Did you encounter any challenges (or difficulties) while doing this task?	Yes.
What parts of this activity were most challenging?	I had trouble organizing the appointments because some appointments had choices, and I had trouble keeping track of where to put them.
Would you do anything differently next time?	Not really.
Are there any other ways that you could approach this task?	Well, maybe I would check off each appointment as I went along. That would have helped.

(Continued)

Exhibit 2.4. After-Task Interview and Rating Scale: Open-Ended Questions, Response Examples, and Probing for More Information *(Continued)*

Examiner Questions (With Probes)	Examinee Responses
Example 4	
Tell me how you went about doing this task. Did you use any strategies or special methods?	At first I just looked for the conflicts and tried to resolve where there were multiple choices that overlap.
I noticed you paused halfway through and took a long look at the appointment list. Tell me more about this.	Yes, because I realized there were some appointments on specific days and times, and I realized carpool could go on any day, so I could leave it to the end.
At one point, it seemed as though you might have changed your approach.	Yes, I put fixed appointments first, then the appointments with multiple choices, and then I did the free appointments that could go on any day.
I noticed you counted the appointments when you were finished. Tell me more about why you did this.	Yes, so I wouldn't miss any, I counted the number of appointments on the list and the number of appointments in the calendar.
Did you encounter any challenges (or difficulties) while doing this task?	Oh yes. Quite challenging.
What parts of this activity were most challenging?	Not taking in the complexity of the problem at first . . . not seeing the conflicts until it was too late. Not being able to do this in pencil
Would you do anything differently next time?	I should have made notes.
What would you make notes about?	I would make notes about the conflicting appointments. I would use the scrap paper. I didn't think it was going to be that hard.

The first 4 questions on the After-Task Interview and Rating Scale are as follows:

1. Do you do tasks like this on a regular basis? _ Yes _ No (*optional:* Do you use a weekly calendar or schedule? How do you go about keeping track of your own appointments or errands?)
2. (a) Tell me how you went about doing this task? [*Wait for response. If necessary, ask.*] (b) Did you use any strategies or special methods? (Did you have a plan or a special approach? How did you manage to keep track of everything or organize everything?) [*If necessary, comment on observations of strategy use.*]
3. Did you encounter (or experience) any challenges (or difficulties) while doing this task? Which parts of this activity were most challenging (hardest)? Which parts were easiest?
4. Would you do anything differently next time? (Would you change the way you went about the task in any way? Are there any other strategies or methods that you could use?)

Additional questions that the examiner might be interested in include the following:

- *If applicable:* How did you manage to remember to tell me the time?
- Did you notice that the calendar had an error? (Did you notice that Saturday and Sunday were out of order?)

Additional guidelines for the After-Task Interview and Rating Scale's open-ended questions include

- Verify strategy use. If the examiner does not understand why the client used a certain strategy, it is important to ask why the client used that strategy and to record the client's explanation, for example, "Tell me why you decided to start with the last appointment."
- Repeat or summarize the client's responses to ensure understanding, which can also encourage the client to provide additional responses.
- Probe any observations that the examiner did not understand, for example, "I noticed that

you put a lot of appointments on Monday. Can you tell me how or why you decided to put __ on Monday?"

- Verify observations or error recognition. If the examiner observed nonverbal indications of error recognition but the client did not verbally acknowledge the error or attempt to correct it, the After-Task Interview and Rating Scale can be used to verify error recognition, for example, "I noticed that after putting in the doctor's appointment, you put your hand on your head and began to go slower; can you tell me more about that?" or "Can you tell me what was going on at that point?"
- If the client reports the use of internal strategies during the interview, the examiner should be sure to go back to the Recording Form after the interview and record the use of internal strategies on the Strategies Observed checklist. The type of internal strategy reported should be specified.

After-Task Interview and Rating Scale Self-Ratings (Optional)

Questions 5, 6, and 7 on the After-Task Interview and Rating Scale include quantitative self-ratings of performance. In general, if the client appears defensive or anxious during the open-ended questions, quantitative self-ratings are not used.

Question 5 on the After-Task Interview and Rating Scale includes 4 statements that are self-rated by the client and are designed to further explore the client's perception of task difficulty. The client can be presented with the scale and asked to complete it himself or herself, or it can be completed as part of the interview. The client is asked to rate his or her level of agreement with 4 statements on a scale ranging from 1 (*agree*) to 4 (*disagree*). Ratings either can be totaled or averaged to summarize the client's perception of task difficulty. A lower rating indicates the task is perceived as easy. In the example provided in Exhibit 2.5, the client's total rating is 6 and the average rating is 1.5 (6/4 = 1.5), indicating that the client perceived the task as easy.

The examiner optionally can rate his or her own responses to these questions and record his or her rating in the last column. The examiner rates the questions on the basis of his or her performance observations and actual performance results (e.g., the task was easy for the client; the client completed the task without difficulty). On the After-Task Interview and Rating Scale (Appendix E.7), the last column is purposely not labeled so that it can be used for either comments or examiner ratings.

The discrepancy between the examiner's rating of perceived difficulty level and the client's self-ratings can be used as an indicator of the client's general self-awareness. The client and examiner ratings are totaled separately (minimum score = 4; maximum score = 16), and the discrepancy between them is assessed. A discrepancy of 0 indicates perfect agreement, or good awareness. For example, if the client and examiner both rate all tasks as easy (rating of 1), the discrepancy between them is 0.

In Exhibit 2.5, the examiner disagrees with all statements, resulting in an examiner total rating of 16. This rating indicates that the examiner perceives the client as having difficulty. The client's total rating

Exhibit 2.5. Sample of After-Task Interview and Rating Scale Self-Ratings

Statement	Agree (1)	Somewhat Agree (2)	Somewhat Disagree (3)	Disagree (4)	Examiner
1. This task was easy for me.	1				4
2. I used efficient methods to complete this task.		2			4
3. I completed this task accurately.	1				4
4. I kept track of everything I needed to do.		2			4
Totals	2	4			16
Average rating	1.5 average rating				4

is 6, indicating that the client perceives the task as easy. The discrepancy between them is 10 (16 − 6 = 10), indicating that the client appears to be unaware of errors or observed difficulties.

After Question 5, the person can be asked to specifically estimate time and performance accuracy.

6. How much time did it take you to complete this task? [*Encourage the person to estimate or guess if he or she is not sure.*]

_ <10 min ✓ 10–15 min _ 16–20 min _ 21–25 min
_ 26–30 min _ >35 min

7. Seventeen appointments needed to be entered into the weekly calendar. Estimate the number of appointments that you entered accurately into the schedule 16/17.

Responses to these questions are compared with the actual total time required for completion and the actual number of accurate appointments. Discrepancies between actual and estimated time or accuracy provide additional indicators of self-awareness.

- *Time awareness:* If the client estimates that he or she required about 10 to 15 minutes to complete the task but actually completed the task in 30 minutes, the difference would be about 15 minutes, indicating that the client was not completely aware of the actual amount of time spent on the task.
- *Accuracy estimation:* Lower accuracy scores reflect lower levels of performance. If the client estimates that he or she entered 16 appointments accurately but actually entered 10 accurately (accuracy score of 10), the difference between them would be 6, indicating that the client overestimated performance by 6 items.

Responses to the After-Task Interview and Rating Scale can also provide information that can be used by a practitioner to make a judgment about the client's overall level of awareness. What follows are general descriptions of awareness levels that may be helpful to broadly describe awareness in clinical practice.

- *Aware:* The client has an accurate or realistic appraisal of his or her performance and is able to provide specific examples of difficulties he or she may have encountered.
- *Some awareness:* The client may vaguely identify challenges or difficulties but is unable to provide specific examples. The client overestimates some aspects of performance or generally minimizes difficulties, even though they are acknowledged.
- *Slight awareness:* The client overestimates performance and may not verbally acknowledge problems; however, some responses or aspects of behavior during the WCPA or After-Task Interview and Rating Scale suggest that the client is aware of at least some task challenges that were encountered (e.g., "The appointment choices were tricky"). The client may vaguely allude to difficulties or only identify task-specific challenges ("The appointment list had a lot of information").
- *Unaware:* The client is completely unaware of errors or task challenges and has a completely unrealistic appraisal of his or her performance.

Optional Observation Form

The examiner can use the optional Observation Form (Appendix E.8) when observing the client's entry of appointments during the task. The sample Observation Form in Exhibit 2.6 and the full form in Appendix E.8 were used in the Hebrew-translated version to record the order in which a client enters appointments as well as observations, comments, or errors specific

Exhibit 2.6. Sample Observation Form

No.	Appointment	Comments
1	Visit with cousin	Client said the cousin lives far away so she needs time to get there.
2	Food shopping	Client said, "My husband is doing that."
3	Hair cut	After a while, client says it is a mistake but does not correct it because he wants to follow the rule of not crossing out appointments

to each appointment (Ben Ari et al., 2012). It provides a more detailed account of the process and methods that the client uses as he or she completes the calendar. This form is particularly helpful in recording verbal and nonverbal signs of error recognition or attempts at self-correction during the task. The observation form is not required, but it may be helpful for interpretation or later scoring. Exhibit 2.6 shows how the examiner could complete the form (R. Kizony, personal communication, August 29, 2014).

Summary

Information needed for administering the WCPA was provided in this chapter. Set-up, instructions, rules, and observations, including strategy ratings, were described and guidelines for completing the WCPA recording form and conducting the after-task interview were presented. Administration of the WCPA requires careful observation of the process and familiarity with the range of strategies that are typically used during the WCPA.

The after-task interview probes strategy use and investigates the person's self-perceptions of performance. Examples of after-task interview scripts and probing questions should be carefully reviewed. Both strategy rating and the after-task interview provide information that is important in interpretation, as described in Chapter 4, "Interpretation." Therapists are encouraged to practice administration of the WCPA by role playing with colleagues or by administering the test to 2–3 healthy people, corresponding to ages of potential clients, prior to clinical use.

CHAPTER
3 Guidelines for Scoring Appointments

The Calendar Scoring Worksheet (Appendixes A–D, specific to which version is selected) is used to identify and score the accuracy of appointments. Although the general format of the Calendar Scoring Worksheet is the same, each appointment list has its own worksheet. In general, appointment accuracy is examined after the session. However, the worksheet is also used to note any errors in appointment entry that the client self-recognizes during the activity.

Self-Recognition of Errors

During the WCPA, the client may indicate verbally or nonverbally that he or she made a mistake. For example, the client may attempt to self-correct or might shake his or her head, whisper, or say out loud that he or she made a mistake. If the client recognizes errors, even though they may remain uncorrected, the examiner should indicate this with a check mark in the Self-Recognition (SR) column on the Calendar Scoring Worksheet. The After-Task Interview and Rating Scale can be used to confirm observations, if necessary, as described in Chapter 2, "Administration."

The SR column should also be checked if the client is observed attempting to fix a mistake, even though the error correction method may be unsuccessful. Common attempts to correct errors include drawing arrows to indicate where the appointment should be, crossing out and reentering the appointment, or attempting to fix the appointment by changing the days of the week in the header.

Appointment Errors

Errors in entering appointments can be generally identified and indicated by an overall error score, or the examiner can analyze and categorize them according to error type (repetition, location, time, and incomplete) with the detailed scoring method. The method used to score errors depends on the purpose and goals of assessment. The detailed error scoring method can be helpful in further differentiating between clinical populations. For example, two clients may obtain the same overall error score for different reasons. Analysis of errors provides an indication of the underlying reasons why a client may have had difficulty with the task. It also provides implications for treatment.

Instructions for Using the Calendar Scoring Worksheet

A total of 17 errands and appointments (18 for the youth versions) should be entered into the weekly calendar. "Taking medications" (Level III) is not counted.

Step 1: Identify Appointments Entered

The first step in scoring is to identify the appointments entered and those that were omitted or are missing.

- *Entered column:* If the appointment was entered, this column is checked, even if there are errors in the entry.
- *Missing column:* If an appointment was omitted or is missing (not entered in the weekly calendar), place an "X" in this column. If an appointment was entered but was crossed out and not rewritten, it is also considered missing.
- *Totals:* The total number of appointments entered plus the total number of missing appointments should equal 17 (adult versions) or 18 (youth versions).

Step 2: Identify Accuracy

After entered and missing appointments are identified, the examiner should go back through the entered appointments and identify those that are accurate and those that have errors. See Exhibit 3.1 for an example.

Exhibit 3.1. Sample of Partial Calendar Scoring Worksheet, Adult/Older Adult (Ages 18–94 Years), Version A

Entered	Missing	Error	Accurate	SR	Appointments
✓			✓		Mon.: Haircut from 11:00 a.m.–12:00 p.m.
	X				Visit with cousin Mon. or Tues. between 1:00 and 2:00 p.m. or 1:30 and 2:30 p.m. or on Thurs. between 2:30 and 3:30 p.m. or 3:00 and 4:00 p.m.
✓		X		✓	Mon. anytime or Tues. a.m.: Call to renew prescription
	X				Tues.: Lunch with friend from 1:00–2:00 p.m.
✓		X		✓	Tues.: Phone conference before 2:00 p.m. (30 minutes)
✓		X			Mon. or Tues.: Medication picked up between 9:00 a.m. and 3:00 p.m. (30 minutes). Must have previously called to renew prescription.
✓			✓		Thurs.: Walk neighbor's dog before 11:00 a.m. (30 minutes)
5	2	3	2	2	**Total all columns**

Error column

The error column can be completed in two ways: (1) general error scoring or (2) detailed error scoring.

General error scoring. The general error scoring method involves indicating each error (in an entered appointment) with an "X" as illustrated in Exhibit 3.1. The number of errors is totaled for an overall error score. Examples of errors include placing an appointment in the wrong location, day, or time slot; repeating an appointment entry; inaccurately or partially entering the appointment name; or incorrectly allotting the time for the appointment.

Examiners should note that appointments that are only 15 minutes off (one gridline) are considered correct for appointments from 7:00 a.m. to 6:00 p.m.; those that are 30 minutes off from 6:00 p.m. on are also correct. This is to accommodate for difficulties in drawing or boxing the appointment. In Exhibit 3.1, 5 appointments were entered, and 2 appointments were missing. Of the 5 appointments entered, only 2 were accurate. Three errors were made, and 2 of these errors were self-recognized.

Detailed error scoring. The detailed error scoring method involves coding the incorrect appointment entry using an error code. In this method, the codes outlined in Table 3.1 are used in the error column to specify and further define the type of error made by the client.

Table 3.1. Types of Task Errors

Error Type	Description
R = Repetition error	Appointment is repeated or entered more than once, and repetition is not an attempt to self-correct a location error.
L = Location error	Appointment is placed in the wrong location, day, or time slot.
T = Time	Appointment is entered in the right location, but the time allotted is incorrect by more than 15 minutes for appointments from 7:00 a.m. to 6:00 p.m. or more than 30 minutes for appointments scheduled from 6:00 p.m. to 9:00 p.m. In other words, the appointment needs to be within 1 grid line of the correct time to be considered correct.
I = Incomplete or inaccurate	Appointment name is entered inaccurately or partially.
Missing appointments or omissions	Appointment is not entered into the weekly calendar. An "X" is placed in the Missing column.
Extraneous; irrelevant information	The individual writes additional appointments (not on the list) or includes irrelevant information. There is no code for this. This error should be noted.

Exhibit 3.2. Sample of Partial Calendar Scoring Worksheet, Adult/Older Adult (Ages 18–94 Years), Version A, Using Error Codes

Entered	Missing	Error	Accurate	SR	Appointments
✓		R			Mon.: Haircut from 11:00 a.m.–12:00 p.m.
	✓				Visit with cousin Mon. or Tues. between 1:00 and 2:00 p.m. or 1:30 and 2:30 p.m. or on Thurs. between 2:30 and 3:30 p.m. or 3:00 and 4:00 p.m.
✓		L		✓	Mon. anytime or Tues. a.m.: Call to renew prescription
	✓				Tues.: Lunch with friend from 1:00–2:00 p.m.
✓		L		✓	Tues.: Phone conference before 2:00 p.m. (30 minutes)
✓			✓		Mon. or Tues.: Medication picked up between 9:00 a.m. and 3:00 p.m. (30 minutes). Must have previously called to renew prescription.
✓		R			Thurs.: Walk neighbor's dog before 11:00 a.m. (30 minutes)

Accurate column

The Accurate column is used to identify appointments that are entered correctly. Exhibit 3.2 illustrates use of error codes in scoring. Of 5 appointments entered, only 1 is accurate. Two appointments are missing, 2 appointments are in the wrong location, and 2 appointments are repeated.

Totals

The last row of the Calendar Scoring Worksheet includes totals for each column, including the total number of appointments entered and missing. For appointments that were entered, add the total number of errors and accurate appointments as well as self-recognized errors. As a double check, the examiner should be sure that the total number of errors plus the total accurate plus the total missing appointments equals 17 (adult versions) or 18 (adolescent versions).

Efficiency score (optional)

In higher-level cognitive tasks, clients sometimes sacrifice accuracy to enhance speed or vice versa, also known as the *speed–accuracy trade-off.* Although the directions indicate that accuracy is more important than speed, some clients may try to perform the task as quickly as possible because they are being timed (regardless of the directions). Therefore, a scoring method was developed to combine speed and accuracy into a measure of efficiency. Total time in seconds is divided by a weighted accuracy score using the score conversions in Table 3.2. The formula is thus efficiency score = total time in seconds/weighted accuracy score. The weighted accuracy score was derived by multiplying the percentage of correct appointments by the total accuracy score.

A lower efficiency score indicates that the client obtained higher accuracy in less time. For example, if the accuracy score is 15 and the total time in seconds is 1,200 (20 minutes), the efficiency score is 1,200 / 13.2 = 91. The accuracy score of 15 is replaced by the weighted score from Table 3.2 (13.2). If the total time was 800 seconds, the efficiency score would be lower, 800/13.2 = 61, indicating a higher degree of efficiency, even though the accuracy score of 15 is exactly the same.

Note that the efficiency score is not meaningful or relevant below certain levels. If both the accuracy score and the time are low (accuracy <7 and time <500 seconds), the efficiency score should not be calculated. In general, the meaningfulness of accuracy scores that are 1.5 standard deviations or more below the mean are questionable because extremely low accuracy scores inherently reflect inefficiencies in performance.

Table 3.2. Weighted Accuracy Score Conversion

Raw Score	Weighted Accuracy Score	Raw Score	Weighted Accuracy Score
17	17	10	5.9
16	15.0	9	4.8
15	13.2	8	3.8
14	11.5	7	2.9
13	9.9	6	2.1
12	8.4	5	1.5
11	7.2	<4	Not calculated (too low)

Guidelines for Detailed Error Scoring and Examples

If one appointment has multiple errors, only 1 error should be scored. When the examiner observes multiple errors within 1 appointment, the examiner should score them in the following order: (1) repetition, (2) location, (3) time, and (4) inaccurate or incomplete. In other words, repetition errors, if present, are always scored first, followed by location errors, and so on. For example, if an appointment is in the wrong location but is repeated, only the repetition appointment is scored. Similarly, if a client writes an appointment inaccurately or incompletely and also allots the incorrect amount of time, only the time error is scored.

Appointments are marked as correct if they are off by only 15 minutes for appointments from 7:00 a.m. to 6:00 p.m. or by only 30 minutes for evening appointments (after 6:00 p.m.). In other words, appointments that are off by just one gridline on the calendar are still correct and are not marked as errors. Exhibit 3.3 shows examples of correct and incorrect appointment entries.

Repetition Errors

- The client repeats an appointment or writes the same appointment twice, and the repeated appointment is not a conscious effort to correct an incorrect location or entry. For example, the client consciously repeats an appointment because he or she wants to avoid breaking a rule (crossing out the appointment) and is attempting to correct an appointment that was placed in the wrong location. In this situation, the error is coded as a location error (L); however, a check mark is also placed in the SR column.

Location Errors

- The client puts the appointment on the wrong day.
- The client puts the appointment on the right day but in the wrong time slot. For example, the appointment is supposed to be from 1:00 to 2:00 p.m., but the client enters it from 1:30 to 2:30 p.m. or from 2:00 to 3:00 p.m. In this case, the appointment is still entered for 1 hour, but it is placed incorrectly. When the placement of the appointment is off by more than 15 minutes or by more than 1 gridline on the calendar from 7:00 a.m. to 6:00 p.m., it is incorrect (30 minutes for appointments scheduled from 6:00 p.m. on; see Example 2b in Exhibit 3.3).
- The client puts the appointment in the wrong place, realizes it, then crosses it out and enters the appointment in the correct location in an attempt to self-correct the location error (as described earlier). The error is coded as L, but a check mark is also placed in the SR column.
- The client puts the appointment in the wrong place, realizes it, and draws an arrow to correct the location. In this situation, the error is coded as L, but a check mark is also placed in the SR column.
- The client puts the appointment in wrong place, verbally acknowledges the mistake, says out loud that the appointment cannot be crossed out, and enters the appointment in the correct location. The error is coded as L, but a check mark is also placed in the SR column.
- The client enters the appointment on a specified free day (Tuesday, Wednesday, or Thursday).
- The client enters Pick up the medicine before Call the pharmacy. Mark the medication pickup as a location error. If the client enters Pick up the medicine but never enters Call in the prescription, the omission of the prescription calling is recorded as a missing appointment (see Example 7 in Exhibit 3.3).
- If appointment states "before" a designated time, an appointment scheduled *at that time* is coded as L (it must be placed before time).

Time Allotment Errors

- The client writes the appointment on the correct day and time slot, but the actual time allotted for the appointment is incorrect by more than 15 minutes for appointments from 7:00 a.m. to 6:00 p.m. or more than 30 minutes for appointments scheduled after 6:00 p.m. In other words, if an appointment is too long or short by more than one gridline on the calendar, it is incorrect (see Example 3a in Exhibit 3.3).
- One exception to the above is if the client writes out the correct time within the time box. In this situation, the appointment is still correct if the time allotted is too long or short by 2 gridlines (see Example 1g in Exhibit 3.3).

- The client does not indicate the movie time correctly; the client must either extend the time past the time slot, or note the time (7:00–11:00 p.m.; see Examples 4a–4c in Exhibit 3.3).
- If an appointment is 45 minutes to 1 hour long and placed in the middle of an hour box, it is considered accurate (see Example 1e in Exhibit 3.3).
- If an appointment is 90 minutes long, it is considered accurate if it is drawn in a box, marked with a line or arrow, or the time is written in.

Inaccurate or Incomplete

- The client enters the appointment name inaccurately, incompletely, or partially and its meaning would not be completely clear if another person viewed it. For example, if the client writes *food* instead of *food shopping* or *lunch* instead of *lunch with cousin,* another person would have to guess what the actual appointment or errand involved. Exhibit 3.4 provides examples of partial or incomplete appointments that are unacceptable for Adult/Older Adult Version A. This list can be used as a guide for the other versions as well.

Extraneous Appointments

- The client enters appointments into the calendar that are not on the list or that are extraneous and irrelevant information. This error type was not observed in healthy populations, but it has been observed in clinical populations. It is not included on the Calendar Scoring Worksheet, but it is included as part of the Error Analysis Profile described in Chapter 4, "Interpretation."

Samples of completed calendars and appointment scoring forms are provided in Exhibits 3.5–3.13. It is suggested that examiners practice scoring each calendar themselves and then check their scoring against the sample calendar scoring worksheet on the following page.

(Text continues on page 41)

Exhibit 3.3. Examples of Appointment Entries That Are Correct and Incorrect

1. Acceptable ways to indicate time

1a: arrows

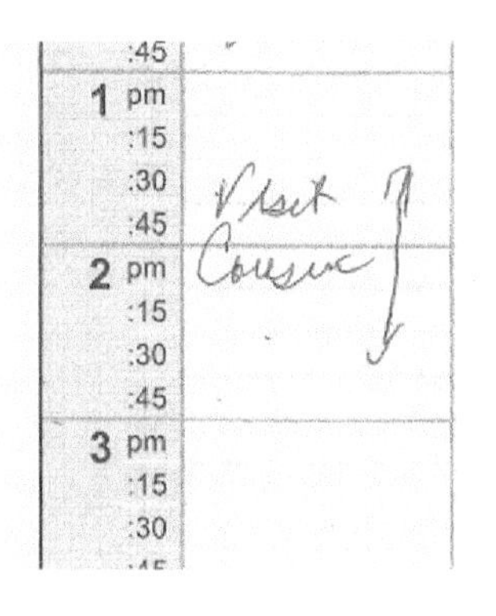

1b: boxes, lines

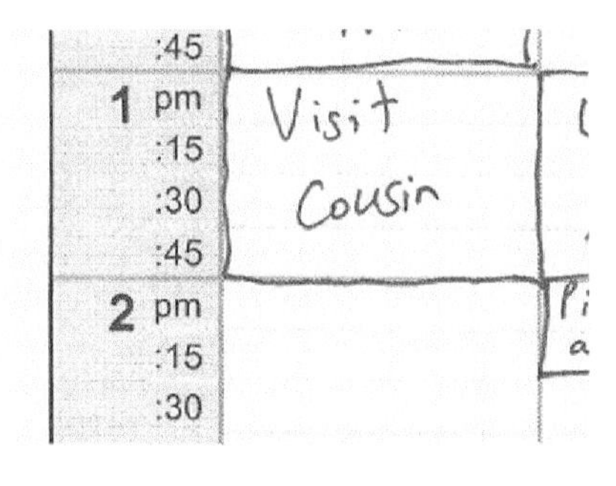

1c: writing time

1d: *Haircut* is accurate because it is only 15 minutes off in the 7:00 a.m.–6:00 p.m. section of the calendar (1 hr, 15 min, vs. 1 hr).

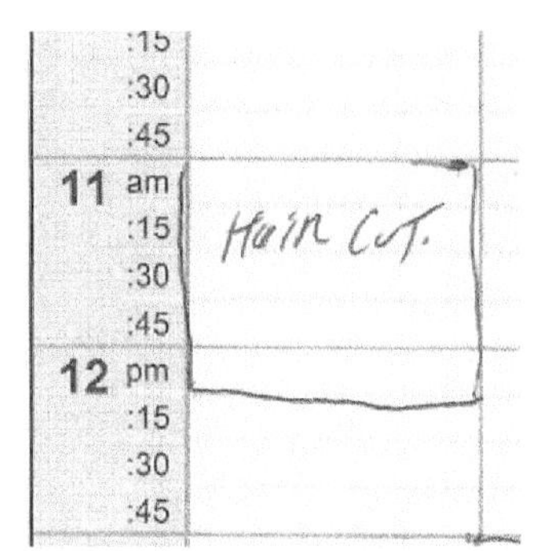

(Continued)

Exhibit 3.3. Examples of Appointment Entries That Are Correct and Incorrect *(Continued)*

1e: Writing an appointment in the middle of an hour box is acceptable for appointments that are 1 hour or 45 minutes long.

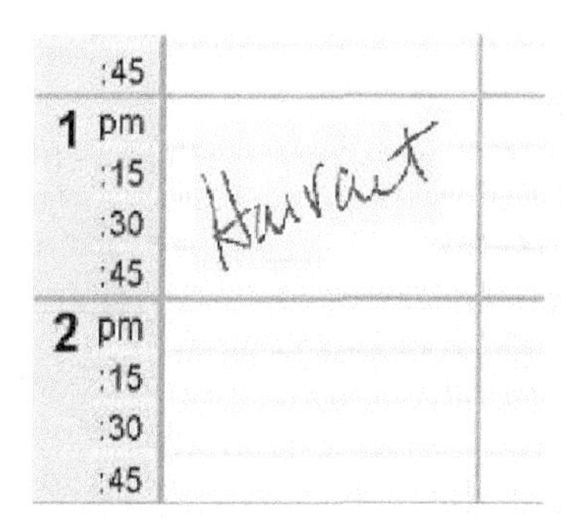

1f: *Doctor's Appointment* is accurate because the correct time of the appointment has been written out and the appointment is placed within the correct hour (however, *Dry Cleaners-Pick up pants* is incorrect because the appointment is not within the correct hour).

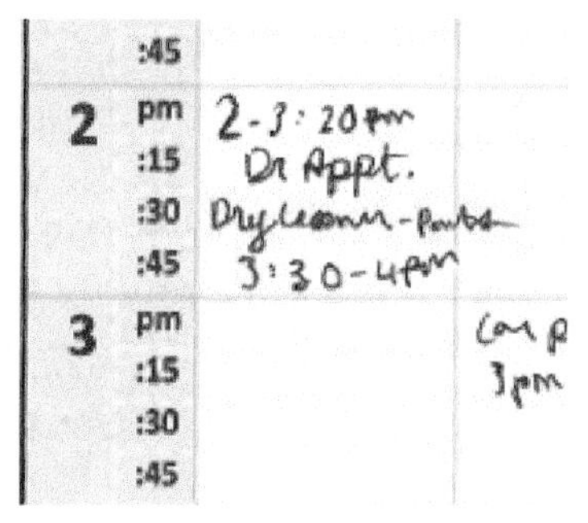

1g: *Volunteer* is accurate because although the boxed time is 9:00–10:00 a.m. (short by 2 gridlines), the correct time has been written out (9:00–10:30 a.m.).

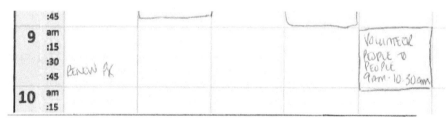

2. Acceptable ways to enter *Dinner With Coworkers* appointment (2 hours; start any time between 6:30 and 8:00 p.m.)

   2a and 2b: Any time slot for 2 hours starting between 6:00 and 8:30 p.m.

   2a: 7:00–9:00 p.m.

7 pm				Movies with Friends	Dinner with co-workers
:30					
8 pm					
:30					

   2b: Only 30 minutes off in the 6:00–9:00 p.m. section of the calendar (starting at 6:00 vs 6:30 p.m.)

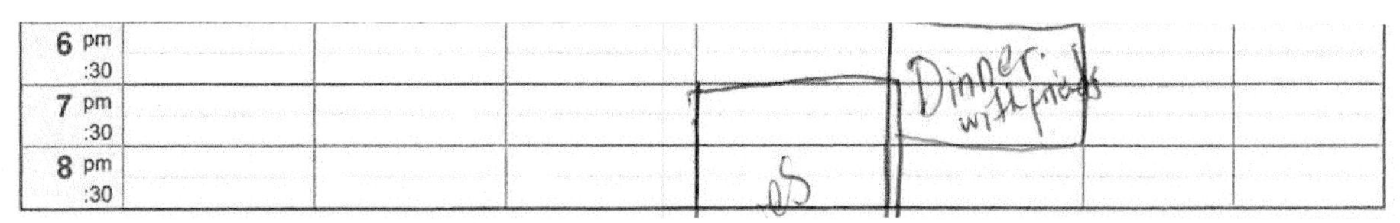

(Continued)

Exhibit 3.3. Examples of Appointment Entries That Are Correct and Incorrect *(Continued)*

2. Acceptable ways to enter *Dinner With Coworkers* appointment (*cont.*)

2c and 2d: Any time slot for 1.5 to 2.5 hours starting between 6:30 and 8:00 p.m.

2c & 2d are accurate because they are only 30 minutes off in the 6:00–9:00 p.m. section of the calendar (7:00–9:30 p.m. vs. 7:00–9:00 p.m.). Extension indicated by an arrow or box past the last line, even when not required, is still considered correct (as the extension is considered one grid line or 30 minutes)

2c:

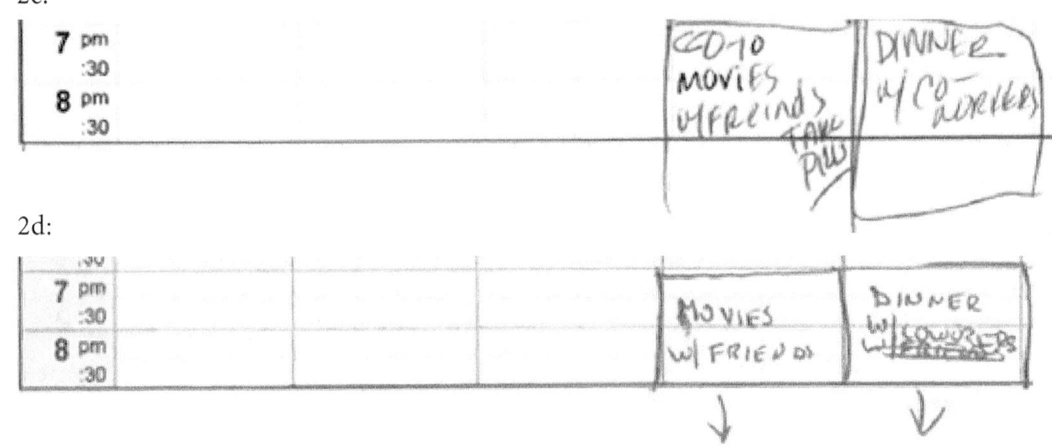

3. Unacceptable ways to enter *Dinner With Coworkers* appointment

3a: More than 30 minutes off in the 6:00–9:00 p.m. section of the calendar (6:00–9:00 p.m.)

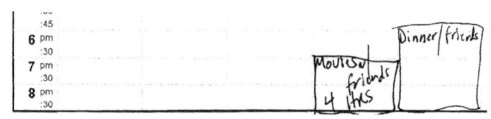

3b: No indication of time

Dinner
co-work

4. Acceptable ways to enter *Movies With Friends* appointment (7:00–11:00 p.m.)

4a. Written indication of time extension past calendar to 11:00 p.m.

Movie with
friends
till 11 P.M.

(Continued)

4. Acceptable ways to enter *Movies With Friends* appointment (*cont.*)

 4b: Indication of time extension with lines

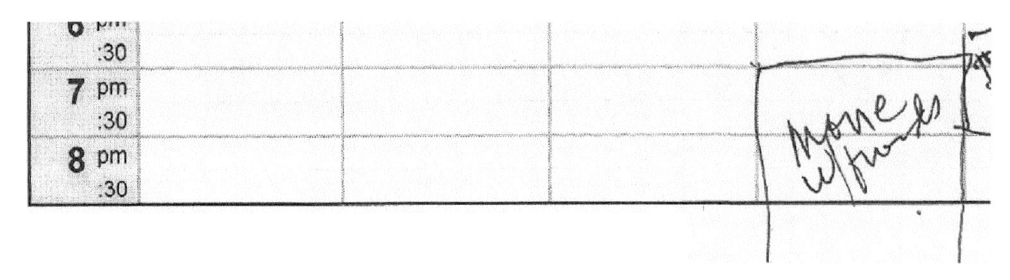

4c: Indication of time extension with arrow

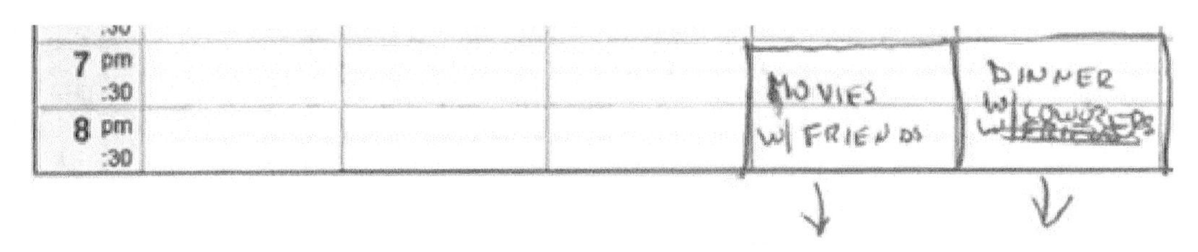

5. Unacceptable ways to enter *Movies With Friends* appointment: No indication of extending time past calendar for 7:00–11:00 p.m. appointment (time error)

:30				
7 pm				Movies
:30				with
8 pm				Friends
:30				

6. Acceptable ways to enter *Renew Prescriptions* and *Pick Up Medication* appointments

6a: Renew is scheduled before pick up (no additional time is required for renew)

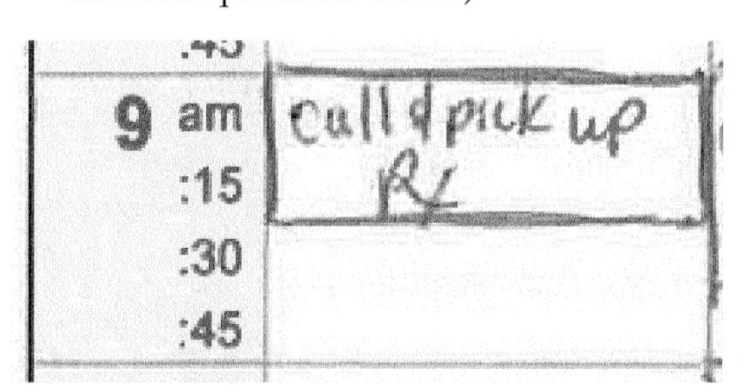

6b: No indication of time is required for renew

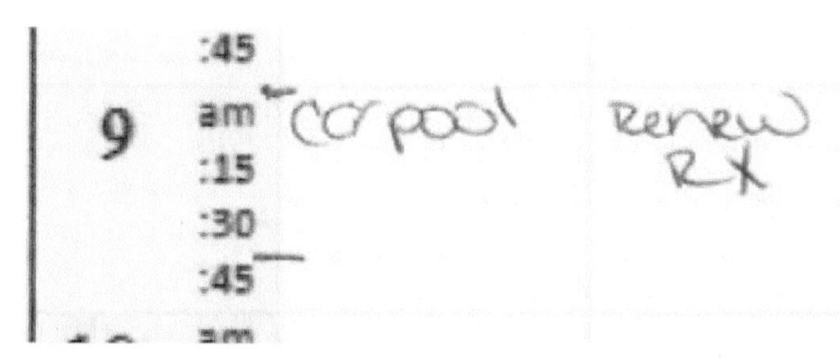

:45
9 am
:15
:30
:45
carpool
Renew
RX

(Continued)

Exhibit 3.3. Examples of Appointment Entries That Are Correct and Incorrect *(Continued)*

7. Unacceptable ways to enter *Renew Prescription* and *Pick Up Medication* appointments: Location error for Pick Up Medication because it is placed before call to renew.

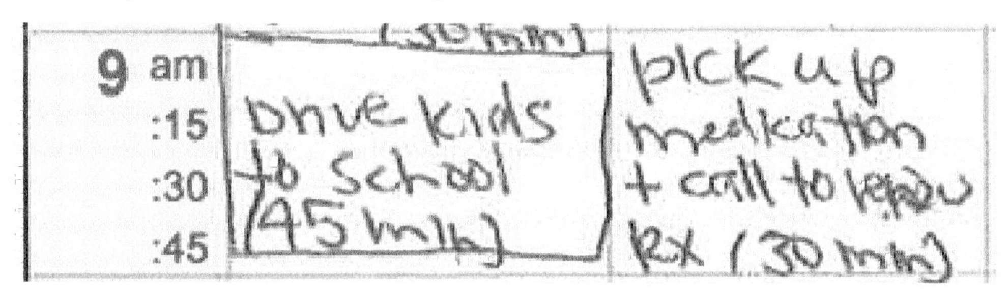

9 am
:15
:30
:45
Drive kids to School (45 min)
pick up medication + call to renew Rx (30 min)

Exhibit 3.4. Examples of Incomplete Errors

Appointments	Unacceptable (Incomplete)	Acceptable
Monday: Haircut from 11:00 a.m.–12:00 p.m.	Hair	Haircut; hairdresser's; salon; cut hair; barber
Visit with cousin	Visit (only); cousin (only)	Visit cousin; meeting with cuz
Call to renew prescription	Prescription; meds	Call drug store or prescription; get script; call in meds; new pres (but examiner needs to probe to determine meaning)
Lunch with friend	Lunch (alone); friend (alone); meet friend	Go out for lunch; lunch appt.; lunch date
Tuesday: Phone conference before 2:00 p.m. for half hour	Phone (alone); telephone or call; conference	Ph. conference; phone call
Medication picked up between 9:00 a.m. and 3:00 p.m. on or before Tues (half hour)	Meds; medicine	Drugstore; pharmacy; pharm; CVS; pick up scrip; P/U Rx; meds pick up
Thursday: Walk neighbor's dog before 11:00 a.m. (half hour)	Dog	Walk dog; walk neighbor's dog; dog sitting; walk pet
Dentist at 3:00 p.m. (1 hour)	Teeth; doctor appt.	Dentist; DDS
Movies with friends from 7:00–11:00 p.m.	Friends; out with friends	Movies; movies—friends
People to People volunteer job	People; meeting	Volunteer job; volunteer; People to People; P to P; PP
Dinner with coworkers	Coworkers; friends; dinner (alone)	Dinner—coworkers; dinner friends; dinner work; dinner reservation; dinner reser; dinner plans
Pick up dry cleaning	Pants (alone); cleaning	Pick up pants; cleaners; P/U pants
Exercise at the gym (45 min)		Gym; exercise; exerc; specific exercise (e.g., "walk for 45 mins")
Doctor—Monday or Friday afternoon at 2:00 p.m. (90 min)		MD; doctor appt.; see doctor; dx; dr.'s; doc; med appt.
Food shopping for 1 hour before Friday	Food (alone); shopping (alone)	Food shopping; food shop; shop grocery; groceries
Carpool	Car (alone); school; pool	Drive kids or pick up kids; kids school; P/U for carpool

Exhibit 3.5. Calendar Sample 1

	Mon	Tues	Wed	Thur	Fri	Sun	Sat
7 am		Phone conference		Food Shopping			Exercise at Gym
:15							
:30							
:45							
8 am					Pick up pants at cleaners		
:15							
:30		Pick up meds at pharmacy					
:45							
9 am	Carpool	Call to renew prescription		Walk neighbor's dog	Volunteer people to people		carpool
:15							
:30							
:45							
10 am							
:15							
:30							
:45							
11 am	Haircut						
:15							
:30							
:45							
12 pm							
:15							
:30							
:45							
1 pm		Lunch with a friend					
:15							
:30	Visit with cousin						
:45							
2 pm					Doctor appointment		
:15							
:30							
:45							
3 pm				Visit Dentist			
:15							
:30							
:45							
4 pm							
:15							
:30							
:45							
5 pm							
:15							
:30							
:45							
6 pm							
:30							
7 pm				movies from 7-11 with friends	Dinner with co-workers		
:30							
8 pm							
:30							

Exhibit 3.6. Sample 1: Calendar Scoring Worksheet for Quick Overall Error Scoring

Calendar Scoring Worksheet: Adult/Older Adult (Ages 18–94), Version A—Wednesday Free

Directions: Place a check mark in the Accurate column if an appointment is entered without errors and an "X" in the Missing column if an appointment is omitted. For quick scoring, place an "X" in the Error column. For detailed error scoring, use one of the following error codes to indicate which type of error was committed.

R = Appointment is repeated or entered more than once, and repetition is not an attempt to self-correct a location error
L = Appointment is placed in the wrong location, day, or time slot
T = Appointment is in the right location, but the time allotted is incorrect by more than 15 minutes (7:00 a.m.–6:00 p.m.) or 30 minutes (6:00–9:00 p.m.)
I = Appointment name is entered inaccurately or partially

Self-Recognition (SR) Column

Place a check mark in this column if the person acknowledges an appointment error or conflict verbally or nonverbally or if you observe the person trying to correct it (e.g., draw lines, cross out).

Entered	Missing	Error	Accurate	SR	Appointments
✓			✓		Mon.: Haircut from 11:00 a.m.–12:00 p.m.
✓			✓		Visit with cousin Mon. or Tues. between 1:00 and 2:00 p.m. or 1:30 and 2:30 p.m. or on Thurs. between 2:30 and 3:30 p.m. or 3:00 and 4:00 p.m.
✓			✓		Mon. any time or Tues. a.m.: Call to renew prescription
✓			✓		Tues.: Lunch with friend from 1:00–2:00 p.m.
✓			✓		Tues.: Phone conference before 2:00 p.m. (30 minutes)
✓		L			Mon. or Tues.: Medication picked up between 9:00 a.m. and 3:00 p.m. (30 minutes). Must have previously called to renew prescription.
✓			✓		Thurs.: Walk neighbor's dog before 11:00 a.m. (30 minutes)
✓			✓		Thurs.: Dentist at 3:00 p.m. (1 hour)
✓			✓		Thurs.: Movies with friends from 7:00–11:00 p.m.
✓			✓		Fri.: Volunteer job from 9:00–10:30 a.m. (90 minutes)
✓			✓		Thurs or Fri.: Dinner, coworkers, starting between 6:30 and 8:00 p.m. (2 hours)
✓			✓		Mon. or Fri.: Pick up dry cleaning between 8:00 a.m. and 4:00 p.m. (30 minutes)
✓			✓		Fri., Sat., or Sun. morning: Exercise at the gym (45 minutes)
✓			✓		Doctor: Mon. or Fri. afternoon at 2:00 p.m. (90 minutes)
✓			✓		Food shopping before Fri. (1 hour)
✓			✓		Carpool: One morning at 9:00 a.m. (45 minutes)
✓		L			Carpool: One afternoon at 3:00 p.m. (45 minutes)
17	0	2	15	0	**Total all columns** The no. of appointments in the missing + accurate + error columns should equal 17

Exhibit 3.7. Sample 1: Explanation of Scoring

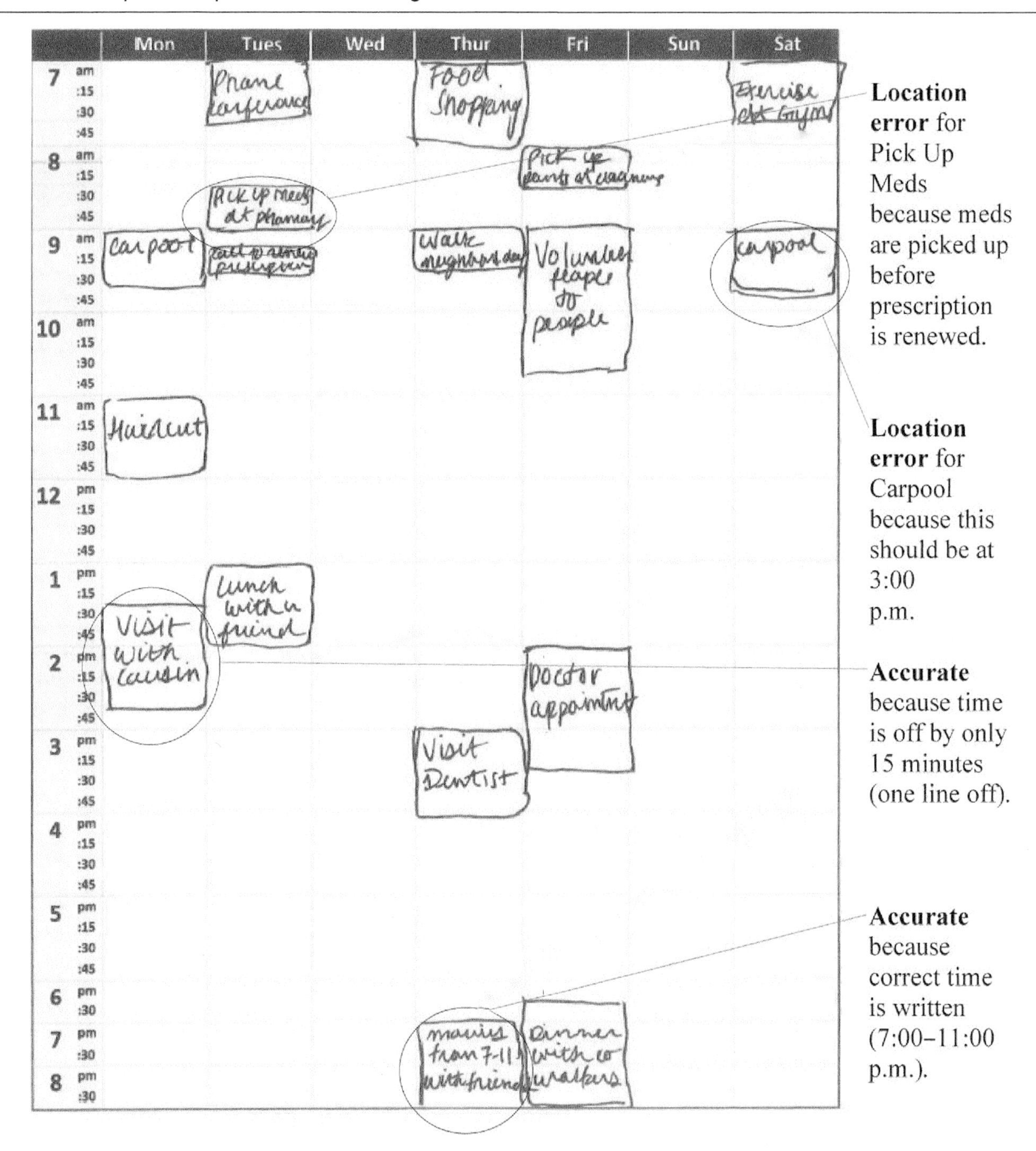

Mon
Tues
Wed
Thur
Fri
Sun
Sat
Location error for Pick Up Meds because meds are picked up before prescription is renewed.
Location error for Carpool because this should be at 3:00 p.m.
Accurate because time is off by only 15 minutes (one line off).
Accurate because correct time is written (7:00–11:00 p.m.).

Exhibit 3.8. Calendar Sample 2

	Mon	Tues	Wed	Thur	Fri	Sun	Sat
7 am							gym
:15							
:30							
:45							
8 am		call to renew pres					
:15							
:30							
:45							
9 am	Carpool	pick up prescription			People to People volunteer	~~People to People volunteer~~	
:15							
:30							
:45							
10 am		phone conference		walk neighbor's dog			
:15							
:30							
:45							
11 am	Hair cut				Dry (pants) cleaner	~~Dry cleaner~~	
:15							
:30							
:45							
12 pm				Food Shopping			
:15							
:30							
:45							
1 pm	visit w/ cousin	Lunch w/a friend					
:15							
:30							
:45							
2 pm					Dr.	~~Dr.~~	
:15							
:30							
:45							
3 pm		carpool		Dentist			
:15							
:30							
:45							
4 pm							
:15							
:30							
:45							
5 pm							
:15							
:30							
:45							
6 pm							
:30							
7 pm				movies w/friends to 11 pm	Dinner w/friends to 9pm		
:30							
8 pm							
:30							

Exhibit 3.9. Sample 2: Calendar Scoring Worksheet for Detailed Error Scoring

Calendar Scoring Worksheet Adult/Older Adult (Ages 18–94), Version A—Wednesday Free

Directions: Place a check mark in the Accurate column if an appointment is entered without errors and an "X" in the Missing column if an appointment is omitted. For quick scoring, place an "X" in the Error column. For detailed error scoring, use one of the following error codes to indicate which type of error was committed.

R = Appointment is repeated or entered more than once, and repetition is not an attempt to self-correct a location error
L = Appointment is placed in the wrong location, day, or time slot
T = Appointment is in the right location, but the time allotted is incorrect by more than 15 minutes (7:00 a.m.–6:00 p.m.) or 30 minutes (6:00–9:00 p.m.)
I = Appointment name is entered inaccurately or partially

Self-Recognition (SR) Column

Place a check mark in this column if the person acknowledges an appointment error or conflict verbally or nonverbally or if you observe the person trying to correct it (e.g., draw lines, cross out).

Entered	Missing	Error	Accurate	SR	Appointments
✓			✓		Mon.: Haircut from 11:00 a.m.–12:00 p.m.
✓			✓		Visit with cousin Mon. or Tues. between 1:00 and 2:00 p.m. or 1:30 and 2:30 p.m. or on Thurs. between 2:30 and 3:30 p.m. or 3:00 and 4:00 p.m.
✓			✓		Mon. any time or Tues. a.m.: Call to renew prescription
✓			✓		Tues.: Lunch with friend from 1:00–2:00 p.m.
✓			✓		Tues.: Phone conference before 2:00 p.m. (30 minutes)
✓			✓		Mon. or Tues.: Medication picked up between 9:00 a.m. and 3:00 p.m. (30 minutes). Must have previously called to renew prescription.
✓			✓		Thurs.: Walk neighbor's dog before 11:00 a.m. (30 minutes)
✓			✓		Thurs.: Dentist at 3:00 p.m. (1 hour)
✓			✓		Thurs.: Movies with friends from 7:00–11:00 p.m.
✓		L		✓	Fri.: Volunteer job from 9:00–10:30 a.m. (90 minutes)
✓			✓		Thurs or Fri.: Dinner, coworkers, starting between 6:30 and 8:00 p.m. (2 hours)
✓		L		✓	Mon. or Fri.: Pick up dry cleaning between 8:00 a.m. and 4:00 p.m. (30 minutes)
✓			✓		Fri., Sat., or Sun. morning: Exercise at the gym (45 minutes)
✓		L		✓	Doctor: Mon. or Fri. afternoon at 2:00 p.m. (90 minutes)
✓			✓		Food shopping before Fri. (1 hour)
✓			✓		Carpool: One morning at 9:00 a.m. (45 minutes)
✓			✓		Carpool: One afternoon at 3:00 p.m. (45 minutes)
17	**0**	**3**	**14**	**3**	**Total all columns** The no. of appointments in the missing + accurate + error columns should equal 17

Exhibit 3.10. Sample 2: Explanation of Scoring

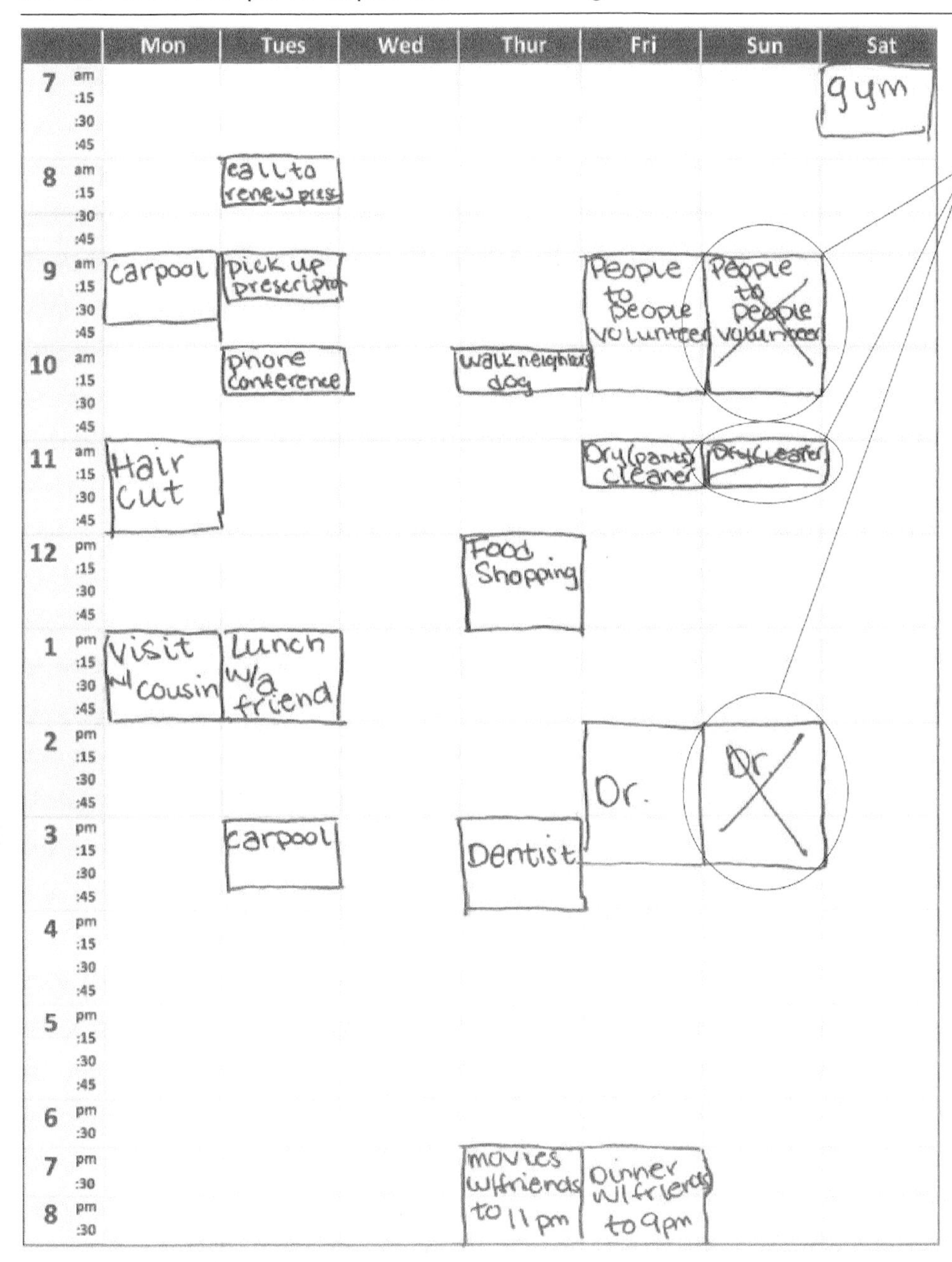

Location error because appointments are crossed out and reentered. This should also be marked as a **rule break** and **self-recognition.**

Exhibit 3.11. Calendar Sample 3

		Mon	Tues	Wed	Thur	Fri	Sun	Sat
7	am							
	:15							
	:30							
	:45							
8	am							
	:15							
	:30							
	:45							
9	am		CALL-5MIN	CARPOOL 9:-9:15	*	CAR-POOL 1HR + ½ [illegible]	WRONG	
	:15							
	:30							
	:45							
10	am	PANTS ½ HR						
	:15							
	:30				10:30- DOG ½			
	:45							
11	am	HAIR CUT 1HR	PHONE ½					GYM 45MIN
	:15							
	:30							
	:45							
12	pm				FOOD SH 1 HR			
	:15							
	:30							
	:45							
1	pm		COUSIN FRIEND LUNCH VISIT					
	:15							
	:30							
	:45							
2	pm	DR. 90 MIN						
	:15							
	:30		PICK UP MED 2:30- 3- ½ HR					
	:45							
3	pm				DENTIST 1 HR	CAR POOL-45		
	:15							
	:30							
	:45							
4	pm							
	:15							
	:30							
	:45							
5	pm							
	:15							
	:30							
	:45							
6	pm				DINNER 2 HRS.			
	:30							
7	pm							
	:30							
8	pm							
	:30							

LATE NIGHT MOVIE

Call P top

Exhibit 3.12. Sample 3: Calendar Scoring Worksheet for Detailed Error Scoring

Calendar Scoring Worksheet Adult/Older Adult (Ages 18–94), Version A—Wednesday Free

Directions: Place a check mark in the Accurate column if an appointment is entered without errors and an "X" in the Missing column if an appointment is omitted. For quick scoring, place an "X" in the Error column. For detailed error scoring, use one of the following error codes to indicate which type of error was committed.

R = Appointment is repeated or entered more than once, and repetition is not an attempt to self-correct a location error
L = Appointment is placed in the wrong location, day, or time slot
T = Appointment is in the right location, but the time allotted is incorrect by more than 15 minutes (7:00 a.m.–6:00 p.m.) or 30 minutes (6:00–9:00 p.m.)
I = Appointment name is entered inaccurately or partially

Self-Recognition (SR) Column

Place a check mark in this column if the person acknowledges an appointment error or conflict verbally or nonverbally or if you observe the person trying to correct it (e.g., draw lines, cross out).

Entered	Missing	Error	Accurate	SR	Appointments
✓			✓		Mon.: Haircut from 11:00 a.m.–12:00 p.m.
✓		L		✓	Visit with cousin Mon. or Tues. between 1:00 and 2:00 p.m. or 1:30 and 2:30 p.m. or on Thurs. between 2:30 and 3:30 p.m. or 3:00 and 4:00 p.m.
✓		I			Mon. any time or Tues. a.m.: Call to renew prescription
✓			✓		Tues.: Lunch with friend from 1:00–2:00 p.m.
✓		I			Tues.: Phone conference before 2:00 p.m. (30 minutes)
✓			✓		Mon. or Tues.: Medication picked up between 9:00 a.m. and 3:00 p.m. (30 minutes). Must have previously called to renew prescription.
✓		I			Thurs.: Walk neighbor's dog before 11:00 a.m. (30 minutes)
✓			✓		Thurs.: Dentist at 3:00 p.m. (1 hour)
✓		L		✓	Thurs.: Movies with friends from 7:00–11:00 p.m.
	✓			✓	Fri.: Volunteer job from 9:00–10:30 a.m. (90 minutes)
✓		I			Thurs or Fri.: Dinner, coworkers, starting between 6:30 and 8:00 p.m. (2 hours)
✓		I			Mon. or Fri.: Pick up dry cleaning between 8:00 a.m. and 4:00 p.m. (30 minutes)
✓			✓		Fri., Sat., or Sun. morning: Exercise at the gym (45 minutes)
✓			✓		Doctor: Mon. or Fri. afternoon at 2:00 p.m. (90 minutes)
✓			✓		Food shopping before Fri. (1 hour)
✓		L		✓	Carpool: One morning at 9:00 a.m. (45 minutes)
✓			✓		Carpool: One afternoon at 3:00 p.m. (45 minutes)
16	**1**	**8**	**8**	**4**	**Total all columns** The no. of appointments in the missing + accurate + error columns should equal 17

Exhibit 3.13 Sample 3: Explanation of Scoring

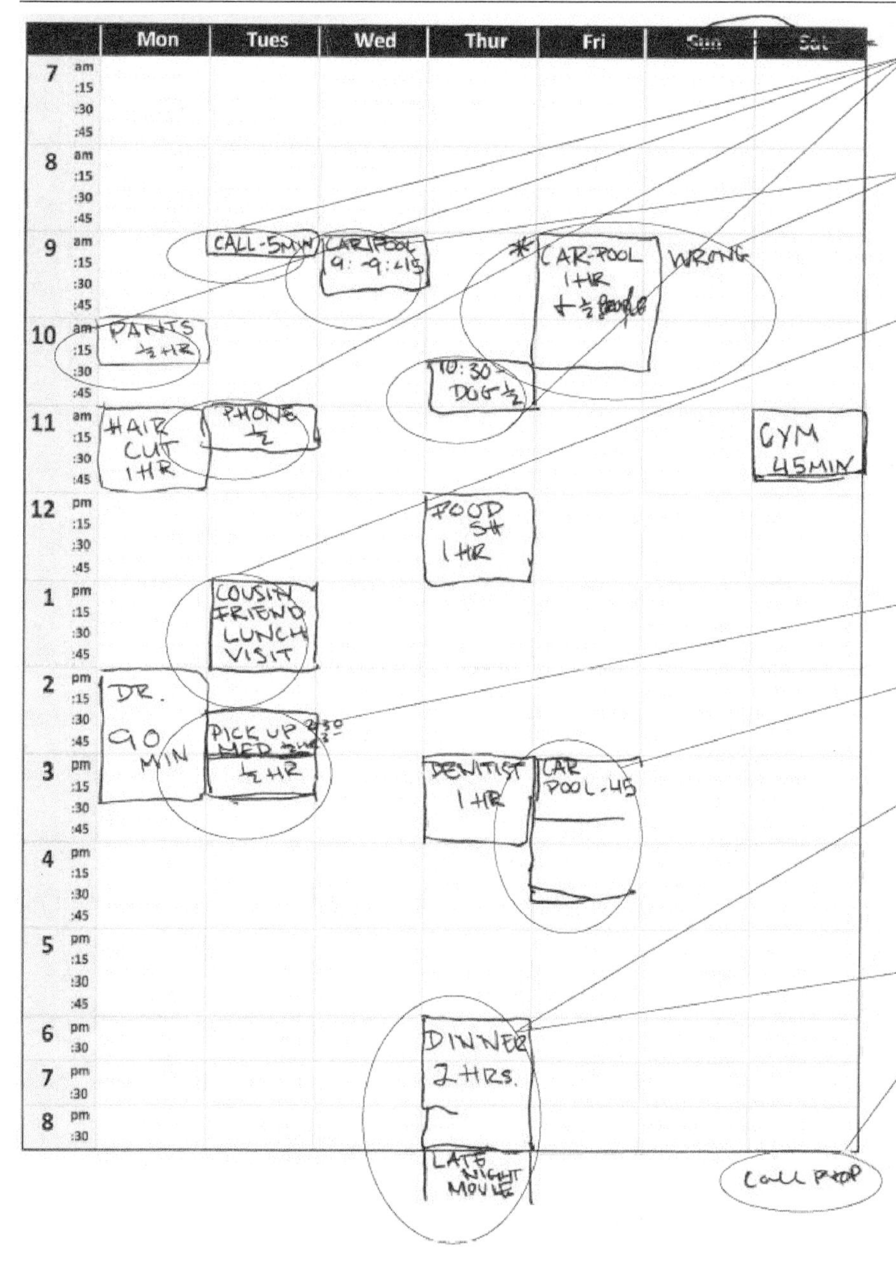

Incomplete errors because there is not enough information entered to be able to identify what the errand is

Location error person recognized error so it is also marked as **Self Recognition.** Person then entered carpool on Wednesday (free day) so this is also a **Rule Break**

Location error for Lunch with Friend and marked as **Self Recognition**. The person tried to correct themselves by putting both appointments in one slot. Give credit for one of the two appointments (Cousin Visit). **Time error** also for Cousin Visit because time marked is 30min too long (more than one gridline).

Accurate because person wrote correct time even though box is drawn incorrectly

Accurate because time is indicated correctly

Location error for Movies with Friends because it is entered starting at 9pm. **Self Recognition** should be checked since person verbalized trying to solve how to enter the appointment

Incomplete error for Dinner with Co-Workers since it does not indicate who the dinner is with

Self Recognition should be checked for Volunteer at People to People because person acknowledged this was left off the calendar

FAQ on Administering the WCPA

Q: Which level should I administer to my client?
A: Level II is recommended for most clients and has been shown to discriminate well between groups. Level III is more complex, contains extraneous material, and can be used with exceptionally high-functioning clients.

Q: What if the client completely misconstrues what the task is and, for example, puts the number of the appointment into the calendar instead of naming the appointment?
A: Stop the client and demonstrate putting an appointment into the sample calendar. If the client persists in doing it his or her way, let the client finish.

Q: What if the client has difficulty with the physical aspect of writing (e.g., because of arthritis or tremor)?
A: The test can be clinically adapted by writing appointments that the client dictates; however, the normative data were not collected in this manner.

Q: What is the purpose of the Saturday/Sunday reversal?
A: The purpose is to observe and document how the client copes with or handles the unexpected. Typically, people do not notice the error or they ignore it. Others cross out the days and write in the correct days. In clinical populations, something unexpected can affect performance because the person may become fixated on the error, even though it is insignificant. The examinee's response is simply observed but not included in scoring.

Q: What if the client asks, "How do I handle conflicts if I can't cross out?"
A: The examiner states, "Handle conflicts in the best way that you can."

FAQ on Scoring the WCPA

Q: What if the client puts 2 appointments into 1 time slot?
A: If 1 appointment is accurate, give the client credit for 1 appointment, and mark the second appointment as a location error.

Q: If there is an appointment scheduled on Wednesday or the specified free day, what type of error is it?
A: The appointment is marked as both a rule break and a location error. Although the appointment list may provide the free day as a choice, the WCPA requires the person to examine the appointment choices carefully and plan ahead because not all appointment choices are correct. Some appointment choices are at the same time as other appointments or on the "free day." A correct appointment requires adherence to the rules and recognition of conflicts.

Q: If the movie time should be 7:00–11:00 p.m. and it is boxed as being from 7:00–9:00 p.m., is that an error?
A: Yes, it should be marked as a time error. To be accurate, there needs to be some kind of indication that time extends beyond 9:00 p.m., for example, with an arrow or by labeling the box "7:00–11:00 p.m." to show the full time.

Q: What if the client enters pick up meds before calling to renew the prescription?
A: The pickup is a location error. The call to renew is considered accurate.

Q: If something is missing but verbalized, should it be considered a self-recognition?
A: Yes, the self-recognition acknowledging the mistake should be recorded.

Q: What if the client places an appointment involving school on a weekend (e.g., carpool to school or walk sibling to school)?
A: The appointment is correct. School appointments are not confined to weekdays.

Q: If a written appointment extends past the allotted time, but the correct time has been indicated, is the appointment still considered correct or would it be a time error?
A: The appointment is correct. As long as the correct time is specified with a box, line, or arrow, or in writing, word overflow does not matter.

Q: If an appointment is in the correct time slot but the client does not box in the appointment according to the correct time, is it still considered correct?
A: Yes. This is also illustrated in the appointment entry samples. If the appointment is 45 minutes or 1 hour and placed in the middle of the correct hour box, it is considered correct. If the correct time frame is written, it is also considered correct.

Q: A client enters an appointment on the right day but in the wrong time slot. Is this a time error or a location error?
A: It is a location error. For a time error, the appointment is placed in the correct day and time slot, but the actual time allotted is too short or too long. For a location error, the amount of time allotted may be correct (for example, 1 hour), but the appointment placement is incorrect. If an appointment time allotment or placement is only off by only 1 calendar gridline (15 minutes for appointments between 7:00 a.m. and 6:00 p.m. and 30 minutes for appointments from 6:00 p.m.–9:00 p.m.), it is still considered correct.

Q: What if a client enters an appointment in the wrong location but then draws an arrow to the correct location?
A: It is a location error, but the SR (self-recognition) column is checked to indicate that the person recognized their errors.

Q: If a person places "Renew prescription" in the same time slot as a different appointment, is this an error?
A: No, it is not an error. No additional time is required for renewing prescription so both appointments are correct. This is also illustrated in samples of appointment entries.

Summary

This chapter focused on scoring the accuracy of appointment entries as well as procedures for obtaining an efficiency score. Efficiency scoring and appointment accuracy is typically examined after test administration. Appointment errors can be coded or analyzed according to the type of error or can be generally identified (without coding error type) for quicker scoring. Detailed analysis of error type may provide additional information that is helpful in treatment planning (described further in Chapter 4, "Interpretation").

Several examples of scoring or determining accuracy of appointments were provided. Therapists should review these examples and the frequently asked questions carefully. This section should be referred to whenever there are questions about scoring the accuracy of appointments.

CHAPTER 4 Interpretation

Interpretation of the WCPA involves analysis of patterns of performance across quantitative scores, qualitative observations, and responses to the After-Task Interview and Rating Scale. Performance on a complex task such as the WCPA can be affected in many ways, which are described in this chapter for each area of the WCPA.

In addition to objective scores, observations, and responses to the after-task interview, results must be considered in the context of the client's prior functioning, personality, culture, and experience. The WCPA is one component of assessment. Results need to be considered and analyzed along with other occupational therapy assessments that examine performance skills, performance patterns, and areas of occupation.

Objective Scores and Normative Comparison

WCPA scores include the number of appointments entered or omitted, accuracy of entered appointments or total number of errors, number of rules adhered to, number of strategies used, planning time, total time required, and efficiency score. A detailed analysis of error types provides additional insight into the nature of performance difficulties.

Normative Comparisons

Comparing the client's scores with those of typical healthy people provides an indication of the extent or degree of performance difficulties. WCPA scores can be compared with a normative sample ages 16 to 94 by examining both means and standard deviations for selected scores or by converting all scores to percentile to aid in interpretation. Percentiles quickly provide an indication of how common or uncommon a score is in the normative sample (Crawford, Garthwaite, & Slick, 2009). Appendix G provides tables for each age group that can be used to convert Level II and Level III scores to percentiles and used to quickly look at average or mean scores. Percentiles provide the most meaningful interpretation for the majority of scores because some scores (rule following and strategy) are ordinal, while other scores (planning time, efficiency, and entered appointments) had score distributions that were skewed or non-normal.

When using these conversion tables, the examiner should first locate the appropriate WCPA level (II or III) and the client's age group. The examiner would then locate each raw score in the vertical columns of the table (number of appointments entered, accuracy, rules followed, number of strategies, planning time, total time, and efficiency score) and read across the row horizontally to find the corresponding percentile in the left-hand column. If the client's exact time or efficiency score is not listed within the table, the examiner chooses the closest score or rounds up to the higher percentile rank. The bottom rows of the tables also include the means, standard deviations, medians, and score ranges for the normative sample.

Interpretation of Percentiles

Percentiles indicate the percentage of scores that occur at or below a particular score. The 50th percentile represents the median or precisely the middle of the score distribution. For example, an accuracy score of 13 in the younger age group is at the 30th percentile (low average), indicating that this score is equal to or greater than 30% of the sample. Another way of interpreting this score is to state that 70% of the normative sample had a score of 13 or more. Similarly, a person with an accuracy score of 16 at the 80th percentile indicates that this score is equal to or better than 80% of the sample.

Several scores, particularly appointments entered and rules followed, have a limited number of items or spread, so the same score values fall across a percentile range. For example, for youth, a score of 4 for the number of rules followed falls between the 20th and 50th percentiles. The lower limit of the percentile range is used to indicate the percentage of scores that fall below this point, while the upper limit indicates the number of scores that are at or below this level. In this example, 20% of the sample scored below a score of 4, whereas 50% of the sample had a score equal to 4 or below. Typically, the upper limit of the percentile range is used in evaluation reports. The upper limit of the score's percentile range also can be used to identify the percentage of scores that score higher than the designated score. For example, if a score of 17 is within a 20th to 40th percentile range, approximately 60% would fall above a score of 17.

Percentiles are calculated assuming high scores represent better performance than lower scores. Because this is not true for time and efficiency scores, a correction was applied by subtracting the percentiles from 100 so they could be interpreted similarly to other scores (Baumgartner, 2009). With this correction, a 42-year-old client requiring 35 minutes to complete the WCPA would be below the 2nd percentile, indicating that his or her total time exceeds or is slower than more than 98% of the population (98% of the sample required less time). Alternatively, a time of 12 minutes falls at the 60th percentile, indicating that this time is faster than that of 60% of the sample (or that 60% required more time).

In some instances, extremely high percentiles do not represent better performance. This is particularly the case for strategies and time. An excessively high number of strategies may contribute to inefficient performance. Similarly, a planning or total time that is too fast or above the 90th percentile is not necessarily better and could suggest that the person rushed through the task (as described in "Total Time and Efficiency Score"). For these reasons, individual scores should not be looked at in isolation. Interpretation requires analysis of performance across WCPA scores.

Table 4.1 offers some general classification of or descriptions for interpretation of percentile ranges. Scores near the extremes of the average range can be classified as low average (25th percentile) or high average (75th percentile).

Mean Scores

In addition to percentiles, the tables in Appendix G provide means, standard deviations, medians, and score ranges in the healthy population for reference. While percentiles provide a quick and simple interpretation of performance and are most appropriate for the majority of scores, means and standard deviations also can be used for normative comparison for accuracy scores and total time.

Table 4.1. Classifications of WCPA Percentile Ranges

Percentile Range	Description
76–99	Above average
25–75	Average
10–24	Low: Below average
<10	Very low: Significantly below average

Note. WCPA = Weekly Calendar Planning Activity.

To interpret means and standard deviations, keep in mind that scores within 1 standard deviation of the mean represent 68% of the sample, or average performance, and those that fall within 2 standard deviations of the mean represent 95% of the sample. Typically, performance that is more than 1.5 standard deviations below the mean represents a significant deviation from expected performance and is observed in less than 10% of the sample (Larsen, Berglund, Joseph, & Pratt, 2011). Scores that are 2 standard deviations or more below the mean provide more conservative criteria for atypical performance because they represent only 2.5% of the population.

As an example, if the mean is 14 and one standard deviation is 2, then 68% of the scores fall between 12 and 16, representing average performance ($14 - 2 = 12$ and $14 + 2 = 16$); 82% of the scores are within 1.5 standard deviations ($2 + 1 = 3$) of the mean, or between 11 and 17; and 95% of the scores fall within 2 standard deviations of the mean, or between 10 and 18. Scores of 10 or 9 are 1.5 and 2 standard deviations below the mean respectively, and are significantly below typical performance. Chapter 5, "Research and Normative Studies," provides additional information on the normative group that can be used for comparison, including more detailed information on error types and additional information on the older age group.

Summarizing WCPA Scores

WCPA objective scores can be summarized in different ways, using tables and charts. Options include a quick summary of raw scores, normative comparison of scores, a performance profile, and an error analysis profile. This section contains examples of these different

Table 4.2. WCPA Quick Summary of Raw Scores

<table>
<tr><th></th><th>Entered Appointment</th><th>Accurate Appointment</th><th>Rules Followed</th><th>Strategy Use</th><th>Awareness</th><th>Total Time</th><th>Planning Time</th><th>Efficiency</th></tr>
<tr><td>High Performance</td><td>16–17</td><td>16–17</td><td>5</td><td>7+</td><td rowspan="2">Aware</td><td><6 min</td><td><10 sec</td><td><40</td></tr>
<tr><td></td><td>14–15</td><td>14–15</td><td></td><td>6</td><td>7–9 min</td><td>10–59 sec</td><td>41–90</td></tr>
<tr><td></td><td>12–13</td><td>12–13</td><td></td><td>6</td><td rowspan="2">Some awareness</td><td>10–15 min</td><td>1 min</td><td>91–125</td></tr>
<tr><td></td><td>10–11</td><td>10–11</td><td>4</td><td>4</td><td>16–20 min</td><td>2 min</td><td>126–150</td></tr>
<tr><td></td><td>8–9</td><td>8–9</td><td>3</td><td>3</td><td rowspan="2">Slight awareness</td><td>21–25 min</td><td>3 min</td><td>151–200</td></tr>
<tr><td></td><td>6–7</td><td>6–7</td><td>2</td><td>2</td><td>26–30 min</td><td>4 min</td><td>201–250</td></tr>
<tr><td></td><td>4–5</td><td>4–5</td><td>1</td><td>1</td><td>No awareness</td><td>31–40 min</td><td>5 min</td><td>251–300</td></tr>
<tr><td>Low Performance</td><td><4</td><td><4</td><td>0</td><td>0</td><td></td><td>40+ min</td><td>6+ min</td><td>300+</td></tr>
</table>

Note. WCPA = Weekly Calendar Planning Activity; min = minutes; sec = seconds.

options for organizing results. The tables and charts are also included in summary worksheets and are integrated into assessment report templates (Appendix F).

Quick Summary of Raw Scores

Table 4.2 provides a quick method to broadly summarize key raw scores. The examiner circles the raw scores in each column that correspond to the client's performance. The Awareness column is based on the examiner's overall judgment of awareness on the basis of responses to the After-Task Interview and Rating Scale (Appendix E.7). This table does not compare scores with the normative sample. It provides a general and quick visual representation of strengths and weaknesses across different areas of WCPA performance for the busy clinician. It can be useful as a screen in some situations; unusually low or high scores can be meaningfully interpreted for purposes of treatment planning without normative comparison. More complete interpretation, however, requires comparison with the normative sample.

Normative Comparison of Scores

Table 4.3 provides a summary of WCPA scores in comparison to the normative sample. Raw WCPA scores are entered in the Score column and converted to percentile rank in the Percentile column. This allows one to view scores against average performance and identify the extent of performance deficits.

Table 4.3 has been completed for a person age 42 for Level II. The table indicates that the number of appointments entered into the calendar and overall time required for completion are just within the average range; however, accuracy, performance efficiency, and ability to adhere to rules are significantly below expected performance. Total strategies used is also below average. The majority of errors were those of location and detail, suggesting that although the person was able to generally handle the number of items on the list, he or she may have had difficulty managing details. Although the type of errors can be compared with average performance using information presented in Chapter 5, "Research and Normative Studies," it is typically not necessary to do so.

WCPA Visual Performance Profile

The WCPA Visual Performance Profile provides a detailed analysis and visual profile of WCPA results. Scores are recorded as percentiles so that the extent to which performance deviates from average performance can be quickly identified. An "X" or a score (or both) corresponding to the percentile is placed in each column of the profile. The 50th percentile row, indicating precisely average performance, is shaded. Higher percentiles reflect higher levels of performance. The performance profile can be used in conjunction with the normative comparison table because they may both be helpful in summarizing results.

Table 4.3. WCPA Normative Comparison

WCPA Scores	Score	Percentile	Comments
Planning time __min __sec	60 sec	50th	Average
Total time: __min __sec	18 min	20th	Low average
No. of rules followed (0–5)	1	<5th	Very low
Total strategies X Partially used __ Consistently used	2	10th	Below average
No. of appointments entered	16/17	30th	Low average
No. of accurate appointments	10/16	5th	Very low
Efficiency score (total seconds/weighted score)	183	<5th	Very low
Error analysis		No percentiles available for these individual error types.	
Appointments missing	1		
Location errors	3		
Time errors	2		
Repetition errors	0		
Incomplete	0		
Total no. of errors	6		
Self-recognition of errors	3		50% of errors made were recognized.

Note. WCPA = Weekly Calendar Planning Activity; min = minutes; sec = seconds.

Table 4.4 shows that a person, age 45, entered 15 of 17 appointments, scoring at the 20th percentile (indicating that 80% of those in this age group entered more appointments), and the appointments that were entered were generally accurate (50th percentile). The ability to adhere to rules and use strategies was also average. Efficiency, planning time, and total time required, however, were less than the 5th percentile, indicating that performance was slower and less efficient than more than 95% of the sample. In this case, the level of accuracy achieved was at the expense of increased time.

Error Analysis Profile

The Error Analysis Profile can be used to provide a quick visual representation of the frequency, number, and pattern of errors. The examiner places an "X" in each column

Table 4.4. Sample WCPA Visual Performance Profile

Percentile	Entered Appointment	Accurate Appointment	Rules Followed	Strategy Use	Efficiency	Planning Time	Total Time	Percentile
≥95								≥95
>75								>75
70								70
60								60
50		X(14)	X(4)					50
40								40
30								30
25				X (3)				25
20	X (15)							20
10								10
<5					X (183)	X (10 min)	X (35 min)	<5

Note. WCPA = Weekly Calendar Planning Activity; min = minutes.

Table 4.5. Error Analysis Profile

	Missing	Repetition	Incomplete	Location	Time	Extraneous	Self-Recognition
0		X		X	X		
1						None	
2	X		X				X
3+							

corresponding to the number of errors listed in the left-hand column. The Extraneous column is included so the examiner can comment on the inclusion of any additional irrelevant or extraneous information. The Self-Recognition column is shaded because in that column a higher score indicates that more errors were recognized, whereas in the other columns, a higher number indicates poorer performance or a greater number of errors.

Table 4.5 indicates that the client had 4 errors: 2 missing appointments and 2 appointments that were incompletely entered. Half of the errors were self-recognized. This pattern suggests that errors of omission, including a tendency to include partial information or miss information or steps, may be influencing performance.

After-Task Interview and Rating Scale: Summarizing Self-Ratings (Optional)

A table can be used to summarize the client's self-ratings of performance. This section is optional. In Table 4.6, the column on the left corresponds to Questions 5, 6, and 7 from the After-Task Interview.

The Self-Rating row corresponds to Question 5 on the After-Task Interview and Rating Scale form. The examiner can include either the total or the average ratings of the examiner or client (separately) and calculate the difference between them as described in Chapter 2, "Administration."

Time estimation corresponds to Question 6 on the After-Task Interview and Rating Scale form. The examiner indicates the total time (in minutes) that the client actually took and the time the client estimated he or she spent on the task to provide a general indication of time awareness.

Accuracy estimation corresponds to Question 7 on the After-Task and Interview and Rating Scale form (Appendix E.7). The actual accuracy score is entered in the first column and the client's estimation of the number of accurate appointments is entered in the second column. A client rating that is better than actual performance or therapist rating by greater than 3 items suggests an overestimation of abilities or decreased awareness of performance. A client rating that is worse than actual performance or therapist rating by greater than 3 items suggests an underestimation of abilities or lack of self-confidence. These are general guidelines based on clinical experience, as discrepancy between self-rating, time, and accuracy estimates was not examined in the normative sample.

In Table 4.6, the client's self-rating score of 4 indicates that he or she rated each of the 4 statements as 1 and perceived the task as easy. The examiner's rating of 10 indicates that the examiner rated the client as having some difficulties. The third column indicates that the discrepancy is 6, indicating that the client overestimated his or her abilities.

In the area of time estimation, the client estimated he or she required 10 minutes, whereas the client actually took 30 minutes, which suggests that time awareness should be carefully examined in other activities or situations to determine whether time awareness is impaired. In the area of accuracy estimation, the client estimated he or she entered 16 accurate appointments when only 9 were actually entered accurately. This represents a large overestimation of abilities and suggests that the client may be unaware of the extent of the performance difficulties.

The tables and charts presented here can be integrated into evaluation reports; however, interpretation of WCPA scores provides only a small piece of the picture. Full interpretation of WCPA performance includes understanding and analyzing the factors influencing performance. The next section provides critical information that is required for complete interpretation of WCPA performance.

Table 4.6. Awareness or Client Perception of Task Difficulty

	Therapist or Actual	Client	Difference	Comments
Self-rating	10	4	6	Overestimation
Time estimation	30 min	10 min	20 min	Poor time awareness
Accuracy estimation	9	16	7	Overestimation

Note. min = minutes.

Interpretation: Performance Analysis and Implications for Treatment

In addition to quantitative scores, the WCPA provides important information on how a client copes with and performs a cognitively challenging task, including the strategies used, types and patterns of performance errors, and the client's self-awareness and self-monitoring skills. This information is particularly relevant for treatment planning.

Because intervention focuses on reducing the effect of performance errors on everyday activities, it is important to understand the frequency and patterns of errors that are occurring. Analysis of errors in a complex activity is important because similar error patterns (e.g., detail-related errors, omissions, repetitions) often interfere with performance in other activities. Different types of performance patterns may also indicate the need for different strategies; thus, the analysis of strategies and the process of how a client goes about an activity is a key aspect of the WCPA.

Interpretation of the WCPA for the purposes of treatment planning requires careful consideration of a combination of both scores and observations. In general, people without cognitive impairments performed the task accurately and efficiently and quickly recognized that some appointments were fixed and others were variable. They typically entered fixed appointments first and then went back and entered variable appointments. People who started at the top of the page and proceeded in order down the page quickly adjusted or changed their approach as they recognized potential conflicts. Common strategies included putting a line through the day on which no appointments were to be scheduled, and checking or crossing off appointments as they were entered. The majority of people maintained and followed all rules without having to refer back to the instruction sheet. In clinical populations, a wide range of performance difficulties were observed.

Considerations for interpretation of results include planning time, time efficiency, following rules, appointments entered and omitted, number of accurate appointments, error type, and after-task interview and self-ratings. This section describes these considerations in each area of the WCPA and analysis of performance patterns across different areas. The same scores can have different implications for treatment depending on self-awareness, self-monitoring skills, and strategy use. The use of the WCPA for intervention planning is also described. Chapter 6, "Dynamic Assessment," also provides additional methods for connecting assessment results to treatment.

Planning Time

The results of initial planning time need to be looked at in the context of how a client proceeds through the task and uses strategies. Many healthy people initially jumped into the activity, but as they started to do the task they recognized potential conflicts and adjusted their performance (e.g., they paused, stopped, reread the list). Initial planning time is, therefore, not as important as the ability to adjust performance in the middle of an activity or to pause and plan when challenges are recognized. The use of two planning times as described in Chapter 2's discussion of the Recording Form may possibly provide a better measure of planning abilities.

It is not surprising, therefore, that initial planning time on the WCPA was unrelated to performance accuracy in healthy adolescents or adults during normative studies. If limited planning time is part of a pattern of impulsive responses and actions observed throughout the activity, however, then it is interpreted differently. For example, if a client shows a planning time of less than 1 minute and also completes the activity quickly, without recognizing conflicts, attending to details, following rules (answers questions, crosses appointments out), or using strategies, it can reflect a pattern of impulsivity or general difficulty in self-regulating performance. Thus, planning time cannot be interpreted in isolation.

Planning time also needs to be considered in the context of a client's cognitive style, personality, experience, and culture. In geographical locations such as large urban cities (e.g., New York City), people are frequently in a hurry, are often under time constraints, and tend to be impatient. It may be more common to observe a tendency to jump into an activity without planning in a large urban city than in a rural area or different culture, depending on living environment, work styles, and social norms.

It is important to understand how the client or others describe the client's work style and personality. A lack of planning time observed in a client who is described as being reflective and thoughtful and as always taking time to review and plan activities indicates a change that may be detrimental to performance.

However, if the client is the type of person who always likes to get things done quickly, the tendency to jump into a task may represent his or her usual task approach. This style, however, requires the ability to think on one's feet and quickly adjust performance at the moment that challenges are encountered. After a brain injury or illness, information may be processed differently, and a client may have difficulty quickly adjusting performance. A client's previous style of jumping into a task may therefore no longer be efficient or effective. In this situation, intervention may involve helping a client let go of previous task approaches and adopt a new, slower, and more methodical method.

Total Time and Efficiency Score

The amount of time a client takes to complete the entire task needs to be looked at in combination with the number of accurate appointments. If the total time is 8 minutes or less for Level II and 12 minutes or less for Level III, it suggests that the person may have rushed through the task. Faster time does not necessarily represent better performance, particularly if speed is associated with errors. Examining both time and accuracy together provides an indication of efficiency (efficiency score = total time [in seconds]/weighted accuracy score). Four combinations of efficiency and accuracy can be observed:

1. *High accuracy and high time:* The client may be accurate but slow. Increased time raises the efficiency score, indicating inefficient performance. The client may require twice as much time as others to achieve an accurate score.
2. *High accuracy and low time:* This pattern represents highly efficient performance. The efficiency score will be low.
3. *Low accuracy and high time:* This pattern represents inefficient performance. If the client's accuracy score is very low or 1.5 standard deviations or more below the mean, then the efficiency score is not meaningful.
4. *Low accuracy and low time*: If accuracy is lower than or equal to 7 and time is 500 seconds or less, then the efficiency score is not meaningful. For example, a client may complete the task in 3 to 4 minutes but enter only 6 of the appointments. In this situation, the efficiency score is not meaningful.

In some situations, observation of the patterns just described provides an immediate indication of performance efficiency (e.g., low accuracy and high time), so an objective efficiency score is not always needed for interpretation. In other situations, however, an objective measure of efficiency and comparison with a normative sample is helpful in identifying and defining the level of performance efficiency. Appendix G provides average efficiency scores and percentiles for healthy adults across the three age groups. Higher efficiency is reflected by lower scores (less time to achieve greater accuracy), and low efficiency is reflected by higher scores (more time to achieve accuracy).

Two people can have the same accuracy score but demonstrate different levels of efficiency. For example, Client A and Client B, both age 42, entered 16 accurate appointments, but Client A completed the task in 42 minutes and has an efficiency score of 168 (below the 5th percentile, indicating that at least 95% of people in this age group were more efficient). Client B completed the task in 8 minutes and has an efficiency score of 32 (above the 90th percentile), indicating that Client B was faster and more accurate than

90% of other people in this age group, reflecting highly efficient performance. Client A was accurate, but at the expense of time. Low efficiency can affect people's ability to complete everything that they need to do and suggests difficulty with tasks that have limited time frames. Although Client A was accurate, the efficiency score suggests that performance may be inadequate to meet work expectations or life demands. Intervention strategies to improve efficiency may be needed to increase overall function and participation.

In addition to the efficiency score itself, it is important to observe how the client uses his or her time. Some people spend an excessive amount of time planning, and others jump right into the activity but then get distracted by irrelevant aspects of the calendar or begin talking about thoughts triggered by the list of appointments. Others become stuck and do not know what to do when they notice that Saturday and Sunday are reversed or that the calendar's evening time ends earlier than the appointment, and others demonstrate generally slowed information processing.

Following Rules

The WCPA has 5 rules that a client is told to follow. The rules are written and placed on the table so that the client can refer to them at any time. It is important that the examiner look at which rules the client had difficulty following to identify any patterns. Several rules require the ability to inhibit impulses or actions such as not answering questions, not crossing out appointments, or not scheduling appointments on a particular day. People who are impulsive will likely have difficulty adhering to these rules.

The rules to not cross out appointments and to leave a specified day free were designed to promote planning and to discourage a trial-and-error approach. In clinical populations, it is not uncommon to observe people ignoring the rules and proceeding with a trial-and-error approach, crossing out appointments all over the page and entering appointments on the specified free day.

During normative studies, some people placed an appointment in the wrong location but immediately self-recognized their errors. In an attempt to correct their mistakes, some drew arrows to the correct location to avoid breaking a rule (crossing out). After self-recognizing their error, they were observed to adjust their pace of performance and proceed more cautiously. In clinical populations, people who self-recognize an error may become stuck and not know what to do because they cannot cross out. Some people restated the rule but crossed out the appointment anyway because they could not generate alternative methods and did not know how else to proceed.

The 3 extraneous questions require the ability to remain goal-focused while ignoring distractions. These questions also interrupt activity flow, so it is important to observe how the client handles the interruption and resumes or continues with the activity. During the normative studies, the majority of healthy adults (78%) ignored all questions; 11% responded to 1 question, but nearly all immediately self-recognized their error. Although a rule is considered broken if any of the questions are answered, the examiner should look at the number of questions that are ignored or responded to.

Some people with neurological impairments not only answered all 3 questions but expanded on the answers and then had difficulty returning to the activity or remembering where they left off. For example, one client with acquired brain injury began telling a story about his pets. When he returned to the calendar, he reentered several appointments because he had lost track of where he left off. The tendency to become easily sidetracked with irrelevant information can have an impact on performance across everyday activities and is an important area to address in treatment.

Two rules (stating the time after a designated length of time and stating when finished) involve *prospective memory,* or the ability to monitor time and keep track of future intentions. If the designated time is not stated, it suggests that memory or the ability to keep track of information may be limited, whereas if the time is stated too late, it suggests that failure to monitor the passage of time, rather than recall, may be contributing to prospective memory failure. Difficulties suggest that prospective memory should be further examined in other activities.

In general, the rules increase the amount of information the client has to keep track of and create a multitasking effect. The client has to keep the rules in mind while simultaneously engaging in the activity.

Although the rules are written, many clients do not refer back to the instruction sheet. As they become engaged in the task, they seem to forget entirely about the rules, indicating difficulty in keeping all aspects of a task or situation in mind.

Appointments Entered and Omissions

The number of appointments entered, regardless of whether they are entered completely or in the correct time and location, provides a general indication of the ability to attend to items on the list. Discrepancies between entered and accurate appointments should be noted. Some people enter a limited number of appointments but enter them all accurately. Others enter all appointments, but fewer than half are accurate, suggesting that they were able to follow and use the list but had difficulty with completeness, details, or handling conflicts.

Scores involving the number of entered appointments and the number of missing appointments overlap. The examiner needs to look at only one of these scores because appointments that are not entered are counted as missing or omission errors. On average, most healthy people did not have missing appointments. Those who did omitted only 1 or 2 appointments. The majority of people entered at least 16 or all 17 appointments. A median of 17 for the younger and middle age groups indicates that at least half of the participants did not have any missing appointments; however, half of the older group (ages 65 or older) was missing 1 appointment (median = 16).

A larger number of missing appointments suggests that the client has difficulty using the list and attending to or handling the number of items presented simultaneously. The number of items on the list (17 or 18) may be above the client's processing capacity. The examiner could consider administering the 10-item WCPA to determine whether fewer items improves performance. In general, a large number of missing appointments suggests that treatment activities may be most effective with a shorter list or fewer items or steps.

In addition to decreasing the number of items, another approach to treatment involves helping the client self-recognize that the number of items presented at once may be too many. The client is then guided in generating and using task simplification strategies or figuring out ways to modify the activity and reduce the number of items (e.g., stimuli reduction methods, such as covering half the items presented to them or using more effective strategies to manage a list, such as crossing out or checking off items as they are entered).

Number of Accurate Appointments

Accuracy, or the number of appointments that were correctly entered and placed in the right time slot and location, is usually interpreted in comparison to the normative sample. However, the examiner needs to understand how or why performance errors occurred. Accuracy needs to be analyzed along with the time required to complete the task (efficiency) and the strategies and task methods used. Examination of the types of performance errors made provides insight into underlying performance difficulties and provides a foundation for treatment planning.

Error Types

Analysis of errors involves determining whether one type of error predominates, for example, missing appointments versus repetitions versus time and location. Error patterns observed on the WCPA should also be examined across different cognitive IADLs. If similar errors are observed across more than one task, intervention should focus on helping the client anticipate, recognize, and monitor the targeted performance error during the task.

For example, if the client has a tendency to miss or leave out key details and steps, activities that help the client monitor and recognize omissions could be emphasized. Disorganized, haphazard, or impulsive approaches to activities typically result in a combination of different error types. In these situations, treatment may focus on pacing the speed of actions or responses, monitoring the tendency to go too quickly, or taking the time to create an organized plan. Effective self-monitoring requires the ability to assess task demands and identify potential challenges.

Repetition

Entering an appointment into the calendar more than once may be related to perseveration, or an inability to shift from one appointment to the next. Decreased cognitive flexibility may be observed along with difficulty accommodating, adjusting to, or coping with unexpected aspects of the task such as the Saturday/ Sunday reversal, an appointment that extends past the calendar time, or the switch from 15-minute to half-hour time slots at the end of the calendar. The client may become stuck or sidetracked by the calendar errors and not know how to proceed. Healthy people either ignored the errors completely or easily adapted to them. Subtle difficulties in shifting may also be identified by a tendency to continue to place appointments on the same day rather than shifting to other days. Repetition can also reflect an inability to keep track of which appointments were already entered (decreased working memory).

The client's awareness of a repeated error is important to observe. On some occasions, the repetition may be an obvious attempt to self-correct an appointment placed in the wrong location. For example, if the client recognizes that the appointment is in the wrong location, he or she may rewrite the appointment in the correct slot, and announce that he or she is correcting the location error. In this case, the repetition is actually an adaptive strategy and is therefore not coded as a repetition error (it is coded as a location error).

Location and time errors

Entering an appointment into a weekly calendar requires mentally holding onto the name of the appointment as well as the time and day of the appointment. Some clients have difficulty simultaneously holding onto all 3 pieces of information. Once they look away from the list or paragraph, they forget some of the information. For example, they may remember the appointment name but not the day and time. Time and location errors may also represent difficulty in attending to detail or an impulsive approach. Correct time entry requires greater attention to detail than does location; however, both types of error often occur together. In some situations, a greater number of location errors (difficulty placing appointments) can suggest visual–spatial or perceptual difficulties.

Incomplete entries

In some cases, an appointment is not entered completely, which may represent a tendency to quickly attend to only part of the appointment and miss key information or details. It could also reflect a tendency to overfocus on pieces of information or details without recognizing the context or whole. For example, the client may write *pants* in the calendar without including that the pants need to be picked up from the dry cleaner. The client may have just focused on the pants without recognizing that picking them up from the dry cleaner was important information. Partial or inaccurate entries may also represent a failure to simultaneously keep multiple aspects of an appointment in mind.

Extraneous appointments

Some clinical populations enter extraneous information or personal appointments that are not on the appointment list. For example, during the activity, some people gradually stopped looking at the appointment list and entered their own appointments. This reflects *goal neglect*, a common manifestation of executive dysfunction (Levine et al., 2011). As the person is engaged in an activity, the goal of the activity fades away and is not maintained. This has been hypothesized to be related to limitations in cognitive resources or working memory. In some cases, the calendar's familiarity triggers an automatic response of writing one's own appointments, and the list is ignored, even though the person can accurately repeat the directions. In other words, environmental stimuli (e.g., the calendar) elicit familiar actions or responses, and the person is unable to use higher-order executive skills to inhibit his or her automatic responses and adhere to the task goals. This has been described as *environment-dependent behavior,* another common symptom of executive dysfunction (Besnard et al., 2011).

Finally, the client may write personal appointments into the weekly schedule because he or she has difficulty understanding or conceptualizing that the task is simulated as a result of limited abstraction abilities or concrete thinking. The client may narrowly focus on one component or aspect of the activity (weekly schedule) and misinterpret the overall goal even though the directions are in front of him or her. Problem solving and coping with new or unfamiliar situations requires the ability to view a situation or task from different perspectives and think flexibly or imagine "what if." This ability is also important in social relationships, in which the capacity to view situations from another person's perspective is important (Toglia, 2011). The responses just described are atypical and were not observed in healthy adolescents or older adults during normative studies.

Self-Monitoring and Self-Awareness

Self-monitoring skills and self-awareness are examined through a combination of direct observation during the task as well as through the After-Task Interview and Self-Ratings. The After-Task Interview and Self-Ratings (if appropriate) provide very important information that is directly relevant to treatment planning. Taking the time to thoroughly investigate and gain an understanding of the client's perception of task demands and performance is critical. The After-Task Interview, Observations, and Self-Ratings should be looked at together and in combination with strategy use and other observations or scores to gain a full understanding of the client's self-monitoring skills and self-perceptions.

Self-recognition of errors

The examiner observes and records self-recognition of errors (acknowledgment of errors or error correction attempts) as well as self-checking behaviors (noted in strategy ratings) during the WCPA to provide an indication of self-monitoring skills within an activity. Self-recognition of errors during task performance was frequently observed in healthy populations and reflects the ability to monitor ongoing actions within the context of an activity.

Identification of challenges

The After-Task Interview and Rating Scale examines the client's self-perceptions of task challenges, ability to identify aspects of the task that were easy versus hard, and overall perception of task difficulty. The ability to specifically identify the most challenging aspects of an activity is an important aspect of self-awareness and reflects understanding of task demands in relationship to one's abilities. During the After-Task Interview and Rating Scale, it is important to probe responses. A client with performance difficulties who states that the task was challenging but cannot provide examples or identify which aspects were challenging may not be fully aware. A lack of specificity in responding to the After-Task Interview questions when probes are provided can suggest limitations in understanding task demands and recognizing performance errors. During normative studies, healthy adults were able to identify at least one specific task challenge. Most people identified the challenges as time conflicts or appointments with too many choices.

Quantitative ratings

Quantitative ratings of performance (e.g., "This task was easy for me" on a scale of 1 = *agree* to 4 = *disagree*) are optional and can further verify information and impressions obtained from the open-ended questions. In the normative sample, self-ratings of younger (ages 18–39) and older (ages 65 or older) adults were not significantly different, even though significant differences were found between groups across nearly all WCPA scores. This finding suggests that some older adults may not be fully aware of performance difficulties. A client's self-ratings can be compared with the client's actual performance on the calendar and with the examiner's judgment.

For example, if the discrepancy between the examiner and client is 0, it indicates that they agree. If the client says that he or she had no difficulty but at the same time made a high number of errors (more than 2 standard deviations away from average performance), it indicates that the client may not be aware of the extent of performance errors. Wide discrepancies between the client's rating and actual performance or the examiner's rating indicate that the client is overestimating his or her abilities and suggest decreased self-awareness. Alternatively, negative discrepancies (e.g., when a client reports having a lot of difficulty with the task even though his or her performance was well within average abilities) indicate that the client underestimates his or her abilities and suggest decreased self-confidence.

Performance estimation

The client can be asked to estimate the number of appointments that he or she accurately entered as well as the amount of time required to complete the task. This question was not included in the initial normative studies; however, comparison of the client's actual scores and time with his or her after-task estimates may provide additional useful information regarding the client's self-perceptions and awareness of time. For example, poor awareness of the amount of time spent on an activity can affect the ability to complete daily activities and meet responsibilities. Time awareness techniques such as breaking activities into time components, predicting and estimating time, and use of timers at specific intervals to provide time monitoring cues can be applied across treatment activities.

One limitation of examining discrepancies between the client's perceptions and actual or examiner ratings is that discrepancy methods are inherently confounded by the severity of performance deficits. For example, if the client estimates a perfect accuracy score of 17, the magnitude of discrepancy between his or her estimation and actual scores depends on his or her performance. For example, if he or she obtained an accuracy score of 14 on the WCPA, the maximum difference between the client's estimated and actual performance would be 3 (17 − 14 = 3), whereas the maximum difference for a person with a WCPA score of 5 would be 12 (17 − 12 = 5). The magnitude of the difference between actual and estimated scores is inherently constrained by performance accuracy. Therefore, calculation of discrepancies as an indicator of awareness may be most useful when a client's score is below average and wide differences are possible.

Another consideration when using prediction and estimation methods is that some people do not like to predict or estimate their performance. Estimation of performance may be perceived as threatening, and responses could be related to self-confidence or personality traits rather than to awareness of performance, as described earlier. Open-ended questions can be more effective in providing information on an individual's self-perceptions than quantitative ratings.

Therefore, the use of quantitative awareness ratings was presented as an option, and use is based on the clinician's judgment. In some situations, it can confirm information obtained from open-ended questions or provide additional information, whereas in other cases, it may not be helpful. If a client appears defensive during open-ended questioning or overrationalizes difficulties, it is recommended that quantitative self-ratings not be used.

Discrepancies between observations and interview or self-ratings

Inconsistencies between observations regarding self-recognition of errors during the task and responses to the After-Task Interview and Rating Scale or self-ratings of task difficulty are important to note. Personality characteristics, cultural factors, and denial reactions may influence verbal responses in the After-Task Interview and Rating Scale. A client may not be willing to verbally acknowledge that a task was difficult, even though the client is aware of his or her performance. Challenges or difficulties can be denied during the interview despite observations, indicating awareness of performance during the activity. For example, a client observed to self-recognize or correct errors during the activity and who initiated multiple strategies demonstrates some level of awareness even though he or she may not verbally acknowledge challenges. If inconsistencies between actions and verbal responses are observed, the responses to the interview may not reflect the client's awareness but may instead reflect psychological mechanisms of coping, denial, or personality and cultural factors.

Implications of Self-Awareness for Strategy Use and Treatment Planning

Clients who are unaware of their own strengths and limitations may misjudge task demands and thus fail to perceive the need to use strategies. If the client perceives a task as very easy, it is unlikely that he or she will initiate use of strategies. When activities are easy, or nonchallenging, few to no strategies are needed. If, during the After-Task Interview and Rating Scale, a client reports that the activity was easy and cannot identify any task challenges, it would not be surprising that the client used few strategies. Strategies are used when a task is challenging. A few healthy people obtained a perfect accuracy score with only one or no strategies. For these people, the task was not adequately challenging, and strategy use was not required for successful performance. Although this was the exception, it illustrates that strategy use depends on both perceived and actual task difficulty relative to the person's abilities.

Effective strategy use requires fully understanding the task's demands and challenges. The implication is that if self-awareness or self-monitoring skills are limited, an initial focus of treatment may need to be helping the client anticipate and recognize task challenges. A client with partial awareness may be fully aware that the activity was challenging yet be unable to identify why or how it was challenging or fail to recognize errors within the activity. General knowledge of strengths and weaknesses may be disassociated from the ability to monitor task performance (Toglia, 2011; Toglia, Johnston, Goverover, & Dain, 2010). In this situation, treatment could be directed at helping the client monitor specific performance errors, such as the tendency to omit or skip information or to become sidetracked or overfocused on details, as a prerequisite to independent strategy use. Complete unawareness of significant performance difficulties across different activities may suggest that treatment approaches such as task-specific training methods that do not require awareness may be more appropriate (Toglia, Golisz, & Goverover, 2013).

Strategy Use

The way in which the client goes about the activity, including how the client begins and proceeds and how he or she handles conflicts or problems that arise, should be carefully observed. The WCPA provides an opportunity to observe the range, frequency, type, and effectiveness of strategies used. Strategies may be directly observed as well as reported by the client during the After-Task Interview and Rating Scale.

Total strategy score

The total strategy score indicates the number of different strategies that were used during the activity but represents only one small aspect of strategy use. The total strategy score provides information on the range of strategies used, but it needs to be examined in the context of the type, efficiency, effectiveness, and quality of strategy use.

Using multiple strategies

Healthy people typically use multiple strategies in a cognitively challenging activity. Most healthy people used approximately 4 strategies in Level II. On one hand, too many strategies (e.g., more than 10) or overly elaborate strategies (e.g., writing out one's own calendar first) may increase effort, time, or use of cognitive resources and decrease performance efficiency and effectiveness. On the other hand, restricted use of strategies can place increased demands on information processing skills and cognitive resources.

For example, if a client does not use any methods to keep track of which appointments from the list have been entered (e.g., checking off each item), more demands are placed on working memory or the ability to internally keep track of information. The total strategy score provides a broad indication of the range of strategies used in comparison to others in the same age group, but this score does not reflect the adequacy of strategy use.

Frequency and timing of strategies

In addition to the total strategy score, the examiner should observe the frequency with which strategies were used during the activity. In the original normative studies, strategies were recorded as used or not used. The Recording Form includes observations regarding frequency of use to differentiate between strategies that are used throughout the task and those that are used partially or inconsistently.

Interpretation of strategy frequency requires careful observation of the timing or temporal patterns of strategy use. Some clients use strategies steadily throughout an activity, and others initially use strategies that gradually fade as they become engaged in the activity.

For example, the client may initially check off each appointment on the list, but as he or she becomes involved in the activity, this strategy may gradually be abandoned. In other situations, the client may initiate strategy use too late or toward the end of the activity, after multiple errors have occurred. Sometimes, a client will use strategies only when conflicts or difficulties are encountered. In this situation, strategy use may appear to be periodic or fluctuating rather than consistent. The client may, however, only use strategies when they are needed, in which case fluctuating strategy use can represent effective performance in some circumstances. A fluctuating strategy pattern, though, can also reflect a random and disorganized approach, so the frequency and timing of strategies needs to be examined in conjunction with other aspects of strategy use.

Type of strategy use

The range, frequency, and timing of strategy use provide important information, but they need to be analyzed in combination with the type of strategy used. The type of strategy used and its effectiveness depend on the type of performance difficulties or cognitive lapses that the client is experiencing. In some cases, clients may use strategies that do not help them control performance errors.

For example, Client A highlighted details throughout the appointment list, but this strategy did not enhance performance because Client A was unable to keep track of what had just been done and what needed to be done next. A strategy such as rehearsal or using a method to keep track of appointments as they were entered would be more effective for this client. In contrast, Client B had difficulty paying attention to details. For Client B, the strategy of highlighting was effective because it helped the client notice and attend to relevant information. Strategies can be effective in controlling performance errors; however, the strategy used needs to be effective for the kind of error or cognitive lapses that are observed. This requires awareness or understanding of one's strengths and weaknesses, as discussed previously.

Switching strategies. The ability to switch strategies when needed and adjust to problems encountered should be carefully observed. Some people use an orderly, sequential approach and go down the appointment list in order. This approach works only until conflicts are encountered, though. The ability to adjust performance and switch strategies when needed in the context of an activity is an important skill and was observed in the majority of adults without cognitive impairment.

Strategy awareness. The After-Task Interview and Rating Scale provides an indication of the client's awareness of the strategies or methods that he or she used during the task. The majority of the normative sample could report and describe the specific strategies and methods they used without difficulty. Some clients use strategies without awareness or let go of strategies prematurely because they were unaware that the strategies they were using were helping performance. Treatment can assist a client in identifying the task methods he or she is using that work best to increase consistency of strategy use.

Strategy generation. The After-Task Interview and Rating Scale also assesses strategy generation by asking the client whether he or she can think of alternative ways to approach the task. The ability to think flexibly and identify alternative task methods is needed to successfully cope with challenges and solve everyday problems. Difficulties in initiation, brainstorming skills, cognitive flexibility, and decreased self-awareness or self-efficacy can affect the ability to generate alternative strategies. Everyday activities that require flexibility of thinking and generation of alternatives such as identifying all the different options for lunch or dinner can be easily incorporated into treatment.

Additional Observations

Emotional reactions such as high anxiety, frustration, or feeling overwhelmed suggest difficulty in coping with cognitively challenging activities. Negative statements such as "I can't do this" and "My brain doesn't work right" suggest low self-efficacy or a decreased sense of control over performance. These statements are typically associated with underestimations of performance during the After-Task Interview and Rating Scale. Increased emotional reactions or negative beliefs can further decrease performance and result in a lack of persistence or withdrawal in the face of challenge.

Intervention may need to begin by helping the client monitor emotional reactions and reframe perceived challenges. Approaches that focus on empowering clients to develop their own strategies to help them effectively cope and manage cognitive challenges may be needed to increase self-confidence and self-efficacy.

Examples of Performance Analysis and Interpretation

WCPA objective scores such as accuracy and efficiency need to be examined in combination with observations regarding adherence to rules, strategy use, error types, and self-recognition of errors, as well as responses to the After-Task Interview and Rating Scale. Interpretation requires careful analysis and consideration of all aspects of performance. The same accuracy or efficiency score may have different implications for treatment depending on the person's awareness, strategy use, and types of performance errors.

This section presents examples of 2 clients who have similar accuracy and efficiency scores; however, differences in other aspects of performance influence interpretation and treatment planning. The case examples provide additional information on how the WCPA can be used in clinical practice to track performance changes and to provide recommendations for intervention.

Example 1: Similar Accuracy and Efficiency Scores but Differences in Awareness

Two clients entered 8 accurate appointments into the weekly calendar within 15 minutes and had similar efficiency scores. Client A perceived the task as easy and did not use any strategies. This client was unable to recognize errors or generate alternative strategies. Client B, however, perceived the task as very difficult. This client attempted to use several strategies, recognized errors, identified aspects of the task that were challenging, and generated alternative strategies for the future.

Client A does not demonstrate prerequisite skills for effective use of strategies. Treatment may attempt to address self-monitoring skills within the context of activities; however, if changes are not observed, other treatment approaches such as task-specific training or adaptation of tasks by others may be more appropriate in improving function than an approach focused on strategy use. Client B needs assistance in using more effective strategies and in anticipating challenges or generating strategies before activities. Client B appears to be a good candidate for an approach focused on optimizing strategy use such as the multicontext approach (Toglia, 2011; Toglia et al., 2010).

Example 2: Similar Accuracy and Efficiency Scores but Differences in Performance Errors

Two clients with similar accuracy and efficiency scores and similar levels of strategy use and awareness demonstrated different types of performance errors. Client A showed little to no planning time, was unable to follow rules, and demonstrated a predominance of errors of omission or detail (time and location). Performance was characterized by impulsivity, disorganization, and a tendency to quickly check off items before they were fully read or entered. Client B showed increased planning time with no errors of omission. This client adhered to all rules and used a sequential, orderly approach but was unable to adjust performance when conflicts or unexpected problems were encountered and became fixated on the Saturday/Sunday error. The examiner observed performance errors of repetition and incompleteness.

In the first situation, intervention strategies could include helping the client to stop and create a plan, use stimuli reduction methods, and pace speed of response. The second situation suggests that the client may have a tendency to get stuck on parts or pieces of a situation and has difficulty shifting set. Treatment strategies may involve helping the client generate alternative methods and to monitor his or her tendency to get stuck on the same step or overfocus on pieces of information. Both of these examples illustrate how all aspects of the WCPA need to be considered simultaneously for full interpretation and treatment planning.

Using the Summary Worksheets and Report Templates

Appendix F presents three worksheets as options for quickly summarizing objective results and observations (Appendixes F.1–F.3). Two sample assessment report templates (Appendix F.4 and Appendix F.5) also are presented to assist in synthesizing and documenting WCPA results. The Report Template: Initial and Follow-Up Comparison (Appendix F.4) is designed to be used when the purpose of the WCPA is to measure change or compare performance over time as well as to compare the client with other people in the same age group.

The Performance Profile and Report Template (Appendix F.5) summarizes performance results for the purpose of treatment planning. This template incorporates the Visual Performance Profile and Worksheet discussed previously. This template includes analysis of additional WCPA components, including examination of error patterns, awareness, and strategy use. The examiner must be familiar with the preceding section on interpretation of performance before using these report templates.

The following 5 case examples illustrate use of the report templates and provide additional information on how the WCPA can be used in clinical practice to track performance changes as well as to provide recommendations for treatment. The first two cases also illustrate completed client calendars as well as the examiner scoring and recording forms.

Case Example 1: Using the WCPA as an Outcome Measure

Anna is a 75-year-old woman who had an embolization of benign bifrontal meningioma and right frontal meningioma resection 2 weeks ago. Before her surgery, she lived with her husband in a condominium. She was independent in all IADLs including managing finances; driving; and using a computer, tablet, and cell phone and was extremely active in her community, including volunteering at the local community center and assisting with coordinating events. She enjoyed going to movies, traveling, gardening, and cooking.

On admission to an inpatient rehabilitation unit, Anna was independent in routine activities such as brushing her teeth and dressing; however, she was observed to have significant difficulties following multiple-step directions. The WCPA was administered as one component of the initial occupational therapy assessment and re-administered 17 days later on discharge from the inpatient setting.

Initial and discharge comparison

The WCPA is a complex performance task that involves entering 17 appointments into a weekly schedule while adhering to rules and avoiding conflicts. It inherently requires integrated use of executive functioning skills including planning, organization, inhibition, self-monitoring, and use of strategies. This report provides results from initial and follow-up assessment and indicates how performance on an integrated EF task compares with that of others. Initial and follow-up scores on the WCPA are presented in Table 4.7. Results demonstrate clear improvements in patterns of errors, strategy use, self-monitoring, and performance accuracy.

Initial evaluation

During the initial WCPA, Anna randomly chose appointments on the list and entered 4 of 17 appointments without regard to time, day, or location, obtaining an accuracy score of 0. The 4th appointment (haircut) was repeated 5 times. Errors included omissions and repetitions as well as failure to enter correct times or locations. No strategy use was observed. An example of the completed initial calendar is shown in Exhibit 4.1. After the activity, Anna indicated that handwriting was challenging but appeared to be unaware of her errors and was therefore unable to identify any challenges or alternative strategies.

Intervention

A multicontext treatment approach was used with an emphasis on structuring activity experiences to facilitate self-recognition of errors. On the basis of initial results, indicating an inability to enter more than 4 items from a list, treatment activities began with a series of activities that involved following simple lists of 5 to 6 items. Examples included using a list to gather items needed for grooming or to make a sandwich. Techniques such as self-assessment worksheets, mediation or questioning to facilitate self-checking, and video feedback were used to help Anna recognize and monitor errors of omission and repetition during simplified activities. As Anna began to use strategies such as marking off each item on a list, activities were expanded to varied contexts. The number of items was gradually increased as performance improvements and carryover of strategies were observed.

Discharge from inpatient setting and changes from initial evaluation (2.5 weeks later)

Follow-up results remained significantly below average; however, strategy use, awareness, accuracy, and

Table 4.7. Summary of Initial and Follow-Up Scores: Case 1, Anna

	Initial		Discharge		
Date:	Score	Percentile	Score	Percentile	Comments
Planning time __min __sec	45 sec	50th	4 min	20th	More time spent planning
Total time: __min __sec	7 min	>90th	30 min	<5th	More time spent on task but slower than average
No. of rules followed (0–5)	3	25th	3	25th	Same
Total no. of strategies	0	<5th	3	40th	Some strategies initiated
No. of appointments entered (0–17)	4	<2nd	17	95th	Much improved; average performance
No. of accurate appointments (0–17)	0	<2nd	7	5th	Much improved but still impaired
Efficiency score (score not applicable)	0	N/A; accuracy score too low	Low; N/A	N/A; accuracy score too low	
Error analysis					
Appointments missing	13		0		Significant change
Location errors	3		6		
Time errors	0		2		
Repetition errors	1 (5×)		1		
Incomplete	0		1		
Total no. of errors	17		10		
Self-recognition of errors	0		4		

Note. min = minutes; sec = seconds.

overall approach to activities improved. On follow-up assessment, Anna entered all 17 appointments into the weekly calendar. She carefully checked off each appointment on the list as she entered it and proceeded in an orderly manner. Errors of omission were no longer observed, and only 1 repetition error occurred. This represented a significant change from the initial evaluation. Nine additional errors reflecting inaccurate entry of time or location were made (see Exhibit 4.1), suggesting continued difficulty keeping track of multiple variables at once (appointment, day, and time) as well as fully attending to all relevant details (see Exhibits 4.2 and 4.3 for scoring).

Anna recognized a few errors during performance; however, she was unaware of the majority of performance errors, indicating that her self-monitoring skills, although improved, remained inadequate in complex tasks. Her ability to identify challenges and generate alternative strategies after the task also demonstrated improvement (see Exhibit 4.4), indicating continued potential to benefit from a strategy-based intervention.

Recommendations for treatment for Anna

The results demonstrate significant improvements in multiple aspects of performance that occurred over the course of inpatient rehabilitation; however, Anna's WCPA scores remain significantly below those of typical performance. Difficulty in managing details and keeping track of all relevant information will affect her ability to successfully engage in former roles and activities such as managing finances, using everyday technologies, coordinating and planning social events, and volunteer work. Outpatient occupational therapy using a multicontext treatment approach is recommended, with a focus on increasing strategy use and self-monitoring skills in cognitive IADL activities.

(Text continues on page 64)

Exhibit 4.1. Calendar Samples Before Treatment and at Discharge: Case 1, Anna

Before treatment:

	Mon	Tues	Wed	Thur	Fri	Sun	Sat
7 am							
:15	Food			Dentist			
:30	Shopping			1hr			
:45				3pm			
8 am					Hair Cut		
:15		45MIN					
:30							
:45		Lunch					
9 am							
:15							
:30							
:45							
10 am					HC		
:15							
:30							
:45					1hr		
11 am							
:15							
:30							
:45							
12 pm							
:15					HC		
:30							
:45					1hr		
1 pm							
:15							
:30							
:45							
2 pm							
:15					HC		
:30							
:45					1hr		
3 pm							
:15							
:30							
:45							
4 pm							
:15					HC		
:30							
:45					1hr		
5 pm							
:15							
:30							
:45							
6 pm					HC		
:30					1hr		
7 pm							
:30							
8 pm							
:30							

Note. Anna entered 4 of 17 appointments, with 13 omissions. 0 appointments were accurate. Notably, Anna perseverated on *Haircut*, entering the errand 5 times. Lunch is scheduled at 8 a.m. The dentist appointment is scheduled at 7 a.m., although the patient writes the appointment as being at 3 p.m.

Exhibit 4.1. Calendar Samples Before Treatment and at Discharge: Case 1, Anna (*Continued*)

Anna at discharge:

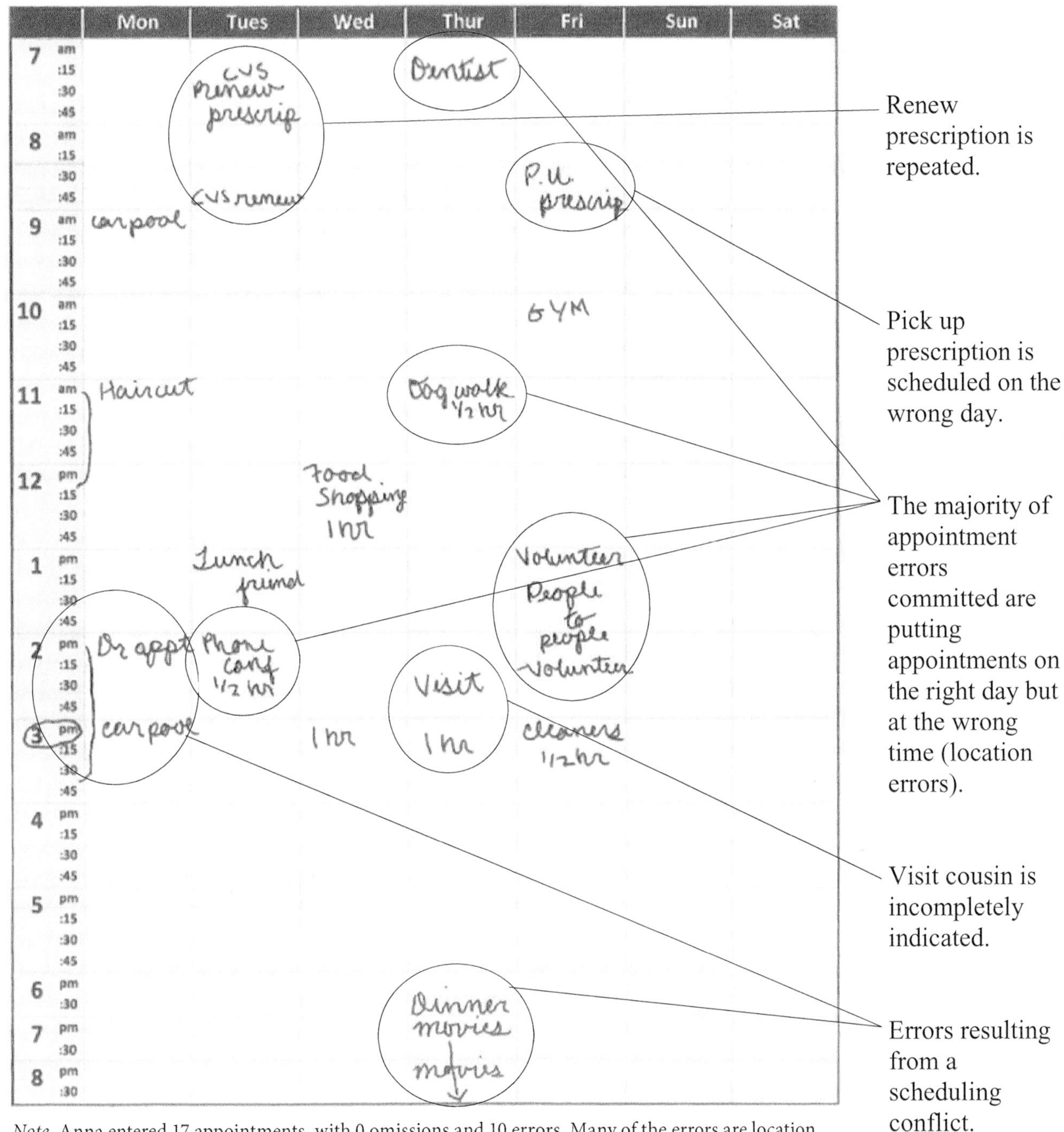

Note. Anna entered 17 appointments, with 0 omissions and 10 errors. Many of the errors are location errors in which the client entered appointments on the right day but at the wrong time or on the wrong day.

Exhibit 4.2. Calendar Scoring Worksheet, Adult/Older Adult (Ages 18–94), Version A (Wednesday Free): Case 1, Anna

Directions: Place a check mark in the Accurate column if an appointment is entered without errors and an "X" in the Missing column if an appointment is omitted. For quick scoring, place an "X" in the Error column. For detailed error scoring, use one of the following error codes to indicate which type of error was committed.

R = Appointment is repeated or entered more than once, and repetition is not an attempt to self-correct a location error

L = Appointment is placed in the wrong location, day, or time slot

T = Appointment is in the right location, but the time allotted is incorrect by more than 15 minutes (7:00 a.m.–6:00 p.m.) or 30 minutes (6:00–9:00 p.m.)

I = Appointment name is entered inaccurately or partially

Self-Recognition (SR) Column

Place a check mark in this column if the person acknowledges an appointment error or conflict verbally or nonverbally or if you observe the person trying to correct it (e.g., draw lines, cross out).

Entered	Missing	Error	Accurate	SR	Appointments
✓			✓		Mon.: Haircut from 11:00 a.m.–12:00 p.m.
✓		I			Visit with cousin Mon. or Tues. between 1:00 and 2:00 p.m. or 1:30 and 2:30 p.m. or on Thurs. between 2:30 and 3:30 p.m. or 3:00 and 4:00 p.m.
✓		R		✓	Mon. any time or Tues. a.m.: Call to renew prescription
✓			✓		Tues.: Lunch with friend from 1:00–2:00 p.m.
✓		L			Tues.: Phone conference before 2:00 p.m. (30 minutes)
✓		L			Mon. or Tues.: Medication picked up between 9:00 a.m. and 3:00 p.m. (30 minutes). Must have previously called to renew prescription.
✓		L			Thurs.: Walk neighbor's dog before 11:00 a.m. (30 minutes)
✓		L			Thurs.: Dentist at 3:00 p.m. (1 hour)
✓		T			Thurs.: Movies with friends from 7:00–11:00 p.m.
✓		L		✓	Fri.: Volunteer job from 9:00–10:30 a.m. (90 minutes)
✓		T		✓	Thurs or Fri.: Dinner, coworkers, starting between 6:30 and 8:00 p.m. (2 hours)
✓			✓		Mon. or Fri.: Pick up dry cleaning between 8:00 a.m. and 4:00 p.m. (30 minutes)
✓			✓		Fri., Sat., or Sun. morning: Exercise at the gym (45 minutes)
✓			✓		Doctor: Mon. or Fri. afternoon at 2:00 p.m. (90 minutes)
✓			✓		Food shopping before Fri. (1 hour)
✓			✓		Carpool: One morning at 9:00 a.m. (45 minutes)
✓		L		✓	Carpool: One afternoon at 3:00 p.m. (45 minutes)
17	**0**	**10**	**7**	**4**	**Total all columns** The no. of appointments in the missing + accurate + error columns should equal 17

Exhibit 4.3. Recording Form: Case 1, Anna

Level 2 Version A

Client Anna Date ________ Examiner ________

Planning time: From "Let's begin" to entering of 1st appointment: 4 min 0 s
Total time: Time from "Let's begin" to completion: 30 min 0 s

Rules

1. Questions answered (Y = *yes;* N = *no*) 1. N 2. N 3. N
2. States time at 7 min (±5 min) __ States time too late ✓ Forgets time completely
3. States when finished: ✓ yes __ no
4. Appointments scheduled on free day (Tues./**Wed.**/Thurs.) : ✓ yes __ no
5. No. of appointments crossed out 0

Total no. of rules followed 3/5

Observations

Refers to Instruction Sheet: __ Never ✓ 1–2 times __ 3–5 times __ >5 times
Calendar error management (Sat./Sun. reversal, evening appointment time format, time ending too early)
✓ Did not affect performance __ Interfered with performance

Strategies Observed (check off whether strategy is observed and how much it is used)

Strategies	Not Observed	Occasionally/ Partially Used	Frequently/ Consistently Used	Inefficient/ Counter-productive
Underlines, circles, or highlights key words or features	✓			
Uses finger	✓			
Verbal rehearsal: Repeats key words or instructions out loud	✓			
Crosses off, checks off, or highlights appointments entered			✓	
Rearrangement of materials	✓			
Categorizes or organizes appointments before entering them (coding system, color codes, highlights, labels)	✓			
Enters fixed appointments first, then flexible appointments	✓			
Uses written plan: Makes a rough draft first or plans out calendar in writing before entering appointments	✓			
Talks out loud about strategy, method, or plan	✓			
Crosses off specified free day	✓			
Self-checks		✓		
Pauses and rereads		✓		
Other:				
Other:				
Total observed strategies		2	1	
Strategies reported (not observed—reported in After-Task Interview) Specify and indicate total no. of strategies:				
Total no. of strategies used: total observed strategies (occasional + frequent) + total strategies reported		3		

Comments and other strategies observed (note any spontaneous statements regarding difficulty while completing task, comment on strategy inefficiencies, and expand on description of strategy use): ________

Exhibit 4.4. After-Task Interview at Initial Evaluation and at Discharge: Case 1, Anna

Question	Initial Evaluation	Discharge From Inpatient Setting
Tell me how you went about doing this task.	I just did it. I didn't think there was need to use any special methods.	I took my time and went slower to increase accuracy.
Did you use any strategies or special methods?	No.	I used a step-by-step approach instead of completing all the activities on a day at once.
Did you encounter any challenges or difficulties?	No, but I don't like my handwriting.	Keeping track and deciding exactly how large a 30-minute box should be.
Would you do anything differently next time?	Write more legibly so that it is clear to me.	I should have put in the appointments that don't have choices first.

Case Example 2: WCPA Report and Treatment Planning

Kathy is a 52-year-old woman who was hit by a car when crossing the street 3 months ago and sustained a traumatic brain injury. She lives with her husband and 12-year-old daughter in a single-story home and was referred for outpatient occupational therapy after inpatient rehabilitation and home care. Before the accident, she worked as an administrative assistant in a busy accounting firm and was proficient in use of the computer, including programs such as Microsoft Word, Excel, and PowerPoint. She describes herself as very efficient, organized, and always on top of things. She previously managed home finances and her daughter's sports and activity schedule and coordinated family and social events.

Kathy is currently independent in self-care activities and is able to prepare routine meals and complete household chores without difficulty. She stated that her mind is not "working right," and she often feels as though things are foggy. Her goal is to be able to think clearly so that she can resume her previous lifestyle and return to work.

The WCPA was administered as one component of the occupational therapy assessment, which also included examination of interests, routines, habits, and goals.

Initial evaluation

The WCPA was administered (Exhibits 4.5–4.7) to provide information on Kathy's ability to cope with a cognitively challenging everyday activity, including the ability to plan ahead, recognize potential conflicts, make performance adjustments, simultaneously keep track of information, restrain impulsive responses, self-monitor performance, and use efficient strategies or methods.

Performance analysis

The results summarized in Exhibit 4.8 demonstrate a pattern of average performance in accuracy, rules followed, and appointments entered, along with excessive time and strategy use. The efficiency and time scores below the 5th percentile indicate that Kathy required considerably more time than more than 95% of people in her age group to achieve low average accuracy and used excessively more strategies.

Strategy use

Strategy frequency. Kathy was observed using numerous ineffective strategies that she quickly abandoned.

Types of strategies. Kathy spent 15 minutes reading and rereading the instructions and appointment list. She then rewrote the list on a different piece of paper, highlighting appointments in different colors and circling key words. She drew arrows connecting different appointments and wrote notes on the page. Appointments were crossed off before she actually entered them into the weekly calendar, creating additional confusion. The appointment list became difficult to read and confusing. Kathy's approach to the WCPA appeared to increase effort and demands on cognitive resources.

(Text continues on page 68)

Exhibit 4.5. Calendar Sample: Case 2, Kathy

	Mon	Tues	Wed	Thur	Fri	Sun	Sat
7 am				FOOD SHOPPING 1HR			GYM 45MS
:15							
:30							
:45							
8 am							
:15					P/U PANTS DRY CLEAN		
:30							
:45							
9 am	CARPOOL				VOLUNTEER PEOPLE 2 PEOPLE		
:15							
:30							
:45							
10 am	CALL PHAR			DOG 1/2 WALK HR			
:15							
:30							
:45							
11 am	HAIRCUT						
:15							
:30							
:45							
12 pm		PHONE CONF					
:15							
:30							
:45							
1 pm	VISIT W/COUSIN 1-2:30	LUNCH W/FRD					
:15							
:30							
:45							
2 pm					DOCTOR APPT 90MIN		
:15							
:30							
:45							
3 pm		CARPOOL					
:15				~~CARPOOL~~			
:30				DDS			
:45							
4 pm							
:15							
:30							
:45							
5 pm							
:15							
:30							
:45							
6 pm					DINNER W/FRIENDS 2HRS		
:30							
7 pm				MOVIES W/FRIEND 7-11			
:30							
8 pm							
:30							

Exhibit 4.6. Calendar Scoring Worksheet, Adult/Older Adult (Ages 18–94), Version A (Wednesday Free): Case 2, Kathy

Directions: Place a check mark in the Accurate column if an appointment is entered without errors and an "X" in the Missing column if an appointment is omitted. For quick scoring, place an "X" in the Error column. For detailed error scoring, use one of the following error codes to indicate which type of error was committed.

R = Appointment is repeated or entered more than once, and repetition is not an attempt to self-correct a location error
L = Appointment is placed in the wrong location, day, or time slot
T = Appointment is in the right location, but the time allotted is incorrect by more than 15 minutes (7:00 a.m.–6:00 p.m.) or 30 minutes (6:00–9:00 p.m.)
I = Appointment name is entered inaccurately or partially

Self-Recognition (SR) Column

Place a check mark in this column if the person acknowledges an appointment error or conflict verbally or non-verbally or if you observe the person trying to correct it (e.g., draw lines, cross out).

Entered	Missing	Error	Accurate	SR	Appointments
✓			✓		Mon.: Haircut from 11:00 a.m.–12:00 p.m.
✓		T			Visit with cousin Mon. or Tues. between 1:00 and 2:00 p.m. or 1:30 and 2:30 p.m. or on Thurs. between 2:30 and 3:30 p.m. or 3:00 and 4:00 p.m.
✓			✓		Mon. any time or Tues. a.m.: Call to renew prescription
✓			✓		Tues.: Lunch with friend from 1:00–2:00 p.m.
✓			✓		Tues.: Phone conference before 2:00 p.m. (30 minutes)
	✓				Mon. or Tues.: Medication picked up between 9:00 a.m. and 3:00 p.m. (30 minutes). Must have previously called to renew prescription.
✓			✓		Thurs.: Walk neighbor's dog before 11:00 a.m. (30 minutes)
✓		T			Thurs.: Dentist at 3:00 p.m. (1 hour)
✓			✓		Thurs.: Movies with friends from 7:00–11:00 p.m.
✓			✓		Fri.: Volunteer job from 9:00–10:30 a.m. (90 minutes)
✓			✓		Thurs or Fri.: Dinner, coworkers, starting between 6:30 and 8:00 p.m. (2 hours)
✓			✓		Mon. or Fri.: Pick up dry cleaning between 8:00 a.m. and 4:00 p.m. (30 minutes)
✓			✓		Fri., Sat., or Sun. morning: Exercise at the gym (45 minutes)
✓			✓		Doctor: Mon. or Fri. afternoon at 2:00 p.m. (90 minutes)
✓			✓		Food shopping before Fri. (1 hour)
✓			✓		Carpool: One morning at 9:00 a.m. (45 minutes)
✓		L		✓	Carpool: One afternoon at 3:00 p.m. (45 minutes)
16	1	3	13	1	**Total all columns** The no. of appointments in the missing + accurate + error columns should equal 17

Exhibit 4.7. Recording Form: Case 2, Kathy

Level 2 Version A

Client Kathy Date ________ Examiner ________
Planning time: "Let's begin" to entering of:
1st appointment 10 min 0 s
Total time: Time from "Let's begin" to completion: 35 min 0 s

Rules

1. Questions answered (Y = *yes;* N = *no*) 1. N 2. N 3. N
2. States time at 7 min (±5 min) ✓ States time too late _ Forgets time completely _
3. States when finished: yes ✓ no _
4. Appointments scheduled on free day (Tues./**Wed.**/Thurs) : yes _ no ✓
5. No. of appointments crossed out 1

Total no. of rules followed 4/5

Observations

Refers to Instruction Sheet: _ Never _ 1–2 times ✓ 3–5 times _ >5 times
Calendar error management (Sat./Sun. reversal, evening appointment time format, time ending too early)
✓ Did not affect performance _ Interfered with performance

Strategies Observed (check off whether strategy is observed and how much it is used)

Strategies	Not Observed	Occasionally/ Partially Used	Frequently/ Consistently Used	Inefficient/ Counter-productive
Underlines, circles, or highlights key words or features		✓		✓
Uses finger		✓		
Verbal rehearsal: Repeats key words or instructions out loud	✓			
Crosses off, checks off, or highlights appointments entered		✓		✓
Rearrangement of materials		✓		
Categorizes or organizes appointments before entering them (coding system, color codes, highlights, labels)		✓		✓
Enters fixed appointments first, then flexible appointments	✓			
Uses written plan: Makes a rough draft first or plans out calendar in writing before entering appointments		✓		✓
Talks out loud about strategy, method, or plan		✓		
Crosses off specified free day	✓			
Self-checks		✓		✓
Pauses and rereads		✓		✓
Other: Draws arrows		✓		✓
Other: Written notes		✓		✓
Total observed strategies		11		8
Strategies reported (Not observed—reported in After-Task Interview) Specify and indicate total no. of strategies:		0		
Total no. of strategies used: total observed strategies (occasional + frequent) + total strategies reported		11		

Comments and other strategies observed (note any spontaneous statements regarding difficulty while completing task, comment on strategy inefficiencies, and expand on description of strategy use): ________

Exhibit 4.8. Visual Performance Profile: Case 2, Kathy

Percentile	Entered Appointment	Accurate Appointment	Rules Followed	Strategy Use	Planning Time	Total Time	Efficiency	Percentile
≥95				**X** (11)				≥95
>75								>75
70								70
60								60
50			**X** (4)					50
40								40
30	**X** (16)	**X** (13)						30
25								25
20								20
10								10
<5					**X** (10 min)	**X** (35 min)	**X** (212)	<5

Error patterns suggest that Kathy had difficulty handling the number of items on the list as well as attending to details as she was performing the activity.

Error Analysis Profile: Case 2, Kathy

	Missing	Repetition	Incomplete	Location	Time	Extraneous	Self-Recognition
0		X	X			None	
1	**X**			X			X
2					X		
3+							

Strategy generation. After the task, Kathy was unable to identify what she would do differently as indicated during the after-task interview (Exhibit 4.9).

Self-monitoring and awareness

During the task. Kathy constantly checked herself; however, she did so in an unsystematic manner and was aware of only one of four errors that she made. Kathy appeared increasingly frustrated, overwhelmed, and anxious during the task, making negative statements such as "My brain is messed up" and "I can't do this" throughout the activity.

After-task awareness of strategies. Kathy was able to identify strategies she used and recognized that they

Exhibit 4.9. After-Task Interview at Initial Evaluation: Case 2, Kathy

Question	Initial Evaluation
Tell me how you went about doing this task?	I tried to make a plan and made a list on this paper and used the highlighter, but everything got confusing and jumbled up.
Then what did you do?	I crossed off appointments and wrote notes as I was going along, but nothing helped.
Why do you think that was?	I have no idea. My brain isn't working right.
Did you encounter any difficulties or challenges while doing this task?	I felt overwhelmed. It was very difficult. My brain is messed up.
What was hardest? Easiest?	Everything was hard. The easy part was writing the appointment.
Would you do anything differently next time?	Not sure what I could do differently.
Are there any other strategies or methods that you could use?	Not really.

Exhibit 4.10. After-Task Perceptions for Case 2, Kathy

	Therapist or Actual	Client	Difference	Comments
Self-ratings	10	16	6	Underestimated
Time estimation	35 min	30 min	5 min	Generally aware of time
Accuracy estimation	13	7	6	Underestimated

Note. min = minutes.

did not work well, but she did not understand why as illustrated during the after-task interview (see Exhibit 4.9).

After-task self-perceptions. Kathy indicated the activity was extremely challenging but could not be more specific. As shown in Exhibit 4.10, she underestimated her performance accuracy and time. Although Kathy was very aware that she experienced difficulties, she did not seem to recognize why she was having difficulty, and this appeared to contribute to increased anxiety and decreased self-efficacy.

Recommendations for treatment for Kathy

Occupational therapy intervention is recommended to improve efficiency of performance, effectiveness of strategies, self-efficacy, and awareness in cognitively challenging activities such as managing schedules, coordinating social events, and work-related tasks. Treatment needs to begin with meaningful activities that are at a just-right challenge level or that have fewer steps or items so that Kathy can experience success.

Recommended techniques include mediation or questioning and self-assessment to promote self-monitoring skills and self-efficacy. Once Kathy has a better understanding of task challenges as she encounters them in an activity, she will likely be more able to select effective strategies that promote success. Treatment should encourage Kathy to carefully select key strategies and assess their effectiveness before abandoning them. In addition, guidance in generating self-regulation strategies such as positive self-talk or visualization may help Kathy control her anxiety and emotional reactions in multitask or complex situations so that she can more effectively cope with challenges.

It is important to focus on empowering Kathy to use strategies that reduce performance errors and manage cognitive symptoms. The ability to recognize and understand challenges that are encountered and use effective strategies across varied higher-level cognitive tasks can decrease anxiety and increase sense of perceived control over performance.

Case Example 3: WCPA Report and Treatment Planning

Charles is a 19-year-old man with a history of ADHD, at-risk behavior, and substance abuse. Charles currently lives with his grandmother and recently reenrolled at a Board of Cooperative Educational Services (BOCES) program in a community college after previously withdrawing from the program. Charles has expressed his desire to be successful in the BOCES program.

Charles acknowledges that he has difficulty concentrating, gets easily frustrated, and gives up quickly. He describes himself as outgoing and friendly, and he enjoys hanging out with his friends, listening to music, and working on cars. He briefly worked at a car repair shop, assisting with mechanical repairs and scheduling appointments, but he was let go after taking a customer's car for a personal errand without asking permission. His goal is to become a car mechanic and get his own apartment.

Initial evaluation

The WCPA Youth Version was administered as one component of the occupational therapy assessment, which also included examination of interests, routines, habits, and goals. It was administered to provide information on Charles's ability to cope with a cognitively challenging everyday activity, including the ability to plan ahead, recognize potential conflicts, make performance adjustments, simultaneously keep track of information, restrain impulsive responses, self-monitor performance, and use efficient strategies or methods.

Overview of performance, strategy use, and self-monitoring skills

Charles's performance on the WCPA was characterized by 12 errors, decreased inhibition, poor strategy use, and decreased self-monitoring skills. Performance was below average in all areas, as shown in the Visual Performance Profile in Exhibit 4.11. Charles jumped into the activity and immediately began putting appointments in the calendar before the examiner even finished instructions. He completed the task in 8 minutes but did not adhere to the rules and exhibited decreased impulse control. For example, he answered all 3 questions, crossed out appointments, and put appointments on a day that was supposed to remain free. He did not refer back to the written instruction sheet, even though it was on the table.

Strategy use

Strategy frequency. Charles was observed to use only 1 strategy; however, its use was transient and incomplete.

Task methods. Charles began the task by randomly selecting appointments in the middle of the page. He initially used his finger to help him focus on the appointments as he read but quickly abandoned this strategy. No other strategies were observed or reported.

Strategy generation (after task). Charles's strategy generation was limited to "concentrating better" and

Exhibit 4.11. Visual Performance Profile: Case 3, Charles

Percentile	Entered Appointment	Accurate Appointment	Rules Followed	Strategy Use	Efficiency	Planning Time	Total Time	Percentile
≥95						X (0)	X (8 min)	≥95
>75								>75
70								70
60								60
50								50
40								40
30								30
25								25
20								20
10								10
<5	X (14)	X (6)	X (0)	X (1)	N/A			<5

Errors were made across all categories as demonstrated in the Error Analysis Profile and appeared to reflect Charles's generally impulsive and scattered approach.

Error Analysis Profile: Case 3, Charles

	Missing	Repetition	Incomplete	Location	Time	Extraneous	Self-Recognition
0						None	X
1		X					
2			X	X			
3+	X (4)				X		

Exhibit 4.12. After-Task Perceptions for Case 3, Charles

	Therapist or Actual	Client	Difference	Comments
Self-ratings	16	6	10	Overestimated
Time estimation	8 min	<10 min	None	
Accuracy estimation	6	16	10	Overestimated

Note. min = minutes.

"focusing," but Charles could not explain this further or provide specific examples of what he would do differently.

Self-monitoring and awareness

During the task. Charles did not appear to recognize or self-correct any of his errors as he was performing the activity (0/12). No self-checking was observed.

After-task awareness of strategies. Charles indicated that he did not use any special methods or strategies. He seemed surprised when the examiner pointed out that he started out the task by using his finger to help him focus.

After-task self-perceptions. Charles stated that the activity initially looked easy but that it got "tricky." Although he acknowledged that it was tricky, he could not provide examples and denied that he encountered any difficulties. His perception of his performance was different from that of the examiner because he overestimated his performance considerably (Exhibit 4.12).

Recommendations for treatment for Charles

Charles's performance was below average in all areas and reflected an impulsive and disorganized approach to the task. Pace of performance was poorly regulated, and effective strategies were not used. Charles did not acknowledge any challenges or difficulties with the task; however, he vaguely acknowledged that he could concentrate better.

The ability to anticipate challenges, plan ahead, restrain impulses, and adjust performance in the face of unexpected challenges is important in building the adaptive capacities necessary for coping with school, work, and other life situations. On the basis of the WCPA results, it is unclear whether Charles could benefit from a metacognitive or strategy-based intervention because his awareness of performance is limited. A trial of a strategy-based intervention is warranted to determine whether self-regulation, self-monitoring skills, or strategy generation and use could be improved. For example, treatment could involve practicing work-related activities, such as scheduling appointments or categorizing auto parts and prices into a table while practicing monitoring and pacing strategies and self-rating performance. Choosing tasks that are relevant and at the appropriate level of challenge will be important. If responsiveness to intervention is limited, an approach that involves task-specific training or repetitive practice in work routines or tasks with fading cues is recommended.

Note: A dynamic test–teach–retest format using Case 3 is presented in Chapter 6, "Dynamic Assessment." This format can provide a better indication of whether a client is a candidate for a strategy-based approach.

Case Example 4: WCPA Report and Treatment Planning

Larry is a 40-year-old man with chronic schizophrenia and moderate negative symptoms. He was diagnosed at age 19 with undifferentiated schizophrenia. Larry currently lives in a large city and manages his own apartment with close supervision from his older sister, who lives in the same apartment building and assists him with managing finances, appointments, shopping, and household tasks. His sister reports that Larry often loses track of his appointments; makes the same meals every day; wears the same clothes unless cued; and needs to be reminded to do the laundry, run the dishwasher, and perform other household tasks. Larry worked in his family's business in a data entry job until his condition deteriorated 3 years ago. His goal is to return to work.

Initial evaluation

The WCPA was administered as one component of the occupational therapy assessment, which also included an occupational profile, observation of IADL and social interaction skills, and exploration of interests and goals. It was administered to provide information on Larry's ability to cope with a cognitively challenging everyday activity, including the ability to plan ahead, recognize potential conflicts, make performance adjustments, simultaneously keep track of information, restrain impulsive responses, self-monitor performance, and use efficient strategies or methods.

Overview of performance

Larry required excessive time to complete the WCPA (40 min), and scores were below the 5th percentile, as illustrated in the performance profile (Exhibit 4.13). Performance was characterized by difficulty getting started, slow processing time, inability to adjust performance when conflicts occurred, concrete interpretations, and a tendency to overfocus on pieces of information.

Larry spent more than 8 minutes reviewing the appointment list and did not appear to know how or where to begin. He had difficulty getting started and was unsure of how to go about handling appointments that involved choices. Several times throughout the activity, he stared at the list or into space for several minutes without any action. At one point, he stopped

Exhibit 4.13. Visual Performance Profile: Case 4, Larry

Percentile	Entered Appointment	Accurate Appointment	Rules Followed	Strategy Use	Efficiency	Planning Time	Total Time	Percentile
≥95								≥95
>75								>75
70								70
60								60
50								50
40								40
30								30
25								25
20								20
10								10
<5	**X** (12)	**X** (5)	**X** (0)	**X** (1)	**N/A**	**X** (8.5 min)	**X** (40 min)	<5

The majority of errors involved omission of appointments (5) and failure to enter appointments completely (4), reflecting an overall tendency to miss information, without awareness. It appears as though some of the missing appointments may have been related to misinterpretations rather than a failure to attend to information. Two extraneous personal appointments that were not on the list were added.

Error Analysis Profile: Case 4, Larry

	Missing	Repetition	Incomplete	Location	Time	Extraneous	Self-Recognition
0		X				Added 2 appointments	
1				X	X		X
2							
3+	X (5)		X (4)				

prematurely and seemed to think he was finished. When the examiner asked whether he was done, he recognized that he had still not entered the majority of appointments.

Inability to handle unexpected problems was observed several times. For example, Larry entered an appointment in the wrong location and did not know what to do because he knew he could not cross it out. He sat there for another several minutes before reentering the appointment. He also became stuck when he realized that the calendar ended at 9:00 p.m. and was unsure how to enter the movie appointment because it ended at 11:00 p.m. In some cases, he became fixated on individual aspects of the appointment. For example, he stated that he did not use a carpool and did not have a volunteer job so he did not want to enter these appointments in the calendar. The simulated nature of the calendar was emphasized; however, Larry continued to leave out appointments that were not in his routine and add other appointments that were not on the list.

Strategy use

Strategy frequency. Larry was observed to use 2 strategies inconsistently, and he used them ineffectively.

Task methods. Larry inconsistently checked off appointments as he was reading them (before they were entered). This created confusion at times because he thought he had entered appointments when he had not. He also inconsistently underlined words, but the words he underlined were often unimportant.

Strategy generation. Larry did not generate any strategies.

Self-monitoring and self-awareness

During the task. Larry immediately self-recognized a location error he made during the activity, but no other spontaneous error recognition or self-checking was observed.

After-task awareness of strategies. Larry was unable to describe any strategies or methods that he used.

After-task self-perceptions. After the task, Larry acknowledged that some appointments were left out; however, he said they were not important anyway and did not need to be included. He rated the task as easy and estimated that he had 17 of 17 correct. He estimated that he had completed the activity in 10 minutes when it fact it required 40 minutes.

Recommendations for treatment for Larry

In summary, Larry demonstrated difficulty in getting started and efficiently moving through a multiple-step activity. Performance was slow and characterized by multiple periods of lack of productivity (staring but not acting). He had difficulty dealing with conflicts or unexpected problems and became stuck on one viewpoint or method, suggesting reduced flexibility and problem-solving skills.

Occupational therapy treatment is recommended to assist Larry in reducing unproductive periods of time within an activity (staring) and increasing initiation and time awareness. The use of external signals such as periodic alarms or self-recorded voice messages on a tablet or cell phone may be helpful in enhancing initiation, time awareness, and persistence of action in multiple-step activities.

Task-specific solutions including adaptations, action scripts, or errorless and repetitive practice are recommended to enhance function. Action scripts involve repetitive rehearsal of a subroutine or action in a specific context. For example, the subroutine "Before getting ready for bed, take out clothes for the next day" can be repeatedly practiced with prompts to prevent errors. As actions become practiced and automated, less executive control and initiation are required.

External cues that trigger alternative solutions, such as a visual schedule with pictures of different dinners for each day of the week, are recommended. As time productivity improves and Larry learns to use external cues, treatment can focus on helping him learn to seek external cues on his own (e.g., set a timer, look at recipe cards when unsure of what to eat).

Case Comparison

Charles and Larry have identical accuracy scores; however, analysis of other aspects of performance provides different implications for intervention. Charles made errors because of an inability to regulate his actions and impulses. Larry had difficulty with initiation and poor time awareness, and he demonstrated concrete, rigid patterns of behavior. Both Charles and Larry demonstrated decreased awareness, but they differed in the quality of their response. Larry acknowledged some errors but rationalized them. Over rationalization suggests that even when errors are identified, the person does not recognize the need to alter performance (possibly because of premorbid personality characteristics or too-rigid thinking patterns). This type of unawareness presents an obstacle to use of a metacognitive or strategy-based approach.

Charles also demonstrated decreased awareness. He did, though, acknowledge that the task was challenging and vaguely indicated that he needed to concentrate better, suggesting that if Charles had a better understanding of his performance, he might be able to alter his responses. A metacognitive or self-regulation approach should thus be attempted.

Case Example 5: WCPA Report and Treatment Planning—Youth (Ages 16–21), Version A

Mary is a 16-year-old girl with postconcussion syndrome, sustained during a soccer game when she hit her head on the field after another player ran into her. Since the accident, she has complained of fatigue and difficulty concentrating and remembering and says that she "can't think." She reports that she is unable to do simple math problems in her head and is unable to keep up with school demands.

Mary finds crowded environments and noisy places overwhelming, and as a result she rarely goes out with groups of friends as she did before the accident. Her parents report that she often watches TV or sleeps during her free time and no longer initiates former activities. She has become increasingly isolated, withdrawn, and depressed.

Initial evaluation

The WCPA was administered as one component of the occupational therapy assessment, which also included examination of interests, activity limitations, participation restrictions, and goals. It was administered to provide information on Mary's ability to cope with a cognitively challenging everyday activity, including the ability to plan ahead, recognize potential conflicts, make performance adjustments, simultaneously keep track of information, restrain impulsive responses, self-monitor performance, and use efficient strategies or methods.

Overview of performance

Mary entered a limited number of appointments (14 of 18); however, 13 of the 14 appointments she entered were accurate, placing her in the low average range for accuracy. The number of appointments entered was less than the number entered by 95% of people in her age range. Total time, efficiency, and rules followed were also significantly below average. In the latter, she lost track of time and forgot about leaving Wednesday free. She never referred back to the instructions, even though they were on the table. The number of strategies used was in the low average range. Mary's performance is summarized in the visual performance profile below (Exhibit 4.14)

Strategy use

Strategy frequency. Mary was observed to use 3 strategies (low average range); however, they appeared to increase rather than decrease effort.

Task methods. Mary initially used a highlighter to color code appointments according to different days of the week, but this method was ineffective because several appointments had choices. She then tried to number the appointments in the order in which she would enter them, but this too became confusing, and she ended up missing several appointments. She was also observed to inconsistently use her finger while reading.

Strategy generation (after task). Strategy generation was limited to "thinking better," and Mary could not explain what she meant by this.

Self-monitoring and self-awareness

During the task. Self-checking was observed during the task. Mary was very careful to ensure that the appointments she entered were in their correct location and time. The one time an error occurred, however, she immediately recognized it and attempted to self-correct it. During the task, she frequently put her hand on her head and appeared overwhelmed. She also put her head down on the table and closed her eyes, saying she was having difficulty focusing and was mentally fatigued.

Exhibit 4.14. Visual Performance Profile: Case 5, Mary

Percentile	Entered Appointment	Accurate Appointment	Rules Followed	Strategy Use	Efficiency	Planning Time	Total Time	Percentile
≥95								≥95
>75								>75
70								70
60								60
50								50
40								40
30		X (13)						30
25				X (3)				25
20						X (2 min)		20
10			X (3)		X (200)			10
<5	X (14)						X (33 min)	<5

The majority of errors were missing appointments, as indicated in the error analysis profile.

Error Analysis Profile: Case 5, Mary

	Missing	Repetition	Incomplete	Location	Time	Extraneous	Self-Recognition
0		X	X	X		None	
1					X		X
2							
3+	X(4)						

After-task awareness of strategies. Mary was able to describe her color coding and numbering methods, but she did not understand why they were ineffective.

After-task self-perceptions. Mary readily acknowledged difficulties and indicated that the number of appointments made the task overwhelming. She also stated that at times she felt overloaded and had difficulty concentrating. Her estimation of time and performance was generally accurate.

Recommendations for treatment for Mary

In summary, Mary demonstrated difficulty managing all of the items on the list and appeared overwhelmed by the amount of information presented simultaneously. Although she omitted several appointments, those that were attended to were generally accurate, reflecting good ability to manage task components and details once information is fully attended to. Mary's performance, however, was excessively slow and effortful, with rest breaks and complaints of fatigue and feeling overloaded.

Occupational therapy treatment is recommended to increase Mary's overall activity level, including engagement in meaningful activities and social participation. Multitasking and dealing with increased information is an inherent part of everyday life for a teenager. Mary could benefit from guidance in effectively managing and coping with everyday tasks and situations that involve multiple steps or increased information presented simultaneously. Initial stages of treatment should include helping Mary recognize situations in which the amount of information presented may be too much.

Once Mary can anticipate or identify situations that may be overwhelming, she can be guided in using methods to simplify tasks herself. Task simplification methods include breaking up tasks into smaller, more manageable components; visually screening out or removing information; and using efficient ways of organizing and categorizing information to reduce the number of stimuli. Higher-level functional activities such as planning a party for a friend, planning a schedule of weekend activities, creating a table or graph of scores of different players in a soccer game, organizing and planning homework assignments, or investigating and learning new apps can be used to practice strategies and recognize or monitor the tendency to skip over or miss task steps and components. Additional strategies such as monitoring attentional lapses, recognizing when breaks are needed, identifying the initial signs and symptoms of feeling overloaded, or asking others to limit the information presented at one time are also recommended.

Summary

Interpretation of WCPA results requires consideration of multiple aspects of performance, including both objective scores and qualitative observations and analysis. The initial section of this chapter describes how WCPA scores (appointments entered, accurate appointments, rules followed, total strategy, efficiency, time) can be compared to the normative sample using the tables presented in Appendix G. This information is particularly important for identifying the presence or extent of performance difficulties. The use of percentiles as well as mean and standard deviations was described. Caution is needed in interpretation of time and strategy scores because faster time or an excessive number of strategies may not be indicative of better performance. Different options for organizing, presenting, and summarizing WCPA results were described and illustrated at the end of this chapter through case examples. Blank summary forms are provided in Appendix F for clinical use.

The majority of this chapter focused on performance analysis and implications of the results of the WCPA for treatment planning. Complete interpretation of the WCPA requires simultaneous integration of information obtained in the After-Task Interview and Rating Scale with objective scores, and qualitative analysis of error types, strategy use, time use, efficiency, adherence to rules, and self-awareness. A tendency to focus on one aspect of performance, such as accuracy of appointments, without considering other aspects of performance can lead to misinterpretations. Clinical examples demonstrated how assessing persons who had similar appointment accuracy scores but differed in other aspects of performance resulted in very different treatment recommendations. The importance of the after-task interview in providing key information related to interpretation and treatment planning was highlighted. Sample evaluation report summaries were provided to illustrate interpretation of results as well to demonstrate how the WCPA can be used across different ages and diagnostic groups to track progress and guide treatment.

CHAPTER 5 Research and Normative Studies

Normative performance on the WCPA Level II has been examined across different ages, ranging from age 16 to 94 years ($N = 435$). Normative studies also have been conducted on WCPA Level III ($N = 175$). The WCPA has been demonstrated to have interrater reliability of scoring (Weiner et al., 2012).

Studies on Youths

The WCPA's discriminative validity has been established between community youths ($n = 49$) and at-risk youths ($n = 113$; Toglia & Berg, 2013). At-risk youths made significantly more errors, followed fewer rules, and used fewer strategies. Moderate relationships were found between academic performance and WCPA performance in youths, suggesting that the skills required to complete the WCPA are also important for academic performance.

This finding was supported by a study examining the WCPA-S with 157 students ages 20–30 enrolled in colleges and universities in Israel ($n = 61$ with ADHD; $n = 96$ without ADHD). Students with ADHD needed significantly more time to complete the task, used fewer strategies, missed more appointments, had more difficulty keeping track of time, and more often expressed that the task was difficult (Lahav & Katz, 2015). Similar to the study by Toglia and Berg (2013), results support discriminative validity and suggest that the WCPA may contribute to prediction of academic success.

The performance of 49 healthy adolescents (ages 16–21) on the WCPA Youth, Level II, Version A (Appendix C.1) is presented in Table 5.1. The majority of participants were female (67%) and White (73%), with an average age of 18.9 years, and were recruited from the community and regular high schools in the St. Louis, Missouri, area.

Participants took an average time of 15.96 minutes ($SD = 6.13$) to complete the task. The average number of accurate appointments was 14.2 ($SD = 2.6$). These average scores are very similar to additional normative data collected for ages 18–39 (see WCPA Level II Normative Sample section) in the New York area, using the WCPA Level II, Version A (see Appendix C). Table 5.2 presents the average number of errors across different error types. Time errors were the most common type, and repetition errors were rarely observed (Toglia & Berg, 2013).

The most common strategies observed in youths were uses finger, crosses out or checks off, fixed appointments first, and self-checks (Table 5.3), with an average of 4.31 strategies used ($SD = 2.01$; Toglia & Berg, 2013). These results are similar to those found with the younger adult population, ages 18–39, described in the WCPA Level II Normative Sample section.

Normative Data for Healthy Adults

Performance of healthy adults was studied for WCPA Levels II and III (Version A). Participants in three age groups (young, middle, and older) were recruited from New York City and surrounding areas or suburbs using snowball sampling techniques. Inclusion criteria for community-dwelling older adults included independent living in the community, English as a primary language, ability to read newspaper print with or without corrective lenses, and normal scores on a mental status screening exam. People with reported learning disabilities, hospitalization for depression or mental health problems, and previous neurological illness or injuries were excluded.

Significant differences on both Level II and Level III of the WCPA were found across younger and older adults. Older adults entered fewer appointments, were less accurate, were slower, used fewer strategies, and broke more rules than younger adults.

Normative studies using Level II also have been conducted in Hebrew in Israel ($N = 280$). The majority of scores, with exception of time and strategy use, were similar to those of U.S. participants, thus extending

Table 5.1. Average Scores on the WCPA Youth (Ages 16–21), Level II ($N = 49$)

WCPA Scores	Score, Mean (*SD*)
Entered appointments	17.4 (0.9)
Total accurate	14.20 (2.6)
Rules followed	4.29 (0.9)
No. of strategies	4.31 (2.0)
Total time	15.96 (6.13)
	Median (Range)
Planning time	0.5 s (0.0–14.0)
Efficiency score	73 (28–316)

Note. SD = standard deviation; WCPA = Weekly Calendar Planning Activity.

From "Performance-Based Measure of Executive Function: Comparison of Community and At-Risk Youth," by J. Toglia & C. Berg, 2013, *American Journal of Occupational Therapy, 67,* p. 519. Copyright © 2013 by the American Occupational Therapy Association. Adapted with permission.

Table 5.3. Most Frequently Used Strategies, WCPA Youth (Ages 16–21), Level II ($N = 49$)

Strategy	*n* (%)
Uses finger	41 (84)
Crosses out or checks off	31 (63)
Fixes first	20 (41)
Self-checks	18 (37)

Note. WCPA = Weekly Calendar Planning Activity.

From "Performance-Based Measure of Executive Function: Comparison of Community and At-Risk Youth," by J. Toglia & C. Berg, 2013, *American Journal of Occupational Therapy, 67,* p. 519. Copyright © 2013 by the American Occupational Therapy Association. Adapted with permission.

the generalizability of some of the findings and suggesting that time and strategy use may be influenced by culture and experiences. Thus, caution should be taken in interpretation of these scores across cultures. The Israeli studies also found that older adults demonstrated a mild decline in performance across the majority of scores (Toglia, Lahav, Kizony, & Ben Ari, 2014).

WCPA Level II Normative Sample: Adults (Ages 18–94)

Normative data for Level II, Version A, were analyzed for 386 healthy adults divided into young, middle, and older age groups (ages 18–39, 40–64, and 65–94, respectively). Average ages for each group are specified in Table 5.4. The majority of participants were female, White, and highly educated. In the area of education, 93% of the younger age group, 81% of the middle age group, and 68% of the older group had more than 12 years of education. No significant differences were found between groups on gender, $\chi^2(2, N = 385) = 0.17, p = .92$. The oldest age group had a significantly greater percentage of White individuals and a lower educational level than the youngest group. Gender and ethnicity did not have an effect on performance; however, educational level had a weak association with accuracy ($r = .20, p = .001$), suggesting that caution should be taken in interpreting results for adults who have lower levels of education, particularly less than 12 years.

Table 5.2. Average Errors on the WCPA Youth (Ages 16–21), Level II ($N = 49$)

Type of Errors	Mean (*SD*)
Missing appointments	0.63 (0.1)
Repetition errors	0.04 (0.3)
Location errors	1.39 (1.4)
Time errors	1.53 (1.4)
Incomplete errors	0.29 (0.6)
Total errors	3.27 (2.4)

Note. SD = standard deviation; WCPA = Weekly Calendar Planning Activity.

From "Performance-Based Measure of Executive Function: Comparison of Community and At-Risk Youth," by J. Toglia & C. Berg, 2013, *American Journal of Occupational Therapy, 67,* p. 519. Copyright © 2013 by the American Occupational Therapy Association. Adapted with permission.

Average WCPA Level II Scores

Table 5.5 presents the means and standard deviations of WCPA scores for each of the three age groups. The average accuracy scores of the younger age group (18–39) are similar to those of the adolescent age group (ages 16–21). Interpretation of means and standard deviations was described in Chapter 4, "Interpretation." The distribution of scores for planning time and efficiency demonstrated significant deviations from the normal distribution, so median scores are presented rather than means.

The percentage of participants following four and five rules are presented in Table 5.6, along with the percentage of participants who answered no questions or one question. The majority of participants followed

Table 5.4. Demographic Characteristics of Level II Adult Participants (N = 386)

Characteristic	Young (Ages 18–39; n = 114) Mean (*SD*)	Middle (Ages 40–64; n = 142) Mean (*SD*)	Older (Ages 65–94; n = 130) Mean (*SD*)
Age, years	28.6 (6.4)	53.1 (8.3)	73.6 (6.2)
Gender, n (%)			
Male	45 (39.5)	53 (37.3)	48 (36.9)
Female	69 (60.5)	89 (62.7)	81 (62.3)
Race, n (%)			
Black/African-American	11 (9.6)	21 (14.8)	22 (16.9)
Asian/Pacific Islander	12 (10.5)	9 (6.3)	3 (2.3)
Caucasian	66 (57.9)	92 (64.8)	96 (73.8)
Hispanic	14 (12.3)	8 (5.6)	3 (2.3)
Other	5 (4.4)	11 (7.7)	6 (4.6)
Education level, years, n (%)			
<12	1 (0.9)	1 (0.7)	5 (3.8)
12	7 (6.1)	26 (18.3)	37 (28.5)
13–15	25 (21.9)	30 (21.1)	28 (21.5)
≥16	81 (71.1)	85 (59.9)	60 (46.2)

Note. SD = standard deviation.

at least 4 of 5 rules, including not answering any of the questions.

Group Differences

Group differences were analyzed using a one-way between-subjects analysis of variance (ANOVA) or the nonparametric equivalent (Kruskal–Wallis test) for all WCPA scores presented in Table 5.5. There were significant differences across age groups for entered appointments, $F(2,383) = 9.3$, $p = .000$; accurate appointments, $F(2,383) = 23.1$, $p = .000$; rules followed, $F(2,383) = 15.5$, $p = .000$; number of strategies, $F = 6.6(2,383)$, $p = .001$; and efficiency, $\chi^2(2, N = 383) = 30.4$, $p = .000$. Post hoc comparisons with Bonferroni correction showed no significant differences between the young and middle age groups across all WCPA scores, with the exception of total time. The middle age group was significantly faster than the younger age group ($p = .02$) and the older age group ($p = .02$). The average WCPA scores of the older group were significantly different from those of the younger and middle age groups for the majority of WCPA tasks.

Table 5.5. Average Scores on the WCPA Level II by Age Group (N = 386)

WCPA Scores	Young (Ages 18–39; n = 114) Mean (*SD*)	Middle (Ages 40–64; n = 142) Mean (*SD*)	Older (Ages 65–94; n = 130) Mean (*SD*)
Entered appointments	16.5 (0.8)	16.4 (0.9)	16.0 (1.3)
Total accurate	14.2 (2.3)	14.0 (2.1)	12.3 (3.0)
Rules followed	4.3 (0.7)	4.3 (0.7)	3.8 (1.0)
No. of strategies	5.0 (2.3)	5.1 (2.4)	4.2 (2.2)
Total time, min	16.3 (6.7)	14.1 (5.0)	16.2 (7.3)
	Median (Range)	**Median (Range)**	**Median (Range)**
Planning time, min	1.0 (0.0–20.5)	1.1 (0.0–14.0)	0.8 (0.0–19.0)
Efficiency score[a]	77.6 (27.9–478.7)	67.8 (17–237)	91.7 (26.8–654.3)

Note. SD = standard deviation; min = minutes; WCPA = Weekly Calendar Planning Activity.

[a]Only includes those with 7 or more accurate (n = 382).

Table 5.6. Percentage of Rules Followed and Questions Answered by Healthy Adults ($N = 386$) on the WCPA, Level II

Rules	Young (Ages 18–39; *n* = 114)		Middle (Ages 40–64; *n* = 142)		Older (Ages 65–94; *n* = 130)		Total	
	%	*n*	%	*n*	%	*n*	%	*n*
Rules followed								
All 5	48.2	55	46.5	66	25.4	33	39.9	154
4 or 5	87.7	100	85.9	122	70.0	91	81.1	313
Questions answered								
0 answered	80.7	92	79.6	113	70.8	92	76.9	297
0 or 1	88.6	101	91.5	130	80.8	105	87.0	336

Note. WCPA = Weekly Calendar Planning Activity.

An exception was planning time, which was similar across all age groups and did not appear to influence performance. Both strategy use and the ability to adhere to rules were associated with performance (*rs* = .26 and .32, respectively, *ps* = .000). This is similar to trends observed with Level III participants

Error Analysis

Table 5.7 presents the means and standard deviations for each error type. The number of errors increased with age, across all types of errors; however, the number of missing appointments appeared to increase the most in older age groups, whereas the number of repetition errors remained low across all age groups. A one-way ANOVA was conducted to evaluate differences in error types between age groups. Results confirmed that repetition errors were not significantly different across age groups; however, significant differences were found for missing appointments, $F(2,383) = 9.9$, $p = .000$; location errors, $F(2,383) = 3.7$, $p = .03$; incomplete or inaccurate appointments, $F(2,383) = 13.5$, $p = .000$; and time errors, $F(2,383) = 5.0$, $p = .007$.

Table 5.8 illustrates the frequency of scores for each error type across the three age groups. The results confirm that repetition errors were infrequent across age groups (<8%), and location errors occurred most frequently. Both missing appointments and incomplete or inaccurate errors appeared to demonstrate the largest percentage increase in the older age group compared with the younger and middle age groups.

Older Adults (Ages 60 or Older)

The means and standard deviations for errors in the older group were further subdivided across each decade (60–69, 70–79, and 80 or older) and are presented in Table 5.9. A one-way ANOVA indicated a significant difference between age groups in accuracy, $F(2,177) = 6.7$, $p = .002$, and rules followed, $F(2,177) = 8.1$, $p = .000$. A follow-up *t* test confirmed this difference

Table 5.7. Average WCPA Level II Errors ($N = 386$)

Error Type	Young (Ages 18–39; *n* = 114) Mean (*SD*)	Middle (Ages 40–64; *n* = 142) Mean (*SD*)	Older (Ages 65–94; *n* = 130) Mean (*SD*)
Missing appointments	0.5 (0.8)	0.6 (0.9)	1.0 (1.2)
Repetition errors	0.1 (0.3)	0.1 (0.3)	0.2 (0.6)
Location errors	1.2 (1.4)	1.4 (1.3)	1.7 (1.5)
Time errors	0.9 (1.1)	0.7 (0.9)	1.2 (1.3)
Incomplete errors	0.2 (0.4)	0.3 (0.7)	0.7 (1.3)
Total errors	2.8 (2.3)	3.0 (2.1)	4.7 (3.0)

Note. SD = standard deviation; WCPA = Weekly Calendar Planning Activity.

Table 5.8. Occurrence of Each Error Type in Healthy Adults (N = 386) on the WCPA, Level II

	Young (Ages 18–39; n = 114)		Middle (Ages 40–64; n = 142)		Older (Ages 65–94; n = 130)	
Errors	%	n	%	n	%	n
Omissions (missing)						
0	67	76	62	88	42	54
1	21	24	25	35	35	45
2	9	10	8	11	12	16
≥3	4	4	6	8	12	15
Location						
0	40	46	33	47	25	33
1	25	28	27	38	26	34
2	18	21	23	32	21	27
≥3	17	19	18	25	28	36
Repeated						
0	94	107	94	133	93	120
1	4	5	5	7	4	5
2	2	2	1	2	3	4
≥3	—	—	—	—	1	1
Incomplete						
0	88	100	84	119	65	85
1	11	12	10	14	16	21
2	1	1	4	5	10	13
≥3	1	1	3	4	9	11
Time						
0	48	55	49	69	36	47
1	32	36	35	50	37	48
2	11	12	12	17	12	16
≥3	10	11	4	6	15	19

Note. — = no occurrence.

Table 5.9. Average WCPA Level II Scores for Older Adults (n = 180)

	Ages 60–69 (n = 85)	Ages 70–79 (n = 70)	Ages 80–94 (n = 25)
WCPA Scores	Mean (*SD*)	Mean (*SD*)	Mean (*SD*)
Entered appointments	16.2 (1.1)	15.9 (1.4)	16.0 (1.2)
Total accurate	13.5 (2.7)	12.2 (3.0)	11.5 (3.0)
Rules followed	4.2 (0.7)	3.8 (1.0)	3.5 (1.1)
No. of strategies	3.8 (2.0)	4.1 (2.2)	4.5 (2.2)
Total time, min	13.8 (5.5)	17.4 (7.9)	14.7 (7.1)
	Median (Range)	Median (Range)	Median (Range)
Planning time, min	1.0 (0.0–17.1)	1.0 (0.0–19.0)	0.3 (0.1–3.0)
Efficiency score[a]	74.3 (17–581)	92.9 (27–654)	101.7 (46–442.4)

Note. SD = standard deviation; min = minutes; WCPA = Weekly Calendar Planning Activity.

[a]Included only for those with 7 or more accurate (n = 382)

Table 5.10. Average WCPA Level II Errors for Older Adults (n = 180)

Error Type	Ages 60–69 (n = 85) Mean (SD)	Ages 70–79 (n = 70) Mean (SD)	Ages 80–94 (n = 25) Mean (SD)
Missing appointments	0.8 (1.1)	1.1 (1.4)	1.1 (1.2)
Repetition errors	0.1 (0.5)	0.2 (0.8)	0.0 (0.0)
Location errors	1.3 (1.5)	1.7 (1.4)	2.1 (1.4)
Time errors	1.0 (1.2)	1.2 (1.4)	1.0 (1.2)
Incomplete errors	0.3 (0.7)	0.6 (1.2)	1.4 (1.7)
Total errors	3.5 (2.7)	4.8 (3.0)	5.6 (3.1)

Note. SD = standard deviation; WCPA = Weekly Calendar Planning Activity.

between the 60–69 age group and the 70–79 age group in both accuracy, $t(153) = 2.8, p = .006$, and rules followed, $t(153) = 3.9, p = .003$. The limited number of participants in the 80–94 age group ($n = 25$) limit statistical comparisons with this group; however, there appeared to be a continued downward trend in accuracy as age increased.

Means and standard deviations for errors in the older age group are presented in Table 5.10 for closer examination. Errors in entering appointment names completely and accurately increased the most across each decade. A one-way ANOVA confirmed significant differences for incomplete or inaccurate entry of appointment names, $F(2,177) = 9.4, p = .000$, and location errors, $F(2,177) = 3.4, p = .04$. A follow-up t test confirmed a significant difference for incomplete or inaccurate errors between the 60–69 age group and the 70–79 age group, $t(153) = 2.0, p < .05$; however, no other significant differences were found between these two age groups. The small number of participants in the 80–94 age group ($n = 25$) limits definitive statistical comparisons with this group; however, incomplete and location errors appeared to significantly decline as age increased. Other errors (time, missing appointments, repetitions) appeared relatively stable as age increased.

Strategies

The average number of strategies used by the younger, middle, and older age groups is presented in Table 5.9. The younger age group (18–39) used significantly fewer strategies than the older age group (65–94). The frequency of each type of strategy is presented in Table 5.11. The three most common strategies used by all age groups (including the adolescent group) were crosses out or checks off, uses finger, and self-checks.

The difference between the older group and all other age groups (including adolescents) is that the older group did not use the strategy of entering fixed appointments first as frequently as the other groups. Entering fixed appointments first is a highly effective strategy for this task; therefore, low usage of this strategy may have contributed to lower levels of accuracy in older adults. In comparison to other age groups, the older group also used the strategy of talking aloud more frequently than the other groups (Table 5.11).

WCPA Level III Data, Adults (Ages 18–87)

Normative data for Level III, Version A, were analyzed for 175 healthy adults divided into three age groups: young (ages 18–39), middle (ages 40–64), and old (ages 65–87). Similar to the demographics for the WCPA Level II sample, the majority of participants were female, White, and highly educated, with the older age group including a significantly higher percentage of White individuals and a lower percentage of participants with high education levels than the younger age group (Table 5.12).

Average Level III Performance

Table 5.13 presents the means and standard deviations for WCPA scores for Level III. The average number of entered appointments and accuracy scores are lower than those for the WCPA Level II across

Table 5.11. Frequency of Strategy Use by Level II Participants (n = 297)

Strategy Used	Younger (Ages 18–39; n = 101) %	Middle (Ages 40–64; n = 102) %	Older (Ages 65–94; n = 94) %
Underlines, highlights, or circles words	35.6	43.1	16.0
Uses finger	67.3	84.3	81.9
Talks aloud or verbal rehearsal	32.7	37.3	46.8
Crosses out or checks off	79.2	78.4	55.3
Categorizes, organizes, or codes appointments	26.7	26.5	12.8
Enters fixed appointments first, then flexible appointments	52.5	69.6	33.0
Written plan or notes to self	27.7	28.4	18.1
Crosses off specified free day	16.8	22.5	8.5
Self-checks	41.6	63.7	51.1
Reports use of internal strategies	21.8	18.6	17.0
Other	16.8	22.5	18.1

all age groups, whereas strategy use, time for completion, and efficiency increased. Because strategy use typically increases with task complexity, it is not surprising that the normative sample used a greater number of strategies in Level III as compared with Level II. The results suggests that regardless of age, WCPA performance was influenced by increased task complexity in Level III. An increase in the amount of extraneous or irrelevant information presented at one time appears to similarly decrease performance across all age groups.

Age Group Differences

Similar to the WCPA Level II findings, the majority of WCPA Level III scores demonstrated significant differences among age groups as measured by either one-way ANOVA or Kruskal–Wallis test. For example, entered appointments, $F(2, 172) = 3.2$, $p = .04$;

Table 5.12. Demographic Characteristics of Level III Adult Participants (N = 175)

Characteristic	Young (Ages 18–39; n = 51) Mean (SD)	Middle (Ages 40–64; n = 83) Mean (SD)	Old (Ages 65–87; n = 41) Mean (SD)
Age, years	28.7 (6.4)	54.6 (8.9)	71.8 (5.3)
Gender, n (%)			
Male	21 (41.2)	23 (27.7)	16 (39.0)
Female	30 (58.8)	60 (72.3)	25 (61.0)
Race, n (%)			
White	30 (58.8)	57 (68.7)	31 (75.6)
Black	13 (25.5)	12 (14.5)	3 (7.3)
Other	8 (15.7)	14 (16.9)	7 (17.1)
Education level, years, n (%)			
9–11	0 (0.0)	3 (3.5)	5 (12.2)
12	2 (3.9)	12 (14.5)	5 (12.2)
13–15	13 (25.5)	18 (21.7)	13 (31.7)
≥16	36 (70.6)	50 (60.2)	18 (43.9)

Note. SD = standard deviation.

Table 5.13. Average Scores on the WCPA Level III by Age Group ($N = 175$)

WCPA Scores	Young (Ages 18–39; $n = 51$)	Middle (Ages 40–64; $n = 83$)	Older (Ages 65–87; $n = 41$)
	Mean (*SD*)	Mean (*SD*)	Mean (*SD*)
Entered appointments	16.0 (0.9)	15.6 (1.2)	15.5 (1.4)
Total accurate	13.2 (2.5)	12.2 (2.6)	11.5 (2.7)
Rules followed	4.4 (0.8)	4.1 (0.9)	3.9 (1.1)
No. of strategies	6.6 (2.4)	5.4 (2.4)	5.5 (2.7)
Total time, min	27.1 (11.2)	23.0 (10.8)	28.1 (13.7)
Efficiency score[a]	176.4 (115.2)	182.4 (161.7)	227.7 (104.2)
	Median (Range)	Median (Range)	Median (Range)
Planning time, min	5.0 (0.2–45.0)	2.3 (0.0–27.0)	4.0 (0.1–40.0)
Efficiency score[a]	146.1 (55–600)	147.1 (59.1–563)	227.3 (85.5–611.7)

Note. SD = standard deviation; min = minutes; WCPA = Weekly Calendar Planning Activity.

[a]Includes only those with seven or more accurate ($n = 173$).

accuracy, $F(2, 172) = 6.8$, $p < .001$; rules followed, $F(2, 172) = 5.3$, $p = .006$; strategies, $F(2, 172) = 3.1$, $p = .05$; and efficiency, $\chi^2(2, N = 175) = 15.6$, $p = .000$, were significantly different. An exception was planning time and total time, which were similar across age groups.

A post hoc analysis using Bonferroni adjustment showed no significant differences between the young and middle age groups in accuracy, appointments entered, and rules followed. Similar to Level II, however, the younger and older groups were significantly different in accuracy, number of entered appointments, and rules followed. Both strategy use and the ability to adhere to rules were significantly associated with performance ($n = 174$; $rs = .40$ and $.37$, respectively, $ps = .000$).

Error Types

Table 5.14 presents the average scores for specific error types. A one-way ANOVA comparing differences in specific errors across age groups found that the average number of errors was significantly different across ages for missing appointments, $F(2, 172) = 3.2$, $p = .04$, and for time errors, $F(2, 172) = 4.5$, $p = .01$. No significant differences were found between other types of errors across age groups.

Strategies

The average number of strategies used in each age group are presented in Table 5.15. Similar to trends observed for the WCPA Level II, the total number of strategies used showed a gradual decline across

Table 5.14. Average WCPA Level III Errors ($N = 175$)

Error Type	Young (Ages 18–39; $n = 51$) Mean (*SD*)	Middle (Ages 40–64; $n = 83$) Mean (*SD*)	Older (Ages 65–87; $n = 41$) Mean (*SD*)
Missing appointments	1.0 (0.9)	1.4 (1.2)	1.5 (1.4)
Repetition errors	0.2 (0.5)	0.2 (0.6)	0.3 (0.7)
Location errors	1.3 (1.3)	1.5 (1.3)	1.5 (1.2)
Time errors	0.8 (1.1)	0.9 (1.1)	1.4 (1.4)
Incomplete errors	0.4 (0.8)	0.9 (1.4)	0.9 (1.5)
Total errors	3.7 (2.5)	4.8 (2.6)	5.4 (2.6)

Note. SD = standard deviation; WCPA = Weekly Calendar Planning Activity.

Table 5.15. Frequency of Strategy Use by Level III Participants ($N = 170$)

	Younger (Ages 18–39; $n = 49$)	Middle (Ages 40–64; $n = 83$)	Older (Ages 64–94; $n = 38$)
Strategy Used	%	%	%
Underlines, highlights, or circles words	56.0	51.8	39.5
Uses finger	70.0	72.3	65.8
Talks aloud or verbal rehearsal	20.0	41.0	42.1
Crosses out or checks off	56.0	43.4	53.7
Categorizes, organizes, or codes appointments	12.0	4.8	0.0
Enters fixed appointments first, then flexible appointments	50.0	48.2	47.4
Written plan or notes to self	58.0	53.0	44.7
Crosses off specified free day	24.0	13.3	31.6
Self-checks	54.0	45.8	34.2
Reports use of internal strategies	30.0	15.7	18.4
Other	16.0	14.5	26.3

different age groups. The most frequently used strategy across all age groups was similar to that of Level II and includes uses finger and crosses out or checks off. The younger age group tended to underline, circle, or highlight key words and write out plans more than the older age group.

Future Research

The normative sample allows for comparison of results; however, the sample reported in this manual was limited to single geographic locations: the St. Louis, Missouri, area for adolescents and the greater New York City area for adults. The younger and older adult groups differed in educational level and ethnicity. Particular caution should be taken in interpreting results in people with less than 12 years of education; in older age groups (ages 80 or older); and in people whose primary language is not English. Preliminary normative studies in Israel have suggested that time and strategy use could be influenced by culture, so care should be taken in interpreting these scores in people of different cultural backgrounds (Toglia et al., 2014). Although there is general support for the stability of accuracy scores across cultures and locations, a wider representative normative sample is desirable across all age groups and levels.

The alternate versions of the WCPA have been constructed with care, including ensuring the same number, order, and length of variable and fixed appointments. However, the alternate versions need to be tested for equivalence. Interrater scoring of appointments has been examined, but future studies should include interrater reliability of strategy ratings. Information in the After-Task Interview and Rating Scale provides important qualitative information, but the responses could be rated in the future by examining the number and specificity of examples compared with controls. Research identifying the minimal or clinically important difference in scores would be useful in providing standard interpretation of the WCPA in measuring changes from pre- to post-intervention in clinical populations.

The WCPA has wide application and is currently being studied in several populations, for example, young adults in a mental health setting in Sweden, adolescents with primary generalized epilepsy in Israel, people with Parkinson's disease and subjective cognitive complaints, and people with stroke and acquired brain injury. The Middle/High School version is currently being tested in youths with concussion and mild traumatic brain injury.

Because subtle impairments in EF have been identified in a wide range of conditions as discussed in the introduction to this manual, the WCPA should prove useful with many different populations. Research examining differences in WCPA performance with particular groups of clients is strongly encouraged.

Results of the WCPA could be compared with those of other measures of EF, IADLs, and participation. Analysis of WCPA components such as strategy use, error patterns, rule following, and self-recognition of errors could be examined to track changes over time or the course of recovery. Use of the WCPA in predicting outcome or risk for functional decline could also be examined. For example, during normative studies of older adults, a subgroup of older adults was observed to have lower performance than others in the same age group, although they were living independently. It would be important to continue to follow older adults with lower scores on the WCPA longitudinally because early EF symptoms have been demonstrated to predict functional and cognitive decline. Finally, therapist perceptions of the WCPA's utility in providing information relevant to treatment could be examined.

The dynamic test–teach–retest version, described in Chapter 6, "Dynamic Assessment," needs further examination to determine whether it provides more information for treatment or whether responsiveness to mediation or observed change is a stronger predictor of outcome than is baseline score.

Future Development

The WCPA is a paper-and-pencil task. Future development includes creating tablet and computerized versions of this instrument with automatic scoring. The WCPA has been used informally with the Google Calendar and the iPad calendar, but challenges included logistics of scoring as well as different levels of familiarity and comfort with the tablet and electronic calendars. This was particularly true for older adults.

CHAPTER 6 Dynamic Assessment: Use of the WCPA in a Test–Teach–Retest Format

The WCPA can also be administered using a test–teach–retest dynamic assessment format, an alternative format that may provide additional information related to treatment. This format has not been formally tested but may be useful in clinical practice when more in-depth information related to treatment is desired.

Test–Teach–Retest

In the test–teach–retest version, the WCPA is administered in the standard manner, and baseline performance is obtained. The therapist reviews results with the client and discusses strategies that could be used, following the guidelines presented in this chapter. An equivalent form of the WCPA is then re-administered within the same session, if possible, to determine learning and carryover of strategies. In essence, an intervention trial is sandwiched between a pre- and post-WCPA to examine learning effects.

The test–teach–retest format provides information on modifiability of performance, or the magnitude and type of performance change possible. Dynamic assessment requires a paradigm shift. Its philosophy, purpose, objectives, and methods are different than those of conventional tests (Toglia, 2011; Toglia & Cermak, 2009).

The test–teach–retest format provides information on the ability to carry over learning or maintain performance when cues are withdrawn, thus providing a direct indication of learning. Many performance-based assessments use graded cues to examine the degree of assistance needed for successful performance. This information can provide useful guidance to caregivers, but it is not always enough to know that performance changes while another person is providing cues. The examiner also needs to analyze performance when the cues are removed because it provides information on the ability to integrate and apply information that has just been taught.

Dynamic Assessment

The intent of dynamic assessment is to supplement findings of static or conventional tests, not to replace them. Dynamic assessment provides information that is directly related to intervention. For example, if a client is unable to carry over learning or modify performance in response to therapist guidance, it suggests that treatment approaches that do not expect learning or changes in the client's skills may be most appropriate. In essence, dynamic assessment looks more like treatment than assessment and provides an indication of responsiveness to intervention. Proponents of dynamic assessment have argued that treatment planning requires tests that more closely resemble the treatment process. Limitations of the test–teach–retest dynamic method include longer administration time, additional therapist training, and the inability to use the WCPA as an outcome measure because mediation occurs within the test. Research using the WCPA dynamic format is needed to determine whether it is predictive of response to treatment or outcome.

The test–teach–retest format has been widely described in the dynamic assessment literature (Haywood & Lidz, 2007; Weingartz, Wiedl, & Watzke, 2008). Studies have found that, compared with static assessments, dynamic assessment predicts rehabilitation outcome (Wiedl, Schottke, Green, & Nuechterlein, 2004) and work skill acquisition (Sergi, Kern, Mintz, & Green, 2005) in people with mental illness, differentiates among people with similar baseline scores (Toglia, 2011; Toglia & Cermak, 2009), and improves outcome prediction in people with brain injury (Uprichard, Kupshik, Pine, & Fletcher, 2009). A recent review of dynamic testing literature in adults supported the added value of dynamic assessment over conventional methods in predicting rehabilitation outcome (Boosman, Bovend'Eerdt, Visser-Meily, Nijboer, & van Heugten, 2014).

Test–Teach–Retest Format

Materials

The test–teach–retest format uses the same forms and materials as described in Chapter 2, "Administration," with the addition of the two optional forms that are at the end of this chapter.

1. The After-Task Interview form can be substituted by the WCPA Dynamic Test–Retest After-Task Awareness Interview (Appendix 6.A). This form is abbreviated and focuses only on assessing awareness. The full After-Task Interview can be done, but it is not necessary with this format.
2. An additional optional form, the Test–Teach–Retest Dynamic Assessment Summary (Appendix 6.B), can be used to assist in summarizing the results of the dynamic testing procedure.

The test–teach–retest format involves the following steps.

Step 1: Test Phase

The examiner obtains baseline performance using usual testing procedures. No cues are provided during performance. The WCPA Dynamic Test–Retest After-Task Awareness Interview form at the end of this chapter can be used, following the guidelines below, instead of the typical After-Task Interview and Rating Scale form in Appendix E.7.

Awareness is explored through a series of structured questions that are asked in order from general to specific to understand the client's perceptions of his or her performance. Adults with acquired brain injury tend to show greater levels of awareness for specific task components than for general questions or questions related to cognitive symptoms.

Dynamic Test–Retest After-Task Awareness Interview

The Dynamic Test After-Task Awareness Interview investigates the client's awareness of his or her performance by using questions that gradually become more specific, as outlined below. The client is initially asked a general awareness question (1) about whether he or she encountered any challenges or difficulties, similar to the usual after-task interview. If the client is able to provide specific examples of challenges or difficulties in response to this general awareness question, questioning stops, and there is no need to probe or ask subsequent questions (2 or 3). If the client does not acknowledge difficulties that were observed, appears unaware of errors, or vaguely acknowledges difficulties but cannot provide examples, a symptom-specific question is then asked, as described next. If the client continues to demonstrate limited awareness, a task-specific question is asked. Awareness questions 1, 2, and 3 are

1. *General awareness questions:* Did you encounter any difficulties or challenges (obstacles) while you were doing this activity? What kinds of difficulties (problems, challenges) did you experience?
2. *Symptom-specific awareness questions:* Did you experience any difficulties keeping track of what you needed to do? Paying attention to details? Staying organized? (The question should be specific to the cognitive symptom observed.)
3. *Task-specific awareness questions:* Did you experience any difficulties in remembering to cross each item off the list? Following the rules? Placing the appointments in the correct location? Indicating the correct amount of time for the appointment? (The question should be specific to the task error observed.)

These questions are asked in order from general to specific. On the basis of the client's responses to these questions, the clinician can assign a rating ranging from 1 (*good awareness*) to 6 (*unaware*) as described in Exhibit 6.1. If the client acknowledges vague difficulties with general questions (rating × 2), the examiner may still proceed with more specific questions; however, the highest level rating is still assigned (2).

Exhibit 6.1. Performance Self-Perception

Rating	Self-Perception of Performance
1	Client acknowledges cognitive difficulties with general questions and can provide 1 or more specific examples.
2	Client acknowledges vague difficulties with general question ("mind didn't work right") but is unable to provide specific examples.
3	Client acknowledges difficulties only with questions directed at specific cognitive problems or symptoms ("Did you have any difficulty keeping track of information? Attending to details?").
4	Client acknowledges difficulties only with task-specific questions ("Did you have any difficulty managing the appointments with choices? Remembering not to schedule appointments on Wednesday? Placing the appointments in the correct place or time slot?").
5	Client blames errors on external sources, identifies problems with task or physical deficits.
	a. Client acknowledges only physical difficulties or difficulties with specific parts of a task (e.g., "It was hard to write or fit the appointments in the box") but does not acknowledge cognitive difficulties.
	b. Client acknowledges some errors but provides a rationale or blames the difficulties on external sources ("Directions were unclear; these are not my appointments; the appointments I left out were unimportant").
6	Client does not acknowledge any errors, challenges, or difficulties with the task.

Source. The Multi-Context Approach to Cognitive Rehabilitation of Executive Dysfunction: Promoting Strategy Use and Awareness Across Functional Activities, by J. P. Toglia, 2010, supplement manual for workshops conducted at various locations. Copyright © 2010 J. P. Toglia. Used with permission.

Step 2: Teach or Mediation Phase (10–15 Minutes)

After the baseline is obtained (without cues) and awareness is assessed, a period of mediation is used if the client experienced task difficulty. The mediation period can be in the same session or in the next session, and it should last approximately 10–15 minutes. Mediation should be specifically targeted toward the symptoms and task errors that were observed on the WCPA. The goals of the mediation phase are to (1) determine whether error awareness and self-monitoring can be enhanced and (2) determine whether strategy generation and use can be facilitated through guidance from an examiner.

The mediation phase requires a supportive and empowering approach, which requires practice and skill on the part of the examiner. The examiner's role is to use questions that guide the client in discovering errors himself or herself as well as to help the client generate alternative methods that can help him or her be successful. Positive feedback and encouragement should be provided whenever possible. The overall message to the client is that once a person can identify and recognize what went wrong, things can be done to stay a step ahead. The focus should not be on what is wrong but on helping the client realize that he or she can do things to improve performance.

Mediation consists of two phases: (1) error awareness and (2) strategy generation. If the client does not recognize errors on the baseline WCPA and After-Task Interview and Rating Scale, mediation begins by facilitating awareness of errors. This facilitation consists of self-questioning to promote self-checking. If the client is already aware of errors, this phase is skipped, and the therapist immediately proceeds to the second phase of mediation, which involves facilitating strategy generation.

The following guidelines and samples of scripts can be modified or used to enhance error awareness and strategy generation. The categories outlined should be followed, but there is flexibility in the script or words that are used because they should be tailored to the client's problems. A Test–Teach–Retest Dynamic Assessment Summary form can be used to organize and record results.

Error awareness

(*Note.* Skip this step and go to strategy generation mediation if the client is aware of the errors.)

If the client is unaware of errors on the weekly calendar, the examiner reviews the calendar with the client again using the sample prompts and questions that follow. The goal is to raise the client's level of awareness and error recognition; however, the client does not need to be aware of every error that occurred. Mediation should follow the categories indicated, but the phrasing should be changed to fit the particular symptoms or task errors observed. Once some changes in awareness or error recognition are observed, the examiner can proceed to strategy generation.

Sample mediation scripts for error awareness

- *General questioning:* "Let's look at the calendar. How can you be sure that the appointments are all in the correct time slots or locations? Is there anything you can do to be sure that everything is complete (or accurate)?"
- *Double check:* "Are there any special methods you can use to check yourself?" or "It might be a good idea to double check yourself to make sure everything is completed (or accurate)." (If the client is unable to detect errors after double checking, move to general feedback.)
- *General feedback*: "It might be a good idea to double check the appointment list one appointment at a time."

Structuring the self-assessment process. If the client is unable to locate his or her errors, the examiner then structures the self-assessment process. Some examples follow.

- *Simplified score sheet:* Provide a list of the appointments that could be entered on Monday or Tuesday so that the client can self-check each appointment himself or herself. In other words, the scoring worksheet can be divided into separate lists for each day and simplified as illustrated in Exhibit 6.2 to structure the self-assessment process.
- *Specific questions (e.g., focusing attention):* "Let's look over here [point]. Do you see anything that you would change?" "Let's look at this appointment and compare it with the list," or "Let's look at this appointment and see if it is in the right time slot? Right place?"
- *Modifications:* "Let's take a look at the list of appointments one at a time, and check each one to make sure they are in the right place" (provide paper to cover other appointments with).

Exhibit 6.2. Self-Assessment

Monday or Tuesday Appointments	Correct	Revision Needed
Mon.: Haircut from 11:00 a.m.–12:00 p.m.		
Visit with cousin Mon. or Tues. between 1:00 and 2:00 p.m. or 1:30 and 2:30 p.m. or on Thurs. between 2:30 and 3:30 p.m. or 3:00 and 4:00 p.m.		
Mon. any time or Tues. a.m.: Call to renew prescription		

Gently point out specific errors. If the preceding methods do not facilitate awareness, the examiner draws attention to the error, for example, "Can you show me where this appointment is on the calendar? This appointment seems to be in [the wrong location, time slot, etc.]. What do you think?" If the client still does not recognize the error or acknowledges the error but makes an excuse, the examiner should not continue to try to facilitate awareness.

Once the client recognizes some errors, he or she is encouraged to generate strategies or different task methods to enhance performance using the following guidelines. If the client does not acknowledge errors, or recognizes errors but is defensive and over rationalizes or makes excuses for them, awareness mediation should stop, and strategy mediation can be attempted. If the client has limited awareness, strategy generation and use will likely be limited; however, it should be attempted because failure to verbally acknowledge errors can be separate from actual awareness.

Strategy generation mediation

During this phase, the examiner encourages self-generation of a strategy through guided questioning. Questions are initially general and gradually become more specific. Mediation is tailored to the error patterns or difficulties observed with each individual client. Sample mediation scripts are provided next, but scripts will vary depending on the performance issues observed.

Sample scripts

- *General mediation:* "Let's think about how you initially approached this task. Tell me how

you went about it. Can you think of a different method or approach that will make things easier or less confusing?" or "Can you think of a different way to go about (or approach) this activity?" "If you did this activity again, what other methods could you use to help make it easier (or less confusing, etc.)?"
- *Sample symptom-specific mediation:* "Let's look at this weekly calendar again. Can you think of anything that you could do to make it easier to keep track of things? Stay organized? Pay attention to details? Stay focused? Slow down?"
- *Sample task-specific mediation (specifically related to task component difficulties that were observed during performance):* "Let's take a look at the appointments. How are they similar? Different? Are there any appointments that have only one day and time? Choices? Do you see any ways to group them?" "Is there anything you can do to help you keep track of which appointments you have just entered?" "Is there anything you can do to help identify which appointments should be entered first?" "Is there anything you could do to help yourself remember that no appointments should be scheduled on Wednesday [or the specified free day]?"
- *Provide strategy suggestion or choice:* If the client cannot generate a strategy, the examiner chooses one of the following strategies or selects another strategy that is hypothesized to be beneficial, given the task error or symptoms, for example, "There may be some methods that can help. Do you think it would be helpful to repeat what you need to do at least 3 times to yourself before you do it?" If after 2 attempts at strategy suggestion are made the client does not agree or resists suggestions, the examiner should discontinue strategy generation methods.

The therapist may provide a choice of strategies to the client, if appropriate, but presenting more than 2 strategies at once should be avoided because it can be overwhelming. No more than 1–2 strategies should be suggested, such as "What about . . . ."

- Talking aloud as you are doing the activity
- Spending more time planning and thinking about what you need to do
- Reading the entire directions to get a sense of everything involved before jumping in
- Slowing yourself down and talking through your actions
- Repeating what you need to do at least 3 times to yourself before you do it or verbally rehearsing key details of appointment out loud before putting it in the calendar
- Using your finger to point to help yourself focus or keep your place
- Using self-cues (e.g., to stay focused)
- Using mental practice (reviewing what you need to do in your mind, picturing what you need to do)
- Pausing or taking breaks when you feel your attention is fading
- Entering fixed appointments first, then flexible appointments
- Breaking directions, activity, or information down into components; simplifying (covering part of page)
- Crossing off each item on the list after you complete it
- Underlining or circling key words in the instructions
- Using highlighters or color coding
- Crossing out or checking off appointments after they are entered
- Making a list or outline (comment on organization)
- Rereading the instructions several times before beginning
- Writing notes to yourself
- Using a finger to keep your place
- Covering other lines when reading
- Rearranging materials
- Self-checking
- Crossing off the specified free day (Tuesday, Wednesday, or Thursday).

It is important that the strategies suggested be consistent with the client's performance difficulties. For example, if the client has difficulty keeping track of which appointments were entered, crossing off each appointment after entering it would be an effective strategy. The examiner should help the client think about why or how a strategy may help. For example, the examiner may say, "How or why do you think talking out loud

Exhibit 6.3. Strategy Rating

Level of Strategy Generation Achieved

_____ Generates 2 or more specific strategies (e.g., "Use list") that are appropriate for the task (Level 6).
_____ Generates 1 specific strategy appropriate for the task (Level 5).
_____ Generates several strategies that are vague or not efficient for the task (Level 4).
_____ Generates only 1 vague response (if strategies generated are redundant, they are counted as one response, e.g., "Pay attention," "Concentrate"; Level 3).
_____ Unable to self-generate a strategy but chooses a strategy when given a choice or agrees that a provided strategy might be helpful (Level 2).
_____ Does not believe a strategy or special method is needed (Level 1).

If the client is rated at Levels 3–6, indicate the level of mediation required to achieve the strategy generation.

_____ Independent (no mediation required; Level 4)
_____ General questioning mediation (Level 3)
_____ Symptom-specific mediation (Level 2)
_____ Task-specific mediation (Level 1)

Source. The Multi-Context Approach to Cognitive Rehabilitation of Executive Dysfunction: Promoting Strategy Use and Awareness Across Functional Activities, by J. P. Toglia, 2010, supplement manual to workshops conducted at various locations.

might help?" If the client is unsure, the therapist can say, "It might help you stay focused on what you need to do." (*Note.* If needed, the therapist may encourage the client to write the strategy on a card as a reminder to use it during a task.) As an option, the examiner can rate responses to strategy questioning using the scale in Exhibit 6.3.

Strategy practice (optional). If needed, the client can be asked to practice the strategy for a few minutes with the baseline calendar task to ensure that he or she can carry out the strategy that was verbally discussed.

Step 3: Retest Phase

In the retest phase, the calendar task (using an alternate version of the WCPA or different appointments) is re-administered in a standardized way, using the same methods as for the initial baseline assessment.

This phase should be used at the end of the same session as the mediation phase, whenever feasible. No cues are provided. If necessary, it can be used at the beginning of the next session, but this should be noted on the retest Recording Form (see the Dynamic Test–Retest After-Task Awareness Interview [Appendix 6.A] and the Test–Teach–Retest Dynamic Assessment Summary [Appendix 6.B]). The goals of the retest phase are to examine carryover or learning transfer and to determine whether improvements are observed when cues are withdrawn.

Carryover of strategy use is observed, as well as any increases or changes in performance. This provides an indication of modifiability of performance or learning potential. Previous dynamic assessment research suggests that clients can be categorized into at least 3 groups on the basis of dynamic testing results: (1) no learners, (2) learners within the task (only during mediation), and (3) learners. Wiedl, Wienobst, Schottke, Green, and Nuechterlein (2001) found that these groups were more effective than static assessments in predicting rehabilitation outcome in people with schizophrenia.

Awareness questions after retest phase (optional). The examiner can again obtain awareness ratings after the retest phase to determine whether changes in self-perception of performance occurred by re-administering the same After-Task Interview questions and using the ratings described in the After-Task Interview section and Exhibit 6.1.

Clinical Case Example

Clinical use of the dynamic test–teach–retest format is illustrated through a case example. The case of Charles (Case Example 3), along with his initial baseline

WCPA results, was first presented in Chapter 4, "Interpretation" (see Exhibits 6.4–6.6) . Following the test results presented in Chapter 4, the dynamic assessment procedure was used and is illustrated though a sample After-Task Awareness Interview and mediation script.

The After-Task Interview indicates that Charles perceived the task as easy and did not acknowledge any difficulties, although he vaguely indicated that he could concentrate better. The mediation script illustrates use of questioning techniques to enhance error awareness and strategy use. The script provides a snapshot of metacognitive strategy intervention. Charles required general questioning to enhance error awareness. The examiner attempted to structure the self-assessment process by suggesting that Charles use a paper guide to help him focus on one appointment at a time, but Charles rejected this suggestion. Error awareness was increased, although not all errors were recognized.

Once partial awareness was observed, mediation focused on strategy use. Mediation to enhance strategy use involved a combination of general, symptom-specific, and task-specific questions. Overall, Charles was able to generate 2 or more specific strategies (e.g., start at top of list, cross off each appointment, cross off Wednesday); however, task-specific mediation was required to achieve this level.

Following the mediation phase, an alternate version of the WCPA was re-administered to Charles, and retest results were compared to initial baseline results presented in Chapter 4. Charles's results are summarized on the Test–Teach–Retest Dynamic Assessment Summary form. The first section of the summary form, "Test phase (baseline score)," summarizes Charles's baseline results (presented in Chapter 4). The teach or mediation phase indicates the level of mediation provided as reflected within the sample mediation script. The assessment of change section presents Charles's retest results and compares these results to initial baseline testing.

Although performance was still below average, carryover of learning was observed through changes in strategy use, rule adherence, self-recognition of errors, and appointment accuracy. The performance changes observed after a brief period of mediation suggest that a metacognitive or strategy-based treatment approach could be beneficial for Charles.

Summary

The dynamic test–teach–retest procedure systematically examines the effects of a brief intervention to assess performance modifiability and learning potential. A brief intervention is provided between a pre- and posttest WCPA to determine if awareness, strategy use, and performance can be modified and whether learning carries over when cues or support are withdrawn. The literature suggests that the test–teach–retest method may provide added value for treatment planning and prediction of outcome over conventional methods; however, additional research and formal testing of dynamic assessment procedures presented in this chapter is needed.

The mediation guidelines and methodology for dynamic assessment described in this chapter require practice and experience. Unlike direct instruction or cueing techniques, this technique requires the clinician to avoid telling the person what to do. Mediation involves questions that encourage the client to discover errors or generate strategies themselves. A clinical example and script was provided and summarized to illustrate clinical applications. Clinicians are encouraged to role play mediation procedures with others to gain familiarity and comfort with the techniques prior to clinical use.

Exhibit 6.4. WCPA Dynamic Test–Retest After-Task Awareness Interview for Charles

1. *General questions:* Did you encounter any challenges (or difficulties) while doing this task? What kinds of difficulties (problems, challenges) did you encounter?

Charles: No problems. It was a little tricky but I didn't have any difficulties.

2. *Symptom-specific questions:* Did you experience any difficulties in keeping track of all of the appointments? Staying organized?

Charles: No.

3. *Task-specific questions:* Did you experience any difficulties in entering all 17 appointments into the calendar? Placing all of the appointments in the correct locations?

Charles: I don't think so. Maybe I might have missed one, if I wasn't concentrating.

Exhibit 6.5. Sample Mediation Script Using Test–Teach–Retest Format for Charles

Examiner Questions	Examinee Responses
Mediation for error awareness	
Let's look at the calendar. How can you be sure that you followed all the instructions?	Charles looks at the instructions and laughs, stating "I forgot all about these."
How could you be sure that the appointments are all in the correct time slots or locations?	Charles begins checking in a random manner.
Let's think about the best way to go about double checking.	"I guess I should start at the top of the list and check each one."
That is a terrific idea [examiner notices Charles is skipping a few lines]. Do you think it could also be helpful to use this paper to screen out the other appointments?	Charles says, "No, it's not necessary" but recognizes and correct several other errors.
You are really doing a great job of double checking yourself.	Charles recognizes that he missed 2 appointments and entered 1 in the wrong location. *Once some awareness is raised (even though it may not be complete), strategy mediation can begin.*
Mediation for strategy use	
Let's think about how you initially approached this task. Tell me how you went about it.	"I just put the appointments in."
How did you begin? Did you have a plan?	"No, I just started to put the appointments in the calendar."
Yes, I notice you jumped right into the activity. Can you think of a different approach?	"No. I always do things quickly."
Is there anything else you could have done before you started?	"No, not really."
Do you think it might help to take some time to stop and plan ?	"No, it's not my style."
(Examiner does not continue and changes to specific questions related to other symptoms.)	

(Continued)

Exhibit 6.5. Sample Mediation Script Using Test–Teach–Retest Format for Charles *(Continued)*

Let's look at this weekly calendar again. Can you think of anything that you could do to make it easier to keep track of things?	"No, not really."
Let's think about some things that you could to do to make sure that every appointment is entered.	"I can concentrate better."
Can you think of way to approach the task so that you can be sure that none of the appointments are missed?	"I could have just started at the top of the list and went in order."
That is a great idea!	
This activity has a lot of appointments and information to keep track of. Can you think of a different approach that could make it easier to keep track of things?	"I could cross off each appointment."
That is terrific! I think that could make it a lot easier to keep track.	
I noticed that you used your finger initially but then you stopped.	"Oh . . . I guess I do sometimes use my finger when I am reading."
How do you think that using your finger might help?	"Not sure."
Do you think that it could help you focus better during reading?	"I guess so."
Is there anything you could do to help make it easier keep track of all the instructions (rules)?	"Not sure."
Let's look at them. For example, what could you do to help you remember not to put appointments on Wednesday?	"I could cross off Wednesday. I could also move the instructions so it would be easier to remember to look at them."
You are coming up with some really good ideas.	
Let's look at the list carefully—can you think of a way to avoid appointment conflicts?	"Not really. I will deal with them as they come up."
You came up with a lot of great strategies. I think they could really help you stay focused and organized	

Analysis and Commentary: Charles recognizes that he missed several appointments; however, he is not aware of all errors. He also remains unaware of difficulties in regulating or pacing the speed of his response, but the examiner does not push awareness. Charles generated a couple of strategies that could help performance, and this is a place to begin. Other strategies could be helpful, but the examiner does not suggest them. Suggesting too many strategies can be confusing or overwhelming for the client and reduces the probability of use. If the client does not agree with an observation or suggestion, the examiner lets it go and does not try to convince the client otherwise. The examiner provides guidance and suggestions, but does not tell the client what to do. An alternate version is then administered to determine whether the client approaches the task differently after mediation. The retest results for Charles are presented in the summary form below.

Exhibit 6.6. Test–Teach–Retest Dynamic Assessment Summary Form for Charles

Test Phase (Baseline Scores)	
6 No. of accurate appointments 4 No. of missing appointments N/A Efficiency Score 8 min Total Time 0 No. of rules followed 1 Total no. of strategies used 6 After-Task Interview awareness rating	
Teach/Mediation Phase	
Mediation for error awareness	_ None ✓ General questioning ✓ Structured self-assessment _ Point out error
Error awareness achieved	_ None ✓ Partial (acknowledges/recognizes some errors) ___ Complete (recognizes all errors) *Comments:* With general questioning, Charles recognized some of his errors (but not all).
Mediation for strategy generation	___ Independent ✓ General ✓ Symptom specific ✓ Task specific ___ Strategy provided/choice
Strategy generation achieved	_ ≥ 2 specific strategies _1 specific strategy ___Several vague or inefficient strategies _1 vague strategy *Comments:* Charles generated some strategies with specific questioning; however, they were not completely efficient (e.g., going down the list in order), and they did not address all of his performance errors.
Describe strategy use during mediation (comment on frequency and efficiency of strategy)	No practice during mediation
Assessment of Change	
Change in no. of accurate appointments	_ No ✓ Yes Retest score: 11 Change: +5
Changes in no. of rules followed	_ No ✓ Yes Retest Score: 3 Change: +3
Change in total no. of strategies	_ No ✓ Yes Retest Score: 4 Change: +3
Change in type or frequency of strategy use	*Comment:* Crossed off Wed., crossed off each appointment when entered, and used his finger and proceeded in order; however, strategy use was inconsistent and not completely efficient.
Change in awareness	_ No ✓ Yes Retest score: Self-recognition/awareness: 3/6 Change: +3 *Comment:* Self-recognized 3 of 6 errors during the task. Continued to have difficulty providing specific examples of challenges after the task.
Overall performance changes	Charles demonstrated increases in accuracy, strategy use, rule adherence, and recognition of errors. Time increased to 13 minutes. Although performance is still below average and characterized by impulsivity, changes in the way Charles approached the activity were observed after mediation.
Responsiveness to mediation	How responsive was client to mediation? _ A lot ✓ Moderately _ A little _ Not at all How intense an effort was required to induce change during mediation? ___ Low or minimal ✓ Moderate ___ High _ Extreme In your judgment, was there any indication of transfer of learning? _ No ✓ Yes *Comments:*
Summary/Conclusion	Charles appears to be a good candidate for strategy intervention because moderate changes in performance were observed with mediation. Charles responded well to a positive and supportive approach.

Appendix 6.A. WCPA Dynamic Test–Retest After-Task Awareness Interview

1. *General questions:* Did you encounter (or experience) any challenges (or difficulties) while doing this task? What kinds of difficulties (problems, challenges) did you encounter?
2. *Symptom-specific questions:* Did you experience any difficulties in ______ (question should be specific to cognitive symptom observed)? Some examples include "keeping track of what you needed to do?" "Paying attention to details?" and "Staying organized?"
3. *Task-specific questions:* Did you encounter or experience any difficulties in ______ (choose a statement that is specific to the task error observed). Some examples include "entering all 17 appointments into the calendar?" "Following the rules?" "Managing appointment conflicts?" "Placing appointments in the correct location?" and "Indicating the correct amount of time for each appointment?"

Appendix 6.B. Test–Teach–Retest Dynamic Assessment Summary Form

Test Phase (Baseline Scores)	
___ No. of accurate appointments ___ No. of missing appointments ___ Efficiency score ___Total time ___ No. of rules followed ___Total no. of strategies used ___ After-Task Interview awareness rating	
Teach/Mediation Phase	
Mediation for error awareness	___ None ___ General questioning ___ Structured self-assessment ___ Point out error
Error awareness achieved	___ None ___ Partial (acknowledges/recognizes some errors) ___ Complete (recognizes all errors) *Comments:*
Mediation for strategy generation	___ Independent ___ General ___ Symptom specific ___ Task specific ___ Strategy provided/choice
Strategy generation achieved	___ ≥2 specific strategies ___ 1 specific strategy ___ Several vague or inefficient strategies ___1 vague strategy *Comments:*
Describe strategy use during mediation (comment on frequency and efficiency of strategy)	
Assessment of Change	
Change in no. of accurate appointments	___ No ___ Yes Retest score: Change:
Changes in no. of rules followed	___ No ___ Yes Retest score: Change:
Change in total no. of strategies	___ No ___ Yes Retest score: Change:
Change in type or frequency of strategy use	*Comment:*
Change in awareness	___ No ___ Yes Retest score: Self-recognition/awareness: Change: *Comment:*
Overall performance changes	
Responsiveness to mediation	How responsive was client to mediation? ___ A lot ___ Moderately ___ A little ___ Not at all How intense an effort was required to induce change during mediation? ___ Low/minimal ___ Moderate ___ High ___ Extreme In your judgment, was there any indication of transfer of learning? ___ No ___ Yes *Comments:*
Summary/Conclusion	

APPENDIX A

Appointment Lists and Scoring Sheets: Adult/Older Adult Population (Ages 18–94)

Appendix A.1. Appointments and Errands to Be Scheduled: Adult/Older Adult Level I (Version A)

☐ Dentist on Thursday at 3:00 p.m. (1 hour)

☐ Lunch with a friend on Tuesday from 1:00–2:00 p.m.

☐ Haircut on Monday from 11:00 a.m.–12:00 p.m.

☐ Volunteer at People to People on Friday from 9:00–10:30 a.m.

☐ Movies with friends on Thursday from 7:00–11:00 p.m.

☐ Walk neighbor's dog on Thursday morning before 11:00 a.m. (half hour)

☐ One-hour visit with cousin who is only available on Thursday between 2:30 and 4:00 p.m. or on Monday or Tuesday between 1:00 and 2:30 p.m.

☐ Doctor appointment Monday or Friday afternoon at 2:00 p.m. (90 minutes)

☐ Carpool: One morning at 9:00 a.m. and one afternoon at 3:00 p.m. (45 minutes)

☐ Call to renew prescription any time before noon on Tuesday

☐ Phone conference on Tuesday before 2:00 p.m. (half hour)

☐ Pick up medication at pharmacy before it closes on Tuesday. Pharmacy is open from 9:00 a.m.–3:00 p.m. daily (half hour)

☐ Pick up pants from dry cleaners Monday, Wednesday, or Friday between 8:00 a.m. and 4:00 p.m. (half hour)

☐ Dinner with coworkers either Thursday or Friday evening. Start dinner any time between 6:30 and 8:00 p.m. (2 hours)

☐ 45-minute exercise at the gym either Friday or Saturday morning

☐ Go food shopping before Friday (1 hour)

Appendix A.2. Calendar Scoring Worksheet: Adult/Older Adult Level I (Version A)

(*Note.* Wednesday is free in this version.)

Directions: Place a check mark in the Accurate column if an appointment is entered without errors and an "X" in the Missing column if an appointment is omitted. For quick scoring, place an "X" in the Error column. For detailed error scoring, use one of the following error codes to indicate which type of error was committed.

R = Appointment is repeated or entered more than once, and repetition is not an attempt to self-correct a location error
L = Appointment is placed in the wrong location, day, or time slot
T = Appointment is in the right location, but the time allotted is incorrect by more than 15 minutes (7:00 a.m.–6:00 p.m.) or 30 minutes (6:00–9:00 p.m.)
I = Appointment name is entered inaccurately or partially

Self-Recognition (SR) Column

Place a check mark in this column if the person acknowledges an appointment error or conflict verbally or nonverbally or if you observe the person trying to correct it (e.g., draw lines, cross out).

Entered	Missing	Error	Accurate	SR	Appointments
					Mon.: Haircut from 11:00 a.m.–12:00 p.m.
					Visit with cousin Mon. or Tues. between 1:00 and 2:00 p.m. or 1:30 and 2:30 p.m. or on Thurs. between 2:30 and 3:30 p.m. or 3:00 and 4:00 p.m.
					Mon. any time or Tues. a.m.: Call to renew prescription
					Tues.: Lunch with friend from 1:00–2:00 p.m.
					Tues.: Phone conference before 2:00 p.m. (30 minutes)
					Mon. or Tues.: Medication picked up between 9:00 a.m. and 3:00 p.m. (30 minutes). Must have previously called to renew prescription.
					Thurs.: Walk neighbor's dog before 11:00 a.m. (30 minutes)
					Thurs.: Dentist at 3:00 p.m. (1 hour)
					Thurs.: Movies with friends from 7:00–11:00 p.m.
					Fri.: Volunteer job from 9:00–10:30 a.m. (90 minutes)
					Thurs or Fri.: Dinner, coworkers, starting between 6:30 and 8:00 p.m. (2 hours)
					Mon. or Fri.: Pick up dry cleaning between 8:00 a.m. and 4:00 p.m. (30 minutes)
					Fri., Sat., or Sun. morning: Exercise at the gym (45 minutes)
					Doctor: Mon. or Fri. afternoon at 2:00 p.m. (90 minutes)
					Food shopping before Fri. (1 hour)
					Carpool: One morning at 9:00 a.m. (45 minutes)
					Carpool: One afternoon at 3:00 p.m. (45 minutes)
					Total all columns The no. of appointments in the missing + accurate + error columns should equal 17

Appendix A.3. Appointments and Errands to Be Scheduled: Adult/Older Adult Level I (Version B)

- ☐ Doctor appointment on Wednesday at 3:00 p.m. (1 hour)
- ☐ Haircut on Thursday from 1:00–2:00 p.m.
- ☐ Book club on Monday from 11:00 a.m.–12:00 p.m.
- ☐ Brunch with a friend on Friday from 9:00–10:30 a.m.
- ☐ Game night with coworkers on Wednesday from 7:00–11:00 p.m.
- ☐ Feed neighbor's cat on Wednesday morning before 11:00 a.m. (half hour)
- ☐ One-hour visit to friend's art show that is only open on Wednesday between 2:30 and 4:00 p.m. or Monday or Thursday between 1:00 and 2:30 p.m.
- ☐ Dentist on Monday or Friday afternoon at 2:00 p.m. (90 minutes)
- ☐ Carpool: One morning at 9:00 a.m. and one afternoon at 3:00 p.m. (45 minutes)
- ☐ Dinner with family either Wednesday or Friday evening. Start dinner any time between 6:30 and 8:00 p.m. (2 hours)
- ☐ Call gas company to dispute late charge any time before noon on Thursday
- ☐ Return library books on Thursday before 2:00 p.m. (half hour)
- ☐ Mail gas bill at post office before it closes on Thursday. Post office is open from 9:00 a.m.–3:00 p.m. daily (half hour)
- ☐ Get car washed Monday, Tuesday, or Friday between 8:00 a.m. and 4:00 p.m. (half hour)
- ☐ 45 minutes to buy groceries either Friday or Saturday morning
- ☐ Call cousin before Friday (1 hour)

Appendix A.4. Calendar Scoring Worksheet: Adult/Older Adult Level I (Version B)

(*Note.* Tuesday is free in this version.)

Directions: Place a check mark in the Accurate column if an appointment is entered without errors and an "X" in the Missing column if an appointment is omitted. For quick scoring, place an "X" in the Error column. For detailed error scoring, use one of the following error codes to indicate which type of error was committed.

R = Appointment is repeated or entered more than once, and repetition is not an attempt to self-correct a location error

L = Appointment is placed in the wrong location, day, or time slot

T = Appointment is in the right location, but the time allotted is incorrect by more than 15 minutes (7:00 a.m.–6:00 p.m.) or 30 minutes (6:00–9:00 p.m.)

I = Appointment name is entered inaccurately or partially

Self-Recognition (SR) Column

Place a check mark in this column if the person acknowledges an appointment error or conflict verbally or nonverbally or if you observe the person trying to correct it (e.g., draw lines, cross out).

Entered	Missing	Error	Accurate	SR	Appointments
					Mon.: Book club from 11:00 a.m.–12:00 p.m.
					Go to art show on Mon. or Thurs. between 1:00 and 2:00 p.m. or 1:30 and 2:30 p.m. or on Wed. between 2:30 and 3:30 p.m. or 3:00 and 4:00 p.m.
					Mon. or Wed. anytime or Thurs. a.m.: Call to update bill
					Wed.: Feed neighbor's cat before 11:00 a.m. (30 minutes)
					Wed.: Doctor at 3:00 p.m. (1 hour)
					Wed.: Game night with coworkers from 7:00–11:00 p.m.
					Mon., Wed., or Thurs.: Gas bill mailed between 9:00 a.m. and 3:00 p.m. (30 minutes). Must have previously called to update bill
					Thurs.: Haircut from 1:00–2:00 p.m.
					Thurs.: Return library books before 2:00 p.m. (30 minutes)
					Fri.: Brunch with friend from 9:00–10:30 a.m. (90 minutes)
					Wed. or Fri.: Family dinner starting between 6:30 and 8:00 p.m. (2 hours)
					Mon. or Fri.: Get car washed between 8:00 a.m. and 4:00 p.m. (30 minutes)
					Fri., Sat., or Sun. morning: Buy groceries (45 minutes)
					Dentist: Mon. or Fri. afternoon at 2:00 p.m. (90 minutes)
					Call cousin before Friday (1 hour)
					Carpool: One morning at 9:00 a.m. (45 minutes)
					Carpool: One afternoon at 3:00 p.m. (45 minutes)
					Total all columns The no. of appointments in the missing + accurate + error columns should equal 17

Appendix A.5. Appointments and Errands to Be Scheduled: Adult/Older Adult Level II (Version A)

Dentist on Thursday at 3:00 p.m. (1 hour)

One-hour visit with cousin who is only available on Thursday between 2:30 and 4:00 p.m. or on Monday or Tuesday between 1:00 and 2:30 p.m.

Carpool: One morning at 9:00 a.m. and one afternoon at 3:00 p.m. (45 minutes)

Phone conference on Tuesday before 2:00 p.m. (half hour)

Doctor appointment Monday or Friday afternoon at 2:00 p.m. (90 minutes)

Volunteer at People to People on Friday from 9:00–10:30 a.m.

Pick up pants from dry cleaners Monday, Wednesday, or Friday between 8:00 a.m. and 4:00 p.m. (half hour)

Lunch with a friend on Tuesday from 1:00–2:00 p.m.

Dinner with coworkers either Thursday or Friday evening. Start dinner any time between 6:30 and 8:00 p.m. (2 hours)

Go food shopping before Friday (1 hour)

45-minute exercise at the gym either Friday or Saturday morning

Pick up medication at pharmacy before it closes on Tuesday. Pharmacy is open from 9:00 a.m.–3:00 p.m. daily (half hour)

Movies with friends on Thursday from 7:00–11:00 p.m.

Haircut on Monday from 11:00 a.m.–12:00 p.m.

Walk neighbor's dog on Thursday morning before 11:00 a.m. (half hour)

Call to renew prescription any time before noon on Tuesday

Appendix A.6. Calendar Scoring Worksheet: Adult/Older Adult Level II (Version A)

(*Note.* Wednesday is free in this version.)

Directions: Place a check mark in the Accurate column if an appointment is entered without errors and an "X" in the Missing column if an appointment is omitted. For quick scoring, place an "X" in the Error column. For detailed error scoring, use one of the following error codes to indicate which type of error was committed.

R = Appointment is repeated or entered more than once, and repetition is not an attempt to self-correct a location error
L = Appointment is placed in the wrong location, day, or time slot
T = Appointment is in the right location, but the time allotted is incorrect by more than 15 minutes (7:00 a.m.–6:00 p.m.) or 30 minutes (6:00–9:00 p.m.)
I = Appointment name is entered inaccurately or partially

Self-Recognition (SR) Column

Place a check mark in this column if the person acknowledges an appointment error or conflict verbally or nonverbally or if you observe the person trying to correct it (e.g., draw lines, cross out).

Entered	Missing	Error	Accurate	SR	Appointments
					Mon.: Haircut from 11:00 a.m.–12:00 p.m.
					Mon. or Tues.: Visit with cousin between 1:00 and 2:00 p.m. or 1:30 and 2:30 p.m. or on Thurs between 2:30 and 3:30 p.m. or 3:00 and 4:00 p.m.
					Mon. any time or Tues. a.m.: Call to renew prescription
					Tues.: Lunch with friend from 1:00–2:00 p.m.
					Tues.: Phone conference before 2:00 p.m. (30 minutes)
					Mon. or Tues.: Medication picked up between 9:00 a.m. and 3:00 p.m. (30 minutes). Must have previously called to renew prescription.
					Thurs.: Walk neighbor's dog before 11:00 a.m. (30 minutes)
					Thurs.: Dentist at 3:00 p.m. (1 hour)
					Thurs.: Movies with friends from 7:00–11:00 p.m.
					Fri.: Volunteer job from 9:00–10:30 a.m. (90 minutes)
					Thurs. or Fri.: Dinner, coworkers, starting between 6:30 and 8:00 p.m. (2 hours)
					Mon. or Fri.: Pick up dry cleaning between 8:00 a.m. and 4:00 p.m. (30 minutes)
					Fri., Sat., or Sun. morning: Exercise at the gym (45 minutes)
					Doctor: Mon. or Fri. afternoon at 2:00 p.m. (90 minutes)
					Food shopping before Fri. (1 hour)
					Carpool: One morning at 9:00 a.m. (45 minutes)
					Carpool: One afternoon at 3:00 p.m. (45 minutes)
					Total all columns The no. of appointments in the missing + accurate + error columns should equal 17

Appendix A.7. Appointments and Errands to Be Scheduled: Adult/Older Adult Level II (Version B)

Haircut on Thursday from 1:00–2:00 p.m.

Go to friend's art show for 1-hour visit; show is open only on Wednesday between 2:30 and 4:00 p.m. or on Monday or Thursday between 1:00 and 2:30 p.m.

Get car washed Monday, Tuesday, or Friday between 8 a.m. and 4 p.m. (half hour)

Return library books on Thursday before 2:00 p.m. (half hour)

Dentist on Monday or Friday afternoon at 2:00 p.m. (90 minutes)

Book club on Monday from 11:00 a.m.–12:00 p.m.

Mail gas bill at post office before it closes on Thursday. Post office is open from 9:00 a.m.–3:00 p.m. daily (half hour)

Doctor appointment Wednesday at 3:00 p.m. (1 hour)

Carpool: One morning at 9:00 a.m. and one afternoon at 3:00 p.m. (45 minutes)

Brunch with a friend on Friday from 9:00–10:30 a.m.

Buy groceries either Friday or Saturday morning (45 minutes)

Dinner with family either Wednesday or Friday evening. Start dinner any time between 6:30 and 8:00 p.m. (2 hours)

Game night with coworkers on Wednesday from 7:00–11:00 p.m.

Call cousin before Friday (1 hour)

Feed neighbor's cat on Wednesday morning before 11:00 a.m. (half hour)

Call gas company to dispute late charge any time before noon on Thursday

Appendix A.8. Calendar Scoring Worksheet: Adult/Older Adult Level II (Version B)

(*Note.* Tuesday is free in this version.)

Directions: Place a check mark in the Accurate column if an appointment is entered without errors and an "X" in the Missing column if an appointment is omitted. For quick scoring, place an "X" in the Error column. For detailed error scoring, use one of the following error codes to indicate which type of error was committed.

R = Appointment is repeated or entered more than once, and repetition is not an attempt to self-correct a location error

L = Appointment is placed in the wrong location, day, or time slot

T = Appointment is in the right location, but the time allotted is incorrect by more than 15 minutes (7:00 a.m.–6:00 p.m.) or 30 minutes (6:00 p.m.–9:00 p.m.)

I = Appointment name is entered inaccurately or partially

Self-Recognition (SR) Column

Place a check mark in this column if the person acknowledges an appointment error or conflict verbally or nonverbally or if you observe the person trying to correct it (e.g., draw lines, cross out).

Entered	Missing	Error	Accurate	SR	Appointments
					Mon.: Book club from 11:00 a.m.–12:00 p.m.
					Go to art show Mon. or Thurs. between 1:00 and 2:00 p.m. or 1:30 and 2:30 p.m. or Wed. between 2:30 and 3:30 p.m. or 3:00 and 4:00 p.m.
					Mon. or Wed. anytime or Thurs. a.m.: Call to update bill
					Wed.: Feed neighbor's cat before 11:00 a.m. (30 minutes)
					Wed.: Doctor at 3:00 p.m. (1 hour)
					Wed: Game night with coworkers from 7:00–11:00 p.m.
					Mon., Wed., or Thurs.: Gas bill mailed between 9:00 a.m. and 3:00 p.m. (30 minutes). Must have previously called to update bill.
					Thurs.: Haircut from 1:00–2:00 p.m.
					Thurs.: Return library books before 2:00 p.m. (30 minutes)
					Fri.: Brunch with friend from 9:00–10:30 a.m. (90 minutes)
					Wed. or Fri.: Family dinner starting between 6:30 and 8:00 p.m. (2 hours)
					Mon. or Fri.: Get car washed between 8:00 a.m. and 4:00 p.m. (30 minutes)
					Fri., Sat., or Sun. morning: Buy groceries (45 minutes)
					Dentist: Mon. or Fri. afternoon at 2:00 p.m. (90 minutes)
					Call cousin before Friday (1 hour)
					Carpool: One morning at 9:00 a.m. (45 minutes)
					Carpool: One afternoon at 3:00 p.m. (45 minutes)
					Total all columns The no. of appointments in the missing + accurate + error columns should equal 17

Appendix A.9. Appointments and Errands to Be Scheduled: Adult/Older Adult Level II–Short (Version A)

Dentist on Thursday at 3:00 p.m. (1 hour)

One-hour visit with cousin who is only available on Thursday between 2:30 and 4:00 p.m. or on Monday or Tuesday between 1:00 and 2:30 p.m.

Carpool: One afternoon at 3:00 p.m. (45 minutes)

Phone conference on Tuesday before 2:00 p.m. (half hour)

Doctor appointment Monday or Friday afternoon at 2:00 p.m. (90 minutes)

Lunch with a friend on Tuesday from 1:00–2:00 p.m.

Dinner with coworkers either Thursday or Friday evening. Start dinner any time between 6:30 and 8:00 p.m. (2 hours)

Pick up medication at pharmacy before it closes on Tuesday. Pharmacy is open from 9:00 a.m.-3:00 p.m. daily (half hour)

Movies with friends on Thursday from 7:00–11:00 p.m.

Call to renew prescription any time before noon on Tuesday

Appendix A.10. Calendar Scoring Worksheet: Adult/Older Adult Level II–Short (Version A)

(*Note.* Wednesday is free in this version.)

Directions: Place a check mark in the Accurate column if an appointment is entered without errors and an "X" in the Missing column if an appointment is omitted. For quick scoring, place an "X" in the Error column. For detailed error scoring, use one of the following error codes to indicate which type of error was committed.

R = Appointment is repeated or entered more than once, and repetition is not an attempt to self-correct a location error

L = Appointment is placed in the wrong location, day, or time slot

T = Appointment is in the right location, but the time allotted is incorrect by more than 15 minutes (7:00 a.m.–6:00 p.m.) or 30 minutes (6:00–9:00 p.m.)

I = Appointment name is entered inaccurately or partially

Self-Recognition (SR) Column

Place a check mark in this column if the person acknowledges an appointment error or conflict verbally or nonverbally or if you observe the person trying to correct it (e.g., draw lines, cross out).

Entered	Missing	Error	Accurate	SR	Appointments
					Visit with cousin Mon. or Tues. between 1:00 and 2:00 p.m. or 1:30 and 2:30 p.m. or on Thurs. between 2:30 and 3:30 p.m. or 3:00 and 4:00 p.m.
					Mon. anytime or Tues a.m.: Call to renew prescription
					Tues.: Lunch with friend from 1:00–2:00 p.m.
					Tues: Phone conference before 2:00 p.m. (30 minutes)
					Mon. or Tues.: Medication picked up between 9:00 a.m. and 3:00 p.m. (30 minutes). Must have previously called to renew prescription.
					Thurs.: Dentist at 3:00 p.m. (1 hour)
					Thurs.: Movies with friends from 7:00–11:00 p.m.
					Thurs. or Fri.: Dinner, coworkers, starting between 6:30 and 8:00 p.m. (2 hours)
					Doctor: Mon. or Fri. afternoon at 2:00 p.m. (90 minutes)
					Carpool: One afternoon at 3:00 p.m. (45 minutes)
					Total all columns The no. of appointments in the missing + accurate + error columns should equal 10

Appendix A.11. Appointments and Errands to Be Scheduled: Adult/Older Adult Level II–Short (Version B)

Haircut on Thursday from 1:00–2:00 p.m.

Go to friend's art show for 1-hour visit that is open only on Wednesday between 2:30 and 4:00 p.m. or on Monday or Thursday between 1:00 and 2:30 p.m.

Return library books on Thursday before 2:00 p.m. (half hour)

Dentist on Monday or Friday afternoon at 2:00 p.m. (90 minutes)

Mail gas bill at post office before it closes on Thursday. Post office is open from 9:00 a.m.–3:00 p.m. daily (half hour)

Carpool: One afternoon at 3:00 p.m. (45 minutes)

Dinner with family either Wednesday or Friday evening. Start dinner any time between 6:30 and 8:00 p.m. (2 hours)

Game night with coworkers on Wednesday from 7:00–11:00 p.m.

Dentist on Wednesday at 3:00 p.m. (1 hour)

Call gas company to dispute late charge any time before noon on Thursday

Appendix A.12. Calendar Scoring Worksheet: Adult/Older Adult Level II–Short (Version B)

(*Note.* Tuesday is free in this version.)

Directions: Place a check mark in the Accurate column if an appointment is entered without errors and an "X" in the Missing column if an appointment is omitted. For quick scoring, place an "X" in the Error column. For detailed error scoring, use one of the following error codes to indicate which type of error was committed.

R = Appointment is repeated or entered more than once, and repetition is not an attempt to self-correct a location error
L = Appointment is placed in the wrong location, day, or time slot
T = Appointment is in the right location, but the time allotted is incorrect by more than 15 minutes (7:00 a.m.–6:00 p.m.) or 30 minutes (6:00–9:00 p.m.)
I = Appointment name is entered inaccurately or partially

Self-Recognition (SR) Column

Place a check mark in this column if the person acknowledges an appointment error or conflict verbally or nonverbally or if you observe the person trying to correct it (e.g., draw lines, cross out).

Entered	Missing	Error	Accurate	SR	Appointments
					Go to art show Mon. or Thurs. between 1:00 and 2:00 p.m. or 1:30 and 2:30 p.m. or Wed. between 2:30 and 3:30 p.m. or 3:00 and 4:00 p.m.
					Mon. or Wed. anytime or Thurs. a.m.: Call to update bill
					Wed.: Doctor at 3:00 p.m. (1 hour)
					Wed.: Game night with coworkers from 7:00–11:00 p.m.
					Mon., Wed., or Thurs.: Gas bill mailed between 9:00 a.m. and 3:00 p.m. (30 minutes). Must have previously called to update bill.
					Thurs.: Haircut from 1:00–2:00 p.m.
					Thurs.: Return library books before 2:00 p.m. (30 minutes)
					Wed. or Fri.: Family dinner starting between 6:30 and 8:00 p.m. (2 hours)
					Dentist: Mon. or Fri. afternoon at 2:00 p.m. (90 minutes)
					Carpool: One afternoon at 3:00 p.m. (45 minutes)
					Total all columns The no. of appointments in the missing + accurate + error columns should equal 17

Appendix A.13. **Appointments and Errands to Be Scheduled: Adult/Older Adult Level III (Version A)**

You have a dentist appointment on Thursday at 3:00 p.m. for an hour. Also, you need to call to renew your prescription and pick up the medication. You take your medication 3 times a day (8:00 a.m., noon, and 9:00 p.m.) and will be out of medication after taking your last pill on Tuesday at noon. Make time to go to the pharmacy; it is open from 9 a.m. to 3 p.m. daily and will take a half hour. You have plans to go out with your friends to the movies on Thursday from 7:00 to 11:00 p.m. You have a nice pair of pants that you would like to wear out to the movies with your friends, but they are at the dry cleaners. The dry cleaners are only open from 8:00 a.m. to 4:00 p.m. on Monday, Wednesday, and Friday, and picking up the pants will take approximately 30 minutes. You need to get to the dry cleaners to pick up your pants before Thursday night. You have made plans to have lunch with an old friend from 1:00 to 2:00 p.m. on Tuesday. You want to make sure that you look great for your lunch, so you made an appointment to have your hair cut on Monday from 11:00 a.m. to 12:00 p.m. You need to schedule a half-hour phone conference sometime on Tuesday before 2:00 p.m. You need to make time to visit your cousin for an hour, and you also need to go food shopping. Your cousin is only available on Thursday between 2:30 and 4:00 p.m. or on Monday or Tuesday between 1:00 and 2:30 p.m. Food shopping takes 1 hour, and it needs to be done before Friday. Your neighbors went away for an overnight trip and have asked you to walk their dog for a half hour on Thursday morning before 11:00 a.m. You need to schedule a doctor's appointment this week. The doctor has appointments on Monday or Friday afternoon at 2:00 p.m. There is often a wait so you will need to set aside 90 minutes. You are actively involved in your community and volunteer with People to People on Friday mornings from 9:00 to 10:30 a.m. Exercise is also important, and you would like to exercise at the gym either Friday or Saturday morning for 45 minutes. To end your long work week, you are going to have dinner at a restaurant with your coworkers either Thursday or Friday evening. You can make dinner reservations that start any time between 6:30 and 8:00 p.m. You choose the day and start time of the reservation, and schedule 2 hours for dinner. You are in a carpool and need to drive the kids to school on one morning at 9:00 a.m. and pick up on one afternoon at 3:00 p.m. The carpool takes about 45 minutes. You can choose the days.

Appendix A.14. Calendar Scoring Worksheet: Adult/Older Adult Level III (Version A)

(*Note.* Wednesday is free in this version.)

Directions: Place a check mark in the Accurate column if an appointment is entered without errors and an "X" in the Missing column if an appointment is omitted. For quick scoring, place an "X" in the Error column. For detailed error scoring, use one of the following error codes to indicate which type of error was committed.

R = Appointment is repeated or entered more than once, and repetition is not an attempt to self-correct a location error
L = Appointment is placed in the wrong location, day, or time slot
T = Appointment is in the right location, but the time allotted is incorrect by more than 15 minutes (7:00 a.m.–6:00 p.m.) or 30 minutes (6:00–9:00 p.m.)
I = Appointment name is entered inaccurately or partially

Self-Recognition (SR) Column

Place a check mark in this column if the person acknowledges an appointment error or conflict verbally or nonverbally or if you observe the person trying to correct it (e.g., draw lines, cross out).

Entered	Missing	Error	Accurate	SR	Appointments
					Mon.: Haircut from 11:00–12:00 p.m.
					Mon. or Tues.: Visit with cousin between 1:00 and 2:00 p.m. or 1:30 and 2:30 p.m. or on Thurs. between 2:30 and 3:30 p.m. or 3:00 and 4:00 p.m.
					Mon. anytime or Tues a.m.: Call to renew prescription
					Tues.: Lunch with friend from 1:00–2:00 p.m.
					Tues.: Phone conference before 2:00 p.m. (30 minutes)
					Mon. or Tues.: Medication picked up between 9:00 a.m. and 3:00 p.m. (30 minutes). Must have previously called to renew prescription.
					Thurs.: Walk neighbors' dog before 11:00 a.m. (30 minutes)
					Thurs.: Dentist at 3:00 p.m. (1 hour)
					Thurs.: Movies with friends from 7:00–11 p.m.
					Fri.: Volunteer job from 9:00–10:30 a.m. (90 minutes)
					Thurs. or Fri.: Dinner, coworkers, starting between 6:30 and 8:00 p.m. (2 hours)
					Mon.: Pick up dry cleaning between 8:00 a.m. and 4:00 p.m. (30 minutes)
					Fri., Sat., or Sun. morning: Exercise at the gym (45 minutes)
					Doctor: Mon. or Fri. afternoon at 2:00 p.m. (90 minutes)
					Food shopping before Fri. (1 hour)
					Carpool: One morning at 9:00 a.m. (45 minutes)
					Carpool: One afternoon at 3:00 p.m. (45 minutes)
					Total all columns The no. of appointments in the missing + accurate + error columns should equal 17

Appendix A.15. **Appointments and Errands to Be Scheduled: Adult/Older Adult Level III (Version B)**

You have a doctor's appointment on Wednesday at 3:00 p.m. for an hour. Also, you need to call to renew your prescription and pick up the medication. You take your medication 3 times a day (8:00 a.m., noon, and 9:00 p.m.) and will be out of medication after taking your last pill on Thursday at noon. Make time to go to the pharmacy; it is open from 9:00 a.m. to 3:00 p.m. daily and will take a half hour. You want to catch up with some old friends and have planned a brunch to get together on Friday morning from 9:00 to 10:30 a.m. You would like to pick up your friends and drive them to brunch this week, but your car is looking very dirty. The car wash is only open from 8:00 a.m. to 4:00 p.m. on Monday, Tuesday, and Friday and will take approximately 30 minutes. You need to get to the car wash to clean your car before Friday morning. You made an appointment to get your hair cut from 1:00 to 2:00 p.m. on Thursday. You are hosting your neighborhood book club this week, which takes place on Mondays from 11:00 a.m. to 12:00 p.m. You borrowed the books for book club from the library, so you need to schedule a half hour to return these books sometime on Thursday before 2:00 p.m. You need to make time to call your cousin, and you also need to go see your friend's art show for an hour. Calling your cousin takes 1 hour and needs to be done before Friday. The art show is only open on Wednesday between 2:30 p.m. and 4:00 p.m. or on Monday or Thursday between 1:00 and 2:30 p.m. Your neighbors went away for an overnight trip and have asked you to feed their cat on Wednesday morning before 11:00 a.m.; this will take a half hour. You need to schedule a dentist appointment this week. The dentist has appointments on Monday or Friday afternoon at 2:00 p.m. There is often a wait, so you will need to set aside 90 minutes. To break up your long work week, you have plans to take part in a game night with your coworkers on Wednesday from 7:00 to 11:00 p.m. Your family is planning dinner at a restaurant with you. They are all available either Wednesday or Friday evening. You can make dinner reservations that start anytime between 6:30 and 8:00 p.m. You choose the day and start time of the reservation, and schedule 2 hours for dinner. At the end of the week, you are running low on groceries and would like to go to the grocery store either Friday or Saturday morning for 45 minutes. You are in a carpool and need to drive the kids to school one morning at 9:00 a.m. and pick up one afternoon at 3:00 p.m. The carpool takes about 45 minutes. You can choose the days.

Appendix A.16. Calendar Scoring Worksheet: Adult/Older Adult Level III (Version B)

(*Note.* Tuesday is free in this version.)

Directions: Place a check mark in the Accurate column if appointment is entered without errors and an "X" in the missing column if an appointment is omitted. For quick scoring, place an "X" in the Error column. For detailed error scoring, use one of the following error codes to indicate which type of error was committed.

R = Appointment is repeated or entered more than once, and repetition is not an attempt to self-correct a location error
L = Appointment is placed in the wrong location, day, or time slot
T = Appointment is in the right location, but the time allotted is incorrect by more than 15 minutes (7:00 a.m.–6:00 p.m.) or 30 minutes (6:00–9:00 p.m.)
I = Appointment name is entered inaccurately or partially

Self-Recognition (SR) Column

Place a check mark in this column if the person acknowledges an appointment error or conflict verbally or nonverbally or if you observe the person trying to correct it (e.g., draw lines, cross out).

Entered	Missing	Error	Accurate	SR	Appointments
					Mon.: Book club from 11:00 a.m.–12:00 p.m.
					Go to art show on Mon. or Thurs. between 1:00 and 2:00 p.m. or 1:30 and 2:30 p.m. or on Wed. between 2:30 and 3:30 p.m. or 3:00 and 4:00 p.m.
					Mon. or Wed. any time or Thurs. a.m.: Call to renew prescription
					Wed.: Feed neighbors' cat before 11:00 a.m. (30 minutes)
					Wed.: Doctor at 3:00 p.m. (1 hour)
					Wed.: Game night with coworkers from 7:00–11:00 p.m.
					Mon., Wed., or Thurs.: Medication picked up between 9:00 a.m. and 3:00 p.m. (30 minutes). Must have previously called to renew prescription
					Thurs.: Haircut from 1:00–2:00 p.m.
					Thurs.: Return library books before 2:00 p.m. (30 minutes)
					Fri.: Brunch with friend from 9:00–10:30 a.m. (90 minutes)
					Wed. or Fri.: Family dinner starting between 6:30 and 8:00 p.m. (2 hours)
					Mon.: Get car washed between 8:00 a.m. and 4:00 p.m. (30 minutes)
					Fri., Sat., or Sun. morning: Buy groceries (45 minutes)
					Dentist: Mon. or Fri. afternoon at 2:00 p.m. (90 minutes)
					Call cousin before Fri. (1 hour)
					Carpool: One morning at 9:00 a.m. (45 minutes)
					Carpool: One afternoon at 3:00 p.m. (45 minutes)
					Total all columns The no. of appointments in the missing + accurate + error columns should equal 17

APPENDIX B

Appointment Lists and Scoring Sheets: Middle/High School (Ages 12–18)

Appendix B.1. Appointments and Errands to Be Scheduled: Middle/High School Level II (Version A)

Dentist on Thursday at 3:00 p.m. (1 hour)

One-hour visit with cousin who is only available on Thursday between 2:30 and 4:00 p.m. or on Monday or Tuesday between 6:30 and 8:00 p.m.

Walk younger sibling to and from school—one morning at 9:00 a.m. and one afternoon at 3:00 p.m. (45 minutes)

Hand in volunteering permission slip on Tuesday before 2:00 p.m. (half hour)

Attend school book fair Monday or Friday at 2:00 p.m. (90 minutes)

Volunteer at People to People on Friday from 10:00–11:45 a.m.

Pick up cell phone from electronics store Monday, Wednesday, or Friday between 4:00 and 8:00 p.m. (half hour)

Talent show practice with a friend on Tuesday from 6:00–7:30 p.m.

Display science fair project either Thursday or Friday at lunch. Start anytime between 11:00 a.m. and 12:00 p.m. (half hour).

Help with grocery shopping for track meet before 5:00 p.m. on Friday (1 hour)

45-minute exercise at the park either Friday or Saturday morning

Sign up as a volunteer for People to People before registration closes on Tuesday. Registration table is open from 9:00 a.m.–3:00 p.m. daily (half hour)

Meet with math study group on Thursday from 7:00–9:30 p.m.

Haircut on Monday from 5:00–6:00 p.m.

Sort and put out recycling on Thursday morning before 10:00 a.m. (half hour)

Attend soccer game on Sunday morning (90 minutes)

Sign up for science fair display in main office any time before 4:00 p.m. on Wednesday

Appendix B.2. Calendar Scoring Worksheet: Middle/High School Level II (Version A)

(*Note.* Wednesday is free in this version.)

Directions: Place a check mark in the Accurate column if an appointment is entered without errors and an "X" in the Missing column if an appointment is omitted. For quick scoring, place an "X" in the Error column. For detailed error scoring, use one of the following error codes to indicate which type of error was committed.

R = Appointment is repeated or entered more than once, and repetition is not an attempt to self-correct a location error
L = Appointment is placed in the wrong location, day, or time slot
T = Appointment is in the right location, but the time allotted is incorrect by more than 15 minutes (7:00 a.m.–6:00 p.m.) or 30 minutes (6:00–9:00 p.m.)
I = Appointment name is entered inaccurately or partially

Self-Recognition (SR) Column

Place a check mark in this column if the person acknowledges an appointment error or conflict verbally or nonverbally or if you observe the person trying to correct it (e.g., draw lines, cross out).

Entered	Missing	Error	Accurate	SR	Appointments
					Mon.: Haircut from 5:00–6:00 p.m.
					Visit with cousin Mon. or Tues. between 6:30 and 7:30 p.m. or 7:00 and 8:00 p.m. or Thurs. between 2:30 and 3:30 p.m. or 3:00 and 4:00 p.m.
					Mon. or Tues.: Sign up for science fair display
					Tues.: Talent show practice 6:00–7:30 p.m.
					Tues.: Hand in volunteering permission slip before 2:00 p.m.
					Mon. or Tues.: Sign up as a volunteer for People to People (30 minutes). Must have previously handed in permission slip.
					Thurs.: Sort and put out recycling before 10:00 a.m. (30 minutes)
					Thurs.: Dentist at 3:00 p.m. (1 hour)
					Thurs.: Meet with math study group from 7:00–9:30 p.m.
					Fri.: Volunteer job from 10:00–11:45 a.m.
					Thurs. or Fri.: Display science fair project anytime between 11:00 a.m. and 12:00 p.m. (30 minutes)
					Mon. or Fri.: Pick up cell phone between 4:00 and 8:00 p.m. (30 minutes)
					Fri., Sat., or Sun. morning: Exercise at the park (45 minutes)
					Sat. or Sun. morning: Attend soccer game (90 minutes)
					Mon. or Fri. afternoon: Book fair at 2:00 p.m. (90 minutes)
					Fri.: Help with grocery shopping before 5:00 p.m. (1 hour)
					Walk sibling to school: One morning at 9:00 a.m. (45 minutes)
					Walk sibling home: One afternoon at 3:00 p.m. (45 minutes)
					Total all columns The no. of appointments in the missing + accurate + error columns should equal 18

Appendix B.3. Appointments and Errands to Be Scheduled: Middle/High School Level II (Version B)

School musical on Thursday from 7:00–10:00 p.m.

One-hour meeting with science group, who are all only available on Thursday between 6:30 and 8:00 p.m. or on Monday or Wednesday between 5:30 and 7:00 p.m.

Walk dog: one morning at 7:00 a.m. and one afternoon at 3:00 p.m. (45 minutes)

Call Grandma on Wednesday before 6:00 p.m. (half hour)

Go to varsity football game Monday or Friday afternoon from 6:30–9:00 p.m.

Sister's birthday dinner on Friday from 5:00–6:30 p.m.

Attend an open study session Monday, Tuesday, or Wednesday between 1:00 and 8:30 p.m. (half hour)

Movies with a friend on Wednesday from 5:00–6:30 p.m.

Make-up quiz either Thursday or Friday at lunch. Start quiz anytime between 11:00 a.m. and 12 p.m. (half hour)

Buy sister a birthday present before Friday (1 hour)

Ninety-minute orthodontist appointment either Friday or Saturday morning

Sign up for Relay for Life walk before registration closes on Wednesday. Registration table is open from 2:00–7:00 p.m. daily (half hour)

Meet with guidance counselor on Thursday from 11:00 a.m.–1:00 p.m.

Haircut on Monday from 4:00–5:00 p.m.

Collect and take out trash Thursday morning before 11:00 a.m. (half hour)

Attend brunch with family on Sunday morning (90 minutes)

Stop by the math room and reschedule missed quiz before 2:00 p.m. on Thursday

Appendix B.4. Calendar Scoring Worksheet: Middle/High School Level II (Version B)

(*Note.* Tuesday is free in this version.)

Directions: Place a check mark in the Accurate column if an appointment is entered without errors and an "X" in the Missing column if an appointment is omitted. For quick scoring, place an "X" in the Error column. For detailed error scoring, use one of the following error codes to indicate which type of error was committed.

R = Appointment is repeated or entered more than once, and repetition is not an attempt to self-correct a location error
L = Appointment is placed in the wrong location, day, or time slot
T = Appointment is in the right location, but the time allotted is incorrect by more than 15 minutes (7:00 a.m.–6:00 p.m.) or 30 minutes (6:00–9:00 p.m.)
I = Appointment name is entered inaccurately or partially

Self-Recognition (SR) Column

Place a check mark in this column if the person acknowledges an appointment error or conflict verbally or nonverbally or if you observe the person trying to correct it (e.g., draw lines, cross out).

Entered	Missing	Error	Accurate	SR	Appointments
					Mon.: Haircut from 4:00–5:00 p.m.
					Meet with science group Mon. or Wed. between 5:30 and 6:30 p.m. or 6:00 and 7:00 p.m. or Thurs. between 6:30 and 7:30 p.m. or 7:00 and 8:00 p.m.
					Mon. or Wed. anytime or Thurs. before 2:00 p.m.: Reschedule missed quiz
					Wed.: Movies with friend from 5:00–6:30 p.m.
					Wed.: Call Grandma before 6:00 p.m. (30 minutes)
					Mon. or Wed: Sign up for Relay for Life between 2:00 and 7:00 p.m. (30 minutes)
					Thurs.: Collect and take out trash before 11:00 a.m. (30 minutes)
					Thurs.: Meeting with guidance counselor at 11:00 a.m. (2 hours)
					Thurs.: School musical from 7:00–10:00 p.m.
					Fri.: Sister's birthday dinner from 5:00–6:30 p.m. (90 minutes)
					Thurs. or Fri.: Make-up quiz between 11:00 a.m. and 12:30 p.m. (30 minutes). Must have previously rescheduled missed quiz.
					Mon. or Wed.: Attend an open-study session between 1:00 and 8:30 p.m. (30 minutes)
					Fri., Sat., or Sun. morning : Orthodontist appointment (90 minutes)
					Sat. or Sun. morning: Attend brunch with family (90 minutes)
					Football game: Mon. or Fri. from 6:30–9:00 p.m.
					Buy sister a birthday gift before Friday (1 hour)
					Walk dog: One morning at 7:00 a.m. (45 minutes)
					Walk dog: One afternoon at 3:00 p.m. (45 minutes)
					Total all columns The no. of appointments in the missing + accurate + error columns should equal 18

APPENDIX C Appointment Lists and Scoring Sheets: Youth (Ages 16–21)

Appendix C.1. Appointments and Errands to Be Scheduled: Youth Level II (Version A)

Dentist on Wednesday at 3:00 p.m. (1 hour)

One-hour visit with cousin who is only available on Wednesday between 2:30 and 4:00 p.m. or on Monday or Tuesday between 1:00 and 2:30 p.m.

Take younger sibling to and from school: One morning at 9:00 a.m. and one afternoon at 3:00 p.m. (45 minutes)

Phone interview on Tuesday before 12:00 p.m. (half hour)

Doctor appointment Monday or Friday afternoon at 2:00 p.m. (90 minutes)

Volunteer at People to People on Saturday from 9:00–10:30 a.m.

Pick up stereo from layaway Tuesday, Wednesday, or Thursday between 8:00 a.m. and 4 p.m. (half hour)

Haircut on Tuesday from 1:00–2:00 p.m.

Dinner with friends either Wednesday or Friday evening. Start dinner any time between 6:30 and 8:00 p.m. (2 hours)

Go food shopping before Friday (1 hour)

45-minute exercise at the park either Friday or Saturday morning

Pick up medication at pharmacy before it closes on Tuesday. Pharmacy is open from 9:00 a.m.-3:00 p.m. daily (half hour)

Movies with friends on Wednesday from 7:00–11:00 p.m.

Lunch with a friend on Monday from 11:00 a.m.–12:00 p.m.

Take care of friend's dog on Wednesday morning before 11:00 a.m. (half hour)

Attend brunch with family on Sunday morning (90 minutes)

Call to make haircut appointment any time before 2:00 p.m. on Tuesday

Appendix C.2. Calendar Scoring Worksheet: Youth Level II (Version A)

(*Note.* Thursday is free in this version.)

Directions: Place a check mark in the Accurate column if an appointment is entered without errors and an "X" in the Missing column if an appointment is omitted. For quick scoring, place an "X" in the Error column. For detailed error scoring, use one of the following error codes to indicate which type of error was committed.

R = Appointment is repeated or entered more than once, and repetition is not an attempt to self-correct a location error
L = Appointment is placed in the wrong location, day, or time slot
T = Appointment is in the right location, but the time allotted is incorrect by more than 15 minutes (7:00 a.m.–6:00 p.m.) or 30 minutes (6:00–9:00 p.m.)
I = Appointment name is entered inaccurately or partially

Self-Recognition (SR) Column

Place a check mark in this column if the person acknowledges an appointment error or conflict verbally or nonverbally or if you observe the person trying to correct it (e.g., draw lines, cross out).

Entered	Missing	Error	Accurate	SR	Appointments
					Mon.: Lunch with friend from 11:00 a.m.–12:00 p.m.
					Visit with cousin Mon. or Tues. between 1:00 and 2:00 p.m. or 1:30 and 2:30 p.m. or Thurs. between 2:30 and 3:30 p.m. or 3:00 and 4:00 p.m.
					Mon. anytime or Tues. before 1:00 p.m.: Make haircut appointment.
					Tues.: Haircut from 1:00–2:00 p.m. Must have previously called to make appointment.
					Tues. morning: Phone interview (30 minutes)
					Mon. or Tues.: Medication picked up between 9:00 a.m. and 3:00 p.m. (30 minutes)
					Wed.: Take care of friend's dog before 11:00 a.m. (30 minutes)
					Wed.: Dentist at 3:00 p.m. (1 hour)
					Wed.: Movies with friends from 7:00–11:00 p.m.
					Sat. or Sun.: Volunteer job from 9:00–10:30 a.m. (90 minutes)
					Doctor appointment: Mon. or Fri. from 2:00–3:30 p.m.
					Wed. or Fri.: Dinner with friends starting between 6:30 and 8:00 p.m. (2 hours)
					Tues. or Wed.: Pick up stereo from layaway 8:00 a.m.–4:00 p.m. (30 minutes)
					Fri., Sat., or Sun. morning: Exercise at park (45 minutes)
					Sat. or Sun. morning: Attend brunch with family
					Go food shopping before Friday (1 hour)
					Take younger sibling to school: One morning at 9:00 a.m. (45 minutes)
					Get younger sibling from school: One afternoon at 3:00 p.m. (45 minutes)
					Total all columns The no. of appointments in the missing + accurate + error columns should equal 18

Appendix C.3. Appointments and Errands to Be Scheduled: Youth Level II (Version B)

Haircut on Monday from 11:00 a.m.–12:00 p.m.

One-hour visit with uncle who is only available on Thursday between 2:30 and 4:00 p.m. or on Monday or Tuesday between 1:00 and 2:30 p.m.

Pay phone bill at store Monday, Wednesday, or Friday between 8:00 a.m. and 4:00 p.m. (half hour)

Phone interview on Tuesday before 2:00 p.m. (half hour)

Doctor appointment Monday or Friday afternoon at 3:00 p.m. (90 minutes)

Lunch with a friend on Tuesday from 1:00–2:00 p.m.

Pick up medication at pharmacy before it closes on Tuesday. Pharmacy is open from 9:00 a.m.–3:00 p.m. daily (half hour)

Dentist on Thursday at 3:00 p.m. (1 hour)

Take younger sibling to and from school: One morning at 9:00 a.m. and one afternoon at 3:00 p.m. (45 minutes)

Volunteer at People to People on Saturday from 9:00–10:30 a.m.

45-minute exercise at the park either Friday or Saturday morning

Dinner with friends either Thursday or Friday evening. Start dinner any time between 6:30 and 8:00 p.m. (2 hours)

Brother's birthday dinner on Thursday from 7:00–11:00 p.m.

Go food shopping before Friday (1 hour)

Take grandmother to bank on Thursday morning before 11:00 a.m. (half hour)

Attend soccer game on Sunday morning (90 minutes)

Buy birthday gift for brother any time before 11:00 p.m. Thursday

Appendix C.4. Calendar Scoring Worksheet: Youth Level II (Version B)

(*Note.* Wednesday is free in this version.)

Directions: Place a check mark in the Accurate column if an appointment is entered without errors and an "X" in the missing column if an appointment is omitted. For quick scoring, place an "X" in the Error column. For detailed error scoring, use one of the following error codes to indicate which type of error was committed.

R = Appointment is repeated or entered more than once, and repetition is not an attempt to self-correct a location error
L = Appointment is placed in the wrong location, day, or time slot
T = Appointment is in the right location, but the time allotted is incorrect by more than 15 minutes (7:00 a.m.–6:00 p.m.) or 30 minutes (6:00–9:00 p.m.)
I = Appointment name is entered inaccurately or partially

Self-Recognition (SR) Column

Place a check mark in this column if the person acknowledges an appointment error or conflict verbally or nonverbally or if you observe the person trying to correct it (e.g., draw lines, cross out).

Entered	Missing	Error	Accurate	SR	Appointments
					Mon.: Haircut from 11:00 a.m.–12:00 p.m.
					Visit with uncle Mon. or Tues. between 1:00 and 2:00 p.m. or 1:30 and 2:30 p.m. or Thurs. between 2:30 and 3:30 p.m. or 3:00 and 4:00 p.m.
					Buy gift for brother before 7:00 p.m. on Thursday
					Tues.: Lunch with friend from 1:00–2:00 p.m.
					Tues.: Phone interview before 2:00 p.m. (30 minutes)
					Mon. or Tues.: Medication picked up between 9:00 a.m. and 3:00 p.m. (30 minutes)
					Thurs.: Take Grandmother to bank before 11:00 a.m. (30 minutes)
					Thurs.: Dentist at 3:00 p.m. (1 hour)
					Thurs.: Brother's birthday dinner 7:00–11:00 p.m. Must have previously bought birthday gift.
					Sat. or Sun.: Volunteer job from 9:00–10:30 a.m. (90 minutes)
					Thurs. or Fri.: Dinner with friends starting between 6:30 and 8:00 p.m. (2 hours)
					Mon. or Fri.: Pay phone bill at store 8:00 a.m. and 4:00 p.m. (30 minutes)
					Fri., Sat., or Sun. morning: Exercise at park (45 minutes)
					Doctor appointment: Mon. or Fri. from 3:00–4:30 p.m.
					Go food shopping before Friday (1 hour)
					Sat. or Sun. morning: Attend soccer game
					Take younger sibling to school: One morning at 9:00 a.m. (45 minutes)
					Pick up younger sibling from school: One afternoon at 3:00 p.m. (45 minutes)
					Total all columns The no. of appointments in the missing + accurate + error columns should equal 18

APPENDIX D Appointment Lists and Scoring Sheets: WCPA–S (College Students Ages 20–34)

Appendix D.1. Appointments and Errands to Be Scheduled: WCPA–S

Private lesson on Thursday from 11:00 a.m.–12:00 p.m.

Dinner with the family on Monday evening or on Wednesday evening. For each occasion, the meal begins between 6:30 and 8:00 p.m. (2 hours)

Performance at the club on Wednesday from 7:00–11:00 p.m.

Tidy up and organize your apartment on one weekday between 12:00 and 4:00 p.m. (2 hours)

Volunteering at telephone help line on Thursday from 9:00–10:30 a.m.

One work shift in the mall. Possible shifts are from Sunday–Thursday, from 10:00 a.m.–4:00 p.m. or from 4:00–10:00 p.m.

Movie at the theater, at one of two showings: Sunday at 5:00 p.m. or Thursday at 6:00 p.m. (2 hours)

Pick up cellular phone from repair at the mall on Sunday, Tuesday, or Thursday from 8:00 a.m.–12:00 p.m. (half hour)

Buy sneakers at the mall before Thursday (1 hour)

Lunch with friend on Monday from 1:00–2:00 p.m.

45-minute exercise at the gym either Thursday or Friday morning

Take the dog to get vaccination at the open clinic on Wednesday morning until 10:00 a.m. (half hour).

Pick up a package from the post office branch at the mall any time before Monday afternoon at 12:00 p.m.

Eye exam on Wednesday at 2:30 p.m. (1 hour)

In addition, this week you must make a 1-hour appointment with the study advisor. The advisor's office hours are Sunday–Wednesday, 3:00–4:00 p.m. To prepare for the meeting, you must read the handbook for 1st-year students. This can take up to 2 hours. You can buy the handbook at the bookstore, which is open every day from 8:00 a.m.–8:00 p.m. (time to buy: half hour).

Appendix D.2. Calendar Scoring Worksheet: WCPA–S

(*Note.* Tuesday is free in this version.)

Directions: Place a check mark in the Accurate column if appointment is entered without errors and an "X" in the Missing column if an appointment is omitted. For quick scoring, place an "X" in the Error column. For detailed error scoring, use one of the following error codes to indicate which type of error was committed.

R = Appointment is repeated or entered more than once, and repetition is not an attempt to self-correct a location error
L = Appointment is placed in the wrong location, day, or time slot
T = Appointment is in the right location, but the time allotted is incorrect by more than 15 minutes (7:00 a.m.–6:00 p.m.) or 30 minutes (6:00–9:00 p.m.)
I = Appointment name is entered inaccurately or partially

Self-Recognition (SR) Column

Place a check mark in this column if the person acknowledges an appointment error or conflict verbally or nonverbally or if you observe the person trying to correct it (e.g., draw lines, cross out).

Entered	Missing	Error	Accurate	SR	Appointments
					Private lesson Thurs. 11:00 a.m.–12:00 p.m.
					Performance at the club Wed. 7:00–11:00 p.m.
					Volunteering at help line Thurs. 9:00–10:30 a.m.
					Lunch with friend Mon. 1:00–2:00 p.m.
					Vaccination for dog at the clinic Wed. morning until 10:00 a.m. (half hour)
					Eye examination Wed. 2:30 p.m. (1 hour)
					Dinner with the family Mon. or Wed. evening. The meal begins between 6:30 and 8:00 p.m. (2 hours)
					Tidy up and organize apartment one weekday between 12:00 and 4:00 p.m. (2 hours)
					Movie at the cinema Sun. 5:00–7:00 p.m. or Thurs. 6:00–8:00 p.m.
					Exercise at gym Thurs. or Fri. morning (45 minutes)
					Cellular phone from repair at the mall—possibilities: Sun., Tues., or Thurs. 8:00 a.m.–12:00 p.m. (half hour)
					Shift at work in the mall—possibilities: Sun.–Thurs., 10:00 a.m.–4:00 p.m. and 4:00–10:00 p.m.
					Buy sneakers at the mall before Thurs. (1 hour)
					Pick up package from the post office at the mall before Monday at 12:00 p.m. (half hour)
					Purchase handbook any day from 8:00 a.m.–8:00 p.m.
					Read the handbook[1] after purchasing it (2 hours)
					Meet with study advisor [2] after reading the handbook. Possibilities: Sun.–Wed., 3:00 p.m.–4:00 p.m. (1 hour)
					Total all columns The no. of appointments in the missing + accurate + error columns should equal 17

[1]If the task "purchase handbook" was not entered, ignore the requirement to "read the handbook."
[2]If either task or one of them was not entered, ignore the requirement to enter the task after reading or purchasing the handbook.

APPENDIX E General Forms for Administration

Appendix E.1. Weekly Calendar Planning Activity Instruction Sheet

Directions

1. Enter the appointments in any order in the weekly schedule.
2. Enter the entire or complete appointment or errand.
3. Mark the exact time needed on the weekly schedule (when it is indicated).
4. It is more important to be accurate than to go too fast.
5. Remember to follow the rules.

Rules to Remember

- Once you have entered an appointment into the calendar, you cannot cross it out.
- Tell me when it is ____________.
- Leave ____________ free. (Do not schedule any appointments or errands on this day.)
- Do not answer questions from the examiner during this activity.
- Tell the examiner when you are finished.

Note. Choose appointment list from Appendixes A, B, C, or D.

Appendix E.2. Weekly Calendar

Weekly Calendar

	Mon	Tues	Wed	Thur	Fri	Sun	Sat
7 am							
:15							
:30							
:45							
8 am							
:15							
:30							
:45							
9 am							
:15							
:30							
:45							
10 am							
:15							
:30							
:45							
11 am							
:15							
:30							
:45							
12 pm							
:15							
:30							
:45							
1 pm							
:15							
:30							
:45							
2 pm							
:15							
:30							
:45							
3 pm							
:15							
:30							
:45							
4 pm							
:15							
:30							
:45							
5 pm							
:15							
:30							
:45							
6 pm							
:30							
7 pm							
:30							
8 pm							
:30							

Appendix E.3. Weekly Calendar Sample 1: How to Enter Time

Weekly Calendar

		Mon	Tues	Wed	Thur	Fri	Sun	Sat
7	am							
	:15							
	:30							
	:45							
8	am	1 hour						
	:15							
	:30							
	:45							
9	am							
	:15		45 minutes					
	:30				half hour			
	:45							
10	am							
	:15							
	:30							
	:45							
11	am					90 minutes		
	:15							
	:30							
	:45							
12	pm							
	:15							
	:30							
	:45							
1	pm							
	:15							
	:30							
	:45							
2	pm							
	:15							
	:30							
	:45							
3	pm							
	:15							
	:30							
	:45							
4	pm							
	:15							
	:30							
	:45							
5	pm							
	:15							
	:30							
	:45							
6	pm							
	:30							
7	pm							
	:30							
8	pm							
	:30							

Appendix E.4. Weekly Calendar Sample 2: How to Enter Appointments

Weekly Calendar

	Mon	Tues	Wed	Thur	Fri	Sun	Sat
7 am							
:15							
:30							
:45							
8 am	Meeting-						
:15	Mary						
:30							
:45	(1 hour)						
9 am							
:15		Mail					
:30		package		Call sister			
:45		(45 minutes)		(half hour)			
10 am							
:15							
:30							
:45							
11 am							
:15					Movies		
:30					with		
:45					friends		
12 pm					(90 minutes)		
:15							
:30							
:45							
1 pm							
:15							
:30							
:45							
2 pm							
:15							
:30							
:45							
3 pm							
:15							
:30							
:45							
4 pm							
:15							
:30							
:45							
5 pm							
:15							
:30							
:45							
6 pm							
:30							
7 pm							
:30							
8 pm							
:30							

Note. The length of time for the tasks is illustrated. In the actual task, there is no need to indicate the length of time for each task if the appointment is marked or outlined.

Appendix E.5. Adult Background Form (Optional)

ID #: __________ Date: __________ Examiner initials: __________

Gender: ☐ Male ☐ Female

Diagnosis: ______________________________ Approximate length since onset: __________

Age: _______ **English preferred language:** ☐ Yes ☐ No

Race: ☐ Caucasian ☐ Black/African-American ☐ Hispanic ☐ Asian/Pacific Islander
☐ Native American ☐ Other

Residence: ☐ Urban ☐ Rural (choose closest category)

Education (in years beginning with 1st grade): __________________________

Past or present occupation: ______________________________

Previous neurological illness or trauma: ☐ Yes ☐ No

Past Medical History—Before Current Illness or Diagnosis		
1. Neurological diagnosis or illness Specify: ____________________________	☐ No (1)	☐ Yes (2)
2. Loss of consciousness of more than a few minutes	☐ No (1)	☐ Yes (2)
3. History of a learning disability	☐ No (1)	☐ Yes (2)
4. Other chronic illness (e.g., systemic lupus erythematosus, rheumatoid arthritis, fibromyalgia, chronic fatigue syndrome)	☐ No (1)	☐ Yes (2)
5. Cardiac disease	☐ No (1)	☐ Yes (2)
6. Hospitalization for a psychiatric illness	☐ No (1)	☐ Yes (2)

Older Adults

Do you have any help with daily activities? ___ Yes ___ No

If yes, who helps you and what do they do? ____

Do you pay your own bills, organize your own medications, and prepare your own meals? ☐ Yes ☐ No

Do you keep your own calendar? ☐ Yes ☐ No

Appendix E.6. WCPA Recording Form

Level: ____ **Version:** ____
Client: ______________________________ Date: _________________ Examiner: __________________

Planning time: From "Let's begin" to entering of
1st appointment: ____ min ____ sec 2nd appointment: ____ min ____ sec (optional)
Total time: Time from "Let's begin" to completion: ____ min ____ sec

Rules

1. Questions answered (Y = *yes;* N = *no*) 1. ____ 2. ____ 3. ____
2. States time at 7 min (±5 minutes) ____ States time too late ____ Forgets time completely ____
3. States when finished: ____ yes ____ no
4. Appointments scheduled on free day (Tues./Wed./Thurs.): ____ yes ____ no
5. No. of appointments crossed out ______

Total no. of rules followed ____/5

Observations

Refers to Instruction Sheet: ____ Never ____ 1–2 times ____ 3–5 times ____ >5 times
Calendar error management (Sat./Sun. reversal, evening appointment time format, time ending too early) ____ Did not affect performance ____ Interfered with performance

Note. This form applies to all versions of the WCPA.

(Continued)

Strategies Observed (check off whether strategy is observed and how much it is used)

Strategies	Not Observed	Occasionally/ Partially Used	Frequently/ Consistently Used	Inefficient/ Counterproductive
Underlines, circles, or highlights key words or features				
Uses finger				
Verbal rehearsal: Repeats key words or instructions out loud				
Crosses off, checks off, or highlights appointments entered				
Rearrangement of materials				
Categorizes or organizes appointments before entering them (coding system, color codes, highlights, labels)				
Enters fixed appointments first, then flexible appointments				
Uses written plan: Makes a rough draft first or plans out calendar in writing before entering appointments				
Talks out loud about strategy, method, or plan				
Crosses off specified free day				
Self-checks				
Pauses and rereads				
Other:				
Other:				
Total observed strategies				
Strategies reported (not observed—reported in After-Task Interview) Specify and indicate total no. of strategies:				
Total no. of strategies used: total observed strategies (occasional + frequent) + total strategies reported				

Comments and other strategies observed (note any spontaneous statements regarding difficulty while completing task, comment on strategy inefficiencies, and expand on description of strategy use): ____________________

____

Appendix E.7. After-Task Interview and Rating Scale

1. **Do you do tasks like this on a regular basis?** ___ Yes ___ No (*Optional:* Do you use a weekly calendar or schedule? How do you go about keeping track of your own appointments or errands?)
2. **(a) Tell me how you went about doing this task (*Wait for response. If necessary, ask.*)** **(b) Did you use any strategies or special methods?** (Did you have a plan or a special approach? How did you manage to keep track of everything or organize everything?) *If necessary, comment on observations regarding strategy use.* (*Note:* If additional strategies are reported, check off reported strategies on the WCPA Recording Form and specify.)

3. **Did you encounter (or experience) any challenges (or difficulties) while doing this task? Which parts of this activity were most challenging (hardest)? Which parts were easiest?**

4. **Would you do anything differently next time?** (Would you change the way you went about the task in any way? Are there any other strategies or methods that you could use?)

5. **Self-Ratings**

Statement	Agree (1)	Somewhat Agree (2)	Somewhat Disagree (3)	Disagree (4)	
1. This task was easy for me.					
2. I used efficient methods to complete this task.					
3. I completed this task accurately.					
4. I kept track of everything I needed to do.					
Totals					
Average rating					

6. **How much time did it take you to complete this task?** (*Encourage the person to estimate or guess if he or she is not sure.*)
   ___ <10 min ___ 10–15 min ___ 16–20 min ___ 21–25 min ___ 26–35 min ___ >35 min
7. **17 or 18 appointments needed to be entered into the weekly calendar. Estimate the number of appointments that you entered accurately into the schedule: ________.**

Appendix E.8. Observation Form (Optional)

Write the order in which appointments are entered during performance as well as comments specific to the appointments.

Number	Appointment	Comments
1		
2		
3		
4		
5		
6		
7		
8		
9		
10		
11		
12		
13		
14		
15		
16		
17		
18		

APPENDIX F Worksheets and Templates for Summarizing Results

Appendix F.1. **Quick Summary of Raw Scores Worksheet (Worksheet 1)**

Name: ______________________ Date of assessment: ______________

WCPA Profile (circle client scores)

	Entered Appointment	Accurate Appointment	Rules Followed	Strategy Use	Awareness	Total Time	Planning Time	Efficiency
High Performance	16–17	16–17	5	7+	Aware	<6 min	<10 sec	<40
	14–15	14–15		6		7-9 min	10–59 sec	41–90
	12–13	12–13		5	Some awareness	10–15 min	1 min	91–125
	10–11	10–11	4	4		16–20 min	2 min	126–150
	8–9	8–9	3	3	Slight awareness	21–25 min	3 min	151–200
	6–7	6–7	2	2		26–30 min	4 min	201–250
	4–5	4–5	1	1	No awareness	31–40 min	5 min	251–300
Low Performance	<4	<4	0	0		40+ min	6+ min	300+
	Entered Appointment	Accurate Appointment	Rules Followed	Strategy Use	Awareness	Total Time	Planning Time	Efficiency

Performance observations:

Strategy use:

Awareness:

Summary:

Appendix F.2. Summary: Normative Comparison Worksheet (Worksheet 2)

Name: ______________________ Date of assessment: ______________

WCPA Scores	Score	Percentile	Comments
Planning time ___ min ___ sec			
Total time: ___ min ___ sec			
No. of rules followed (0–5)			
Total strategies ___ Partially used ___ Consistently used			
No. of appointments entered			
No. of accurate appointments			
Efficiency score (total seconds/weighted score)			
Error analysis			
Appointments missing			
Location errors			
Time errors			
Repetition errors			
Incomplete			
Total no. of errors			
Self-recognition of errors			

Performance observations:

Strategy use:

Awareness:

Summary:

Appendix F.3. Visual Performance Profile and Worksheet

Name: ____________________ Date of Assessment: ____________________

Visual Performance Profile

Percentile	Entered Appointment	Accurate Appointment	Rules Followed	Strategy Use	Efficiency	Planning Time	Total Time	Percentile
≥95								≥95
>75								>75
70								70
60								60
50								50
40								40
30								30
25								25
20								20
10								10
<5								<5
	Entered Appointment	Accurate Appointment	Rules Followed	Strategy Use	Efficiency	Planning Time	Total Time	

Error Analysis Profile

	Missing	Repetition	Incomplete	Location	Time	Extraneous	Self-Recognition
0							
1							
2							
3+							

Awareness/Client Perception of Task Difficulty

	Therapist or Actual	Client	Difference	Comments
Self-ratings				
Time estimation				
Accuracy estimation				

Comments/observations:

Appendix F.4. Report Template: Initial and Follow-Up Comparison

The Weekly Calendar Planning Activity (WCPA) is a complex performance task that involves entering __ appointments into a weekly schedule while adhering to rules and avoiding conflicts. It inherently requires integrated use of executive functioning skills, including planning, organization, inhibition, self-monitoring, and use of strategies. This report provides results from initial and follow-up assessments and indicates how performance on an integrated executive function task compares with that of others.

Overview of Performance

Initial assessment:

Follow-up and performance changes from initial assessment:

	Initial		Follow-Up		
Date:	Score	Percentile	Score	Percentile	Comments
Planning time: ___ min ___ s					
Total time: ___ min ___ s					
No. of rules followed (0–5)					
Total no. of strategies					
No. of appointments entered (0–17 or 0–18)					
No. of accurate appointments (0–17 or 0–18)					
Efficiency score					
Error analysis					
Appointments missing					
Location errors					
Time errors					
Repetition errors					
Incomplete					
Total no. of errors					
Self-recognition of errors					

Summary and recommendations:

Appendix F.5. Performance Profile and Report Template (Treatment Planning)

Name: ______________________________ Date of Assessment: ____________________

The Weekly Calendar Planning Activity (WCPA) is a complex performance task that involves entering 17 or 18 appointments into a weekly schedule while adhering to rules and avoiding conflicts. It was administered to provide information on the ability to cope with a cognitively challenging everyday activity, including the ability to plan ahead, recognize potential conflicts, make performance adjustments, simultaneously keep track of information, restrain impulsive responses, self-monitor performance, and use efficient strategies or methods.

Visual Performance Profile

Percentile	Entered Appointment	Accurate Appointment	Rules Followed	Strategy Use	Planning Time	Total Time	Efficiency	Percentile
≥95								≥95
>75								>75
70								70
60								60
50								50
40								40
30								30
25								25
20								20
10								10
<5								<5
	Entered Appointment	Accurate Appointment	Rules Followed	Strategy Use	Planning Time	Total Time	Efficiency	

Error Analysis Profile

	Missing	Repetition	Incomplete	Location	Time	Extraneous	Self-Recognition
0							
1							
2							
3+							

Performance analysis:

(Continued)

Appendix F.5. Performance Profile and Report Template (Treatment Planning) (*Continued*)

Strategy Use

Strategy frequency (partial/consistent):

Task methods or type of strategies used:

Strategy generation (after-task interview):

Self-Monitoring and Awareness

During task (self-recognition of errors [SR]; self-checking):

After task (awareness of strategies used; identification of challenges/difficulties; after task interview):

Awareness: Client Perception of Task Difficulty

	Therapist or Actual	Client	Difference	Comments
Self-ratings				
Time estimation				
Accuracy estimation			—	

Summary and treatment recommendations:

APPENDIX G

Raw Score to Percentile Conversions

The tables in this appendix are used for normative reference and are organized according to age group and level (2 or 3). First, locate the appropriate age group and level. Second, locate the client's raw score(s) in the vertical columns and find the corresponding percentile rank, located horizontally, in the left-side column. When the same score falls across several percentiles, choose the upper limit of the percentile range to identify the percentage falling *at* or below the designated score. This is the percentile that should be used in evaluation reports. The lower limit of the range indicates the percentage of the sample falling below the designated score. For example, in the table below, a score of 17 for appointments entered falls between the 20th and 40th percentiles, indicating that only 20% of the sample obtained scores less than 17 and approximately 40% scored had a score equal to or below 17.

The tables are color-coded for ease in interpretation. The tables also include the means, standard deviations, medians, and score ranges to aid in interpretation. Please refer to Chapter 4, "Interpretation," for a full explanation of the tables and how they should be used.

Youth Level II, Version A: Percentiles for Youths, Ages 16–21 (*N* = 49)

Percentile	Appointments Entered	Accuracy	Rules Followed	Strategies[a]	Planning time, sec	Time, min	Efficiency[b]
95	18	18	5	9	2	8	36
90	18	17	5	7–8	5	9	42
80	18	16	5	6	8	11	50
75	18	16	5	6	10	12	55
70	18	16	5	5	12	12	60
60	18	15	5	4	19	13	65
50	18	14	4	4	31	14	73
40	17	14	4	4	40	15	76
30	17	13	4	3	54	17	95
25	17	13	4	3	67	19	100
20	17	12	4	3	120	20	117
10	16	10–11	3	2	437	25	140
5	15	9	2	2	739	30	250
2	14	8	1	1	745	31	310
Mean	17.4	14.2	4.3	4.3	—[c]	16	—[c]
Standard deviation	0.9	2.6	0.9	2.0	—[c]	6.1	—[c]
Median	18	14	4	4	31	14	73
Range	14–18	8–18	2–5	1–10	0–818	7.0–32.0	28–316

Note. The 25th to the 75th percentile range represents average performance. Sec = seconds; min = minutes.

[a]High strategy use or lower time is not always representative of better performance (see Chapter 4 for interpretation).

[b]Only include those with ≥7 accurate (*N* = 45).

[c]Score distribution deviates significantly from normality; therefore, the median is a better measure of central tendency than the mean.

Above average (95–80)
Average (75–25)
Below average (20–10)
Significantly below average (5–2)

Adults Level II: Percentiles for Adults, Ages 18–39 (N = 114)

Percentile	Appointments Entered	Accuracy	Rules Followed	Strategies[a]	Planning time, sec	Time, min	Efficiency[b]
>95	17	17	5	9–10		8	39
90	17	17	5	8	10	9	43
80	17	16	5	7	20	10	50
75	17	16	5	7	27	11	54
70	17	16	5	6	33	12	56
60	17	15	5	6	50	13	65
50	17	15	4	5	61	15	78
40	17	14	4	4	115	17	83
30	16	13	4	4	160	19	94
25	16	13	4	3	180	20	100
20	16	12	4	3	200	21	112
10	15	11	3	2	520	25	149
5	14	9–10	3	1	605	27	194
>2	13	8	2	0	700	35	230
Mean	16.5	14.2	4.3	5.0	—[c]	16.3	—[c]
Standard deviation	0.8	2.3	0.7	2.3	—[c]	6.7	—[c]
Median	17	15	4	5	61	15	77.6
Range	13–17	6–17	2–5	0–12	1–1,230	5.0–42.0	27.9–478.7

Note. The 25th to the 75th percentile range represents average performance. Sec = seconds; min = minutes.

[a]High strategy use or lower time is not necessarily representative of better performance (see Chapter 4 for interpretation).

[b]Only those with ≥7 accurate (n = 45) are included (N = 113).

[c]Score distribution deviates significantly from normality; therefore, the median is a better measure of central tendency than the mean.

- Above average
- Average
- Below average
- Significantly below average

Adults Level II: Percentiles for Adults, Ages 40–64 (N = 142)

Percentile	Appointments Entered	Accuracy	Rules Followed	Strategies[a]	Planning time, sec	Time, min	Efficiency[b]
95	17	17	5	9–10	5	6	31
90	17	16	5	8	10	8	40
80	17	16	5	7	18	9	50
75	17	16	5	7	27	10	52
70	17	15	5	7	30	11	55
60	17	15	5	6	50	12	62
50	17	14	4	5	65	13	68
40	17	14	4	4	115	14–15	80
30	16	13	4	4	130	16	90
25	16	13	4	3	160	17	93
20	15	12	4	3	192	18–20	102
10	15	11	3	2	360	21	117
5	14	10	2	1	500	22–23	148
<2	13	9	2	0	650	24–26	205
Mean	16.4	14.0	4.3	5.1	—[c]	14.1	—[c]
Standard deviation	0.9	2.1	0.7	2.4	—[c]	5.0	—[c]
Median	17	14	4	5	65	13.3	67.8
Range	13–17	8–17	2–5	0–11	0–840	4–28	17–237

Note. The 25th to the 75th percentile represents average performance. Sec = seconds; min = minutes.

[a]High strategy use or lower time is not necessarily representative of better performance (see Chapter 4 for interpretation).

[b]Only those with ≥7 accurate (n = 142) are included.

[c]Score distribution deviates significantly from normality; therefore, the median is a better measure of central tendency than the mean.

Above average
Average
Below average
Significantly below average

Adults Level II: Percentiles for Adults, Ages 65–94 (*N* = 130)

Percentile	Appointments Entered	Accuracy	Rules Followed	Strategies[a]	Planning time, sec	Time, min	Efficiency[b]
>95	17	17	5	8–9	4	6	45
90	17	16	5	7	5	8	53
80	17	15	5	6	10	9	61
75	17	15	5	6	13	10	68
70	17	14	4	5	15	11	77
60	17	13	4	5	28	13	83
50	16	13	4	4	50	14	92
40	16	12	4	3	65	17	108
30	16	11	4	3	120	20	130
25	16	10	3	2	140	21	146
20	15	9	3	2	185	22	106
10	14	8	3	1	302	26	295
5	13	7	2	0	455	30	422
<2	12	6	1	0	700	32	520
Mean	16.0	12.2	3.8	4.2	—[c]	16.2	—[c]
Standard deviation	1.3	3.0	1.0	2.2	—[c]	7.3	—[c]
Median	16	12.5	4	4	50	14.3	91.7
Range	10–17	5–17	1–5	0–10	0–1,140	4.5–41.0	26.8–654.3

Note. The 25th to the 75th percentile range represents average performance. Sec = seconds; min = minutes.

[a]High strategy use or lower time is not necessarily representative of better performance (see Chapter 4 for interpretation).

[b]Only those with ≥7 accurate (*n* = 127) are included.

[c]Score distribution deviates significantly from normality; therefore, the median is a better measure of central tendency than the mean.

Above average
Average
Below average
Significantly below average

Adults Level III: Percentiles for Adults, Ages 18–39 (*N* = 51)

Percentile	Appointments Entered	Accuracy	Rules Followed	Strategies[a]	Planning time, sec	Time, min	Efficiency[b]
>95	17	17	5	11	21	13	60
90	17	16	5	11	51	14	75
80	17	15	5	10	63	17	100
75	16	15	5	8–9	80	18	110
70	16	15	5	8–9	120	20	114
60	16	14	5	7	180	22	125
50	16	14	5	6	300	25	145
40	16	13	4	6	400	28	160
30	16	12	4	5	600	29	185
25	16	12	4	5	730	31	200
20	16	11	4	4	900	32	240
10	15	9	3	3	1,200	42	262
5	14	8	2	2	1,400	50	400
<2	13	7	1	1	1,600	57	560
Mean	16.0	13.2	4.5	6.6	—[c]	26.8	—[c]
Standard deviation	0.9	2.5	0.8	2.4	—[c]	11.2	—[c]
Median	16.0	14.0	5.0	6.0	300.0	25.0	146.1
Range	13–17	7–17	3–5	2–11	10–1,660	10.6–58.0	55.0–600.0

Note. The 25th to 75th percentile range represents average performance. Sec = seconds; min = minutes.

[a]High strategy use or lower time is not necessarily representative of better performance (see Chapter 4 for interpretation).

[b]Only include those with ≥7 accurate (*n* = 51) are included.

[c]Score distribution deviates significantly from normality; therefore, the median is a better measure of central tendency than the mean.

- Above average
- Average
- Below average
- Significantly below average

Adults Level III: Percentiles for Adults, Ages 40–64 ($N = 83$)

Percentile	Appointments Entered	Accuracy	Rules Followed	Strategies[a]	Planning time, sec	Time, min	Efficiency[b]
95	17	16–17	5	10	7	9	66
90	17	15	5	9	23	10	74
80	17	15	5	7	47	13	80
75	16	14	5	7	60	14	87
70	16	14	5	7	63	15	95
60	16	14	4	6	115	18	115
50	16	13	4	5	135	20	147
40	16	12	4	4	250	25	160
30	15	11	4	4	375	29	190
25	15	10	3	3	640	30	205
20	15	9	3	3	900	32	223
10	14	8	3	3	1,207	37	330
5	13	8	2	2	1,320	40	460
2	12	7	1	1	1,400	44	540
Mean	15.6	12.2	4.1	5.4	—[c]	23.0	—[c]
Standard deviation	1.2	2.6	0.9	2.4	—[c]	10.8	—[c]
Median	16.0	12.0	4.0	5.0	137.0	20.4	147.1
Range	11–17	7–17	2–5	1–11	0–1,620	7.1–60.9	59.1–563

Note. The 25th to 75th percentile range represents average performance. Sec = seconds; min = minutes.

[a]High strategy use or lower time is not necessarily representative of better performance (see Chapter 4 for interpretation).

[b]Only those with ≥7 accurate ($n = 83$) are included.

[c]Score distribution deviates significantly from normality; therefore, the median is a better measure of central tendency than the mean.

Legend: Above average (rows 95–80); Average (rows 75–25); Below average (rows 20–10); Significantly below average (rows 5–2)

Adults Level III: Percentiles for Adults, Ages 65–94 ($N = 41$)

Percentile	Appointments Entered	Accuracy	Rules Followed	Strategies[a]	Planning time, sec	Time, min	Efficiency[b]
95	17	16–17	5	10	11	12	110
90	17	15	5	9	23	13	115
80	17	14	5	8	32	16	123
75	16	14	5	7	62	17	133
70	16	14	5	7	75	18	150
60	16	13	4	6	125	20	188
50	16	12–13	4	5	220	25	235
40	15	11	4	4	270	27	267
30	15	11	4	4	340	30	273
25	15	10	3	4	385	33	313
20	15	9	3	3	470	36	315
10	14	8	3	2	1,124	50	338
5	12	7	2	1	1,200	55	385
2	10	6	1	0	1,450	61	545
Mean	15.4	11.2	3.9	5.5	—[c]	27.4	227.7
Standard deviation	1.4	2.9	1.1	2.7	—[c]	13.6	104.2
Median	16.0	11.5	4.0	5.0	240.0	25.7	227.3
Range	10–17	5–16	1–5	0–13	5–2,400	11.3–62.0	83.5–611.7

Note. The 25th to 75th percentile range represents average performance. Sec = seconds; min = minutes.

[a]High strategy use or lower time is not necessarily representative of better performance (see Chapter 4 for interpretation).

[b]Only those with ≥7 accurate ($n = 39$) are included.

[c]Score distribution deviates significantly from normality; therefore, the median is a better measure of central tendency than the mean.

Above average
Average
Below average
Significantly below average

References

Achi, E. Y., & Rudnicki, S. A. (2012). ALS and frontotemporal dysfunction: A review. *Neurology Research International, 2012,* 806306. http://dx.doi.org/10.1155/2012/806306

Alderman, N., Burgess, P. W., Knight, C., & Henman, C. (2003). Ecological validity of a simplified version of the multiple errands shopping test. *Journal of the International Neuropsychological Society, 9*(1), 31–44.

American Occupational Therapy Association. (2013). Cognition, cognitive rehabilitation, and occupational performance. *American Journal of Occupational Therapy, 67*(Suppl.), S9–S31. http://dx.doi.org/ajot.2013.67S9

American Occupational Therapy Association. (2014). Occupational therapy practice framework: Domain and process (3rd ed.). *American Journal of Occupational Therapy, 68*(Suppl. 1), S1–S48. http://dx.doi.org/10.5014/ajot.2014.682006

Baum, C. M., Tabor Connor, L., Morrison, T., Hahn, M., Dromerick, A. W., & Edwards, D. F. (2008). Reliability, validity, and clinical utility of the executive function performance test: A measure of executive function in a sample of people with stroke. *American Journal of Occupational Therapy, 62,* 446–455. http://dx.doi.org/10.5014/ajot.62.4.446

Baumgartner, T. A. (2009). Tutorial: Calculating percentile rank and percentile norms using SPSS. *Measurement in Physical Education and Exercise Science, 13*(4), 227–233. http://dx.doi.org/10.1080/10913670903262769

Ben Ari, E., Lahav, O., & Kizony, R. (2012). *Weekly calendar planning activity* (Hebrew version). Unpublished manuscript.

Besnard, J., Allain, P., Aubin, G., Chauvire, V., Etcharry-Bouyx, F., & Le Gall, D. (2011). A contribution to the study of environmental dependency phenomena: The social hypothesis. *Neuropsychologia, 49,* 3279–3294. http://dx.doi.org/10.1016/j.neuropsychologia.2011.08.001

Best, J. R., Miller, P. H., & Naglieri, J. A. (2011). Relations between executive function and academic achievement from ages 5 to 17 in a large, representative national sample. *Learning and Individual Differences, 21,* 327–336. http://dx.doi.org/10.1016/j.lindif.2011.01.007

Boosman, H., Bovend'Eerdt, T. J., Visser-Meily, J. M., Nijboer, T. C., & van Heugten, C. M. (2014). Dynamic testing of learning potential in adults with cognitive impairments: A systematic review of methodology and predictive value. *Journal of Neuropsychology.* http://dx.doi.org/10.1111/jnp.12063

Boyle, P. A., Paul, R. H., Moser, D. J., & Cohen, R. A. (2004). Executive impairments predict functional declines in vascular dementia. *Clinical Neuropsychology, 18,* 75–82.

Bueno, V. F., da Silva, M. A., Alves, T. M., Louza, M. R., & Pompeia, S. (2014). Fractionating executive functions of adults with ADHD. *Journal of Attention Disorders.* Advance online publication. http://dx.doi.org/10.1177/1087054714545537

Buracchio, T. J., Mattek, N. C., Dodge, H. H., Hayes, T. L., Pavel, M., Howieson, D. B., & Kaye, J. A. (2011). Executive function predicts risk of falls in older adults without balance impairment. *BMC Geriatrics, 11,* 74. http://dx.doi.org/10.1186/1471-2318-11-74

Burgess, P. W., Alderman, N., Forbes, C., Costello, A., Coates, L., Dawson, D. R., . . . Channon, S. (2006). The case for the development and use of "ecologically valid" measures of executive function in experimental and clinical neuropsychology. *Journal of the International Neuropsychological Society, 12,* 194–209.

Campiglia, M., Seegmuller, C., Le Gall, D., Fournet, N., Roulin, J. L., & Roy, A. (2014). Assessment of everyday executive functioning in children with frontal or temporal epilepsies. *Epilepsy and Behavior: E&B, 39C,* 12–20. http://dx.doi.org/S1525-5050(14)00276-5

Chan, R. C., Shum, D., Toulopoulou, T., & Chen, E. Y. (2007). Assessment of executive functions: Review of instruments and identification of critical issues. *Archives of Clinical Neuropsychology, 23,* 2-1–2-216. http://dx.doi.org/10.1016/j.acn.2007.08.010

Chaytor, N., Schmitter-Edgecombe, M., & Burr, R. (2006). Improving the ecological validity of executive functioning assessment. *Archives of Clinical Neuropsychology, 21,* 217–227.

Cicerone, K., Levin, H., Malec, J., Stuss, D., & Whyte, J. (2006). Cognitive rehabilitation interventions for executive function: Moving from bench to bedside in patients with traumatic brain injury. *Journal of Cognitive Neuroscience, 18,* 1212–1222.

Clément, F., Gauthier, S., & Belleville, S. (2012). Executive functions in mild cognitive impairment: Emergence and breakdown of neural plasticity. *Cortex, 49,* 1268–1279.

Cramm, H. A., Krupa, T. M., Missiuna, C. A., Lysaght, R. M., & Parker, K. H. (2013). Executive functioning: A scoping review of the occupational therapy literature. *Canadian Journal of Occupational Therapy/Revue Canadienne d'Ergotherapie, 80,* 131–140.

Crawford, J. R., Garthwaite, P. H., & Slick, D. J. (2009). On percentile norms in neuropsychology: Proposed reporting standards and methods for quantifying the uncertainty over the percentile ranks of test scores. *The Clinical Neuropsychologist, 23*(7), 1173–1195. http://dx.doi.org/10.1080/13854040902795018

Crean, R. D., Tapert, S. F., Minassian, A., Macdonald, K., Crane, N. A., & Mason, B. J. (2011). Effects of chronic, heavy cannabis use on executive functions. *Journal of Addiction Medicine, 5,* 9–15. http://dx.doi.org/10.1097/ADM.0b013e31820cdd57

Dawson, D. R., Anderson, N. D., Burgess, P., Cooper, E., Krpan, K. M., & Stuss, D. T. (2009). Further development of the multiple errands test: Standardized scoring, reliability, and ecological validity for the Baycrest version. *Archives of Physical Medicine and Rehabilitation, 90*(1), 41–51. http://dx.doi.org/10.1016/j.apmr.2009.07.012

Dybedal, G. S., Tanum, L., Sundet, K., Gaarden, T. L., & Bjolseth, T. M. (2013). Neuropsychological functioning in late-life depression. *Frontiers in Psychology, 4,* 381. http://dx.doi.org/10.3389/fpsyg.2013.00381

Eriksson, G., Tham, K., & Borg, J. (2006). Occupational gaps in everyday life 1–4 years after acquired brain injury. *Journal of Rehabilitation Medicine, 38,* 159–165.

Fisher, A. G., & Bray Jones, K. (2010a). *Assessment of Motor and Process Skills: Vol. 1. Development, standardization, and administration manual* (7th ed.). Fort Collins, CO: Three Star Press.

Fisher, A. G., & Bray Jones, K. (2010b). *Assessment of Motor and Process Skills: Vol. 2. User manual* (7th ed.). Fort Collins, CO: Three Star Press.

Foster, E. R., Cunnane, K. B., Edwards, D. F., Morrison, M. T., Ewald, G. A., Geltman, E. M., & Zazulia, A. R. (2011). Executive dysfunction and depressive symptoms associated with reduced participation of people with severe congestive heart failure. *American Journal of Occupational Therapy, 65,* 306–313. http://dx.doi.org/ajot.2011.000588

Foster, E. R., & Hershey, T. (2011). Everyday executive function is associated with activity participation in Parkinson disease without dementia. *OTJR: Occupation, Participation and Health, 31,* 16–22. http://dx.doi.org/10.3928/15394492-20101108-04

Ganz, P. A., Kwan, L., Castellon, S. A., Oppenheim, A., Bower, J. E., Silverman, D. H., . . . Belin, T. R. (2013). Cognitive complaints after breast cancer treatments: Examining the relationship with neuropsychological test performance. *Journal of the National Cancer Institute, 105,* 791–801. http://dx.doi.org/10.1093/jnci/djt073

Glanz, B. I., Healy, B. C., Rintell, D. J., Jaffin, S. K., Bakshi, R., & Weiner, H. L. (2010). The association between cognitive impairment and quality of life in patients with early multiple sclerosis. *Journal of the Neurological Sciences, 290,* 75–79. http://dx.doi.org/10.1016/j.jns.2009.11.004

Haywood, H. C., & Lidz, C. S. (2007). *Dynamic assessment in practice: Clinical and educational applications.* New York: Cambridge University Press.

Hofmann, W., Schmeichel, B. J., & Baddeley, A. D. (2012). Executive functions and self-regulation. *Trends in Cognitive Sciences, 16,* 174–180. http://dx.doi.org/10.1016/j.tics.2012.01.006

Hommel, M., Miguel, S. T., Naegele, B., Gonnet, N., & Jaillard, A. (2009). Cognitive determinants of social functioning after a first ever mild to moderate stroke at vocational age. *Journal of Neurology, Neurosurgery, and Psychiatry, 80,* 876–880. http://dx.doi.org/10.1136/jnnp.2008.169672

Houston, R. J., Derrick, J. L., Leonard, K. E., Testa, M., Quigley, B. M., & Kubiak, A. (2014). Effects of heavy drinking on executive cognitive functioning in a community sample. *Addictive Behaviors, 39,* 345–349.

Howell, D., Osternig, L., Van Donkelaar, P., Mayr, U., & Chou, L. S. (2013). Effects of concussion on attention and executive function in adolescents. *Medicine and Science in Sports and Exercise, 45,* 1030–1037. http://dx.doi.org/10.1249/MSS.0b013e3182814595

Hsu, N. S., Novick, J. M., & Jaeggi, S. M. (2014). The development and malleability of executive control abilities. *Frontiers in Behavioral Neuroscience, 8,* 221. http://dx.doi.org/10.3389/fnbeh.2014.00221

Insel, K., Morrow, D., Brewer, B., & Figueredo, A. (2006). Executive function, working memory, and medication adherence among older adults. *Journals of Gerontology, Series B: Psychological Sciences and Social Sciences, 61,* P102–P107.

Laes, J. R., & Sponheim, S. R. (2006). Does cognition predict community function only in schizophrenia? A study of schizophrenia patients, bipolar affective disorder patients, and community control subjects. *Schizophrenia Research, 84,* 121–131.

Lahav, O., & Katz, N. (2015). Weekly calendar planning activity for university students: Comparison of individuals with and without ADHD by gender. *Journal of Attention Disorders, 19,* 1–11. http://dx.doi.org/10.1177/1087054714564621

Larsen, M. A., Berglund, E. T., Joseph, R., & Pratt, H. D. (2011). Psychological assessment and testing. In D. R. Patel, D. E. Greydanus, H. A. Omar, & J. Merrick (Eds.), *Neurodevelopmental disabilities: Clinical care for children and young adults* (pp. 29–52). New York: Springer. http://dx.doi.org/10.1007/978-94-007-0627-9_3

Levine, B., Schweizer, T. A., O'Connor, C., Turner, G., Gillingham, S., Stuss, D. T., . . . Robertson, I. H. (2011). Rehabilitation of executive functioning in patients with frontal lobe brain damage with goal management training. *Frontiers in Human Neuroscience, 5,* 1–9.

Lewin, A. B., Larson, M. J., Park, J. M., McGuire, J. F., Murphy, T. K., & Storch, E. A. (2014). Neuropsychological functioning in youth with obsessive compulsive disorder: An examination of executive function and memory impairment. *Psychiatry Research, 216,* 108–115. http://dx.doi.org/10.1016/j.psychres.2014.01.014

Lyons, K. E., & Zelazo, P. D. (2011). Monitoring, metacognition, and executive function: Elucidating the role of self-reflection in the development of self-regulation. *Advances in Child Development and Behavior, 40,* 379–412.

Marshall, G. A., Rentz, D. M., Frey, M. T., Locascio, J. J., Johnson, K. A., & Sperling, R. A.; Alzheimer's Disease Neuroimaging Initiative. (2011). Executive function and instrumental activities of daily living in mild cognitive impairment and Alzheimer's disease. *Alzheimer's and Dementia: The Journal of the Alzheimer's Association, 7,* 300–308. http://dx.doi.org/10.1016/j.jalz.2010.04.005

Meltzer, L. J. (2010). *Promoting executive function in the classroom.* New York: Guilford Press.

Mitchell, A. J., Kemp, S., Benito-Leon, J., & Reuber, M. (2010). The influence of cognitive impairment on health-related quality of life in neurological disease. *Acta Neuropsychiatrica, 22,* 2–13.

Morrison, M. T., Giles, G. M., Ryan, J. D., Baum, C. M., Dromerick, A. W., Polatajko, H. J., & Edwards, D. F. (2013). Multiple Errands Test–Revised (MET–R): A performance-based measure of executive function in people with mild cerebrovascular accident. *American Journal of Occupational Therapy, 67*(4), 460–468. http://dx.doi.org/10.5014/ajot.2013.007880

Muir, S. W., Gopaul, K., & Montero Odasso, M. M. (2012). The role of cognitive impairment in fall risk among older adults: A systematic review and meta-analysis. *Age and Ageing, 41,* 299–308.

Orellana, G., & Slachevsky, A. (2013). Executive functioning in schizophrenia. *Frontiers in Psychiatry, 4,* 35. http://dx.doi.org/10.3389/fpsyt.2013.00035

Osorio, R., de Lozar, B. G., Ramos, I., & Aguera, L. (2009). Disfuncion ejecutiva en pacientes con depresion de inicio tardio [Executive function in patients with late onset depression]. *Actas Espanolas de Psiquiatria, 37,* 196–199.

Ownsworth, T., & Shum, D. (2008). Relationship between executive functions and productivity outcomes following stroke. *Disability and Rehabilitation, 30,* 531–540. http://dx.doi.org/10.1080/09638280701355694

Pandharipande, P. P., Girard, T. D., Jackson, J. C., Morandi, A., Thompson, J. L., Pun, B. T., . . . Ely, E. W.; BRAIN-ICU Study Investigators. (2013). Long-term cognitive impairment after critical illness. *New England Journal of Medicine, 369,* 1306–1316. http://dx.doi.org/10.1056/NEJMoa1301372

Poulin, V., Korner-Bitensky, N., Dawson, D. R., & Bherer, L. (2012). Efficacy of executive function interventions after stroke: A systematic review. *Topics in Stroke Rehabilitation, 19,* 158–171. http://dx.doi.org/10.1310/tsr1902-158

Prencipe, A., Kesek, A., Cohen, J., Lamm, C., Lewis, M. D., & Zelazo, P. D. (2011). Development of hot and cool executive function during the transition to adolescence. *Journal of Experimental Child Psychology, 108,* 621–637. http://dx.doi.org/10.1016/j.jecp.2010.09.008

Puig, O., Penades, R., Baeza, I., Sanchez-Gistau, V., De la Serna, E., Fonrodona, L., . . . Castro-Fornieles, J. (2012). Processing speed and executive functions predict real-world everyday living skills in adolescents with early-onset schizophrenia. *European Child and Adolescent Psychiatry, 21,* 315–326. http://dx.doi.org/10.1007/s00787-012-0262-0

Reid-Arndt, S. A., Yee, A., Perry, M. C., & Hsieh, C. (2009). Cognitive and psychological factors associated with early posttreatment functional outcomes in breast cancer survivors. *Journal of Psychosocial Oncology, 27,* 415–434. http://dx.doi.org/10.1080/07347330903183117

Ritsner, M. S. (2007). Predicting quality of life impairment in chronic schizophrenia from cognitive variables. *Quality of Life Research, 16,* 929–937. http://dx.doi.org/10.1007/s11136-007-9195-3

Royall, D. R., Palmer, R., Chiodo, L. K., & Polk, M. J. (2004). Declining executive control in normal aging predicts change in functional status: The Freedom House Study. *Journal of the American Geriatrics Society, 52,* 346–352.

Royall, D. R., Palmer, R., Chiodo, L. K., & Polk, M. J. (2005). Executive control mediates memory's association with change in instrumental activities of daily living: The Freedom House Study. *Journal of the American Geriatrics Society, 53,* 11–17.

Semrud-Clikeman, M., Fine, J. G., & Bledsoe, J. (2014). Comparison among children with children with autism spectrum disorder, nonverbal learning disorder and typically developing children on measures of executive functioning. *Journal of Autism and Developmental Disorders, 44,* 331–342. http://dx.doi.org/10.1007/s10803-013-1871-2

Sergi, M. J., Kern, R. S., Mintz, J., & Green, M. F. (2005). Learning potential and the prediction of work skill acquisition in schizophrenia. *Schizophrenia Bulletin, 31,* 67–72.

Shallice, T., & Burgess, P. W. (1991). Deficits in strategy application following frontal lobe damage in man. *Brain: A Journal of Neurology, 114*(2), 727–741.

Stilley, C. S., Bender, C. M., Dunbar-Jacob, J., Sereika, S., & Ryan, C. M. (2010). The impact of cognitive function on medication management: Three studies. *Health Psychology, 29,* 50–55. http://dx.doi.org/10.1037/a0016940

Tarricone, P. (2011). *The taxonomy of metacognition.* New York: Psychology Press.

Toglia, J. (2011). The dynamic interactional model of cognition in cognitive rehabilitation. In N. Katz (Ed.), *Cognition, occupation and participation across the life span: Neuroscience, neurorehabilitation and models of intervention in occupational therapy* (3rd ed., pp. 161–201). Bethesda, MD: AOTA Press.

Toglia, J., & Berg, C. (2013). Performance-based measure of executive function: Comparison of community and at-risk youth. *American Journal of Occupational Therapy, 67,* 515–523. http://dx.doi.org/10.5014/ajot.2013.008482

Toglia, J., & Cermak, S. A. (2009). Dynamic assessment and prediction of learning potential in clients with unilateral neglect. *American Journal of Occupational Therapy, 63,* 569–579. http://dx.doi.org/10.5014/ajot.63.5.569

Toglia, J. P., Golisz, K. M., & Goverover, Y. (2013). Cognition, perception, and occupational performance. In B. A. Boyt Schell, G. Gillen, M. E. Scaffa, & E. S. Cohn (Eds.), *Willard and Spackman's occupational therapy* (12th ed., pp. 779–807). Philadelphia: Lippincott Williams & Wilkins.

Toglia, J., Johnston, M. V., Goverover, Y., & Dain, B. (2010). A multicontext approach to promoting transfer of strategy use and self regulation after brain injury: An exploratory study. *Brain Injury, 24,* 664–677. http://dx.doi.org/10.3109/02699051003610474

Toglia, J., Lahav, O., Kizony, R., & Ben Ari, E. (2014, June). *A new performance measure of executive function: Cross-cultural comparison.* Paper presented at the 16th International Congress of the World Federation of Occupational Therapists, Yokohama, Japan.

Toglia, J., Rodger, S. A., & Polatajko, H. J. (2012). Anatomy of cognitive strategies: A therapist's primer for enabling occupational performance. *Canadian Journal of Occupational Therapy/Revue Canadienne d'Ergotherapie, 79,* 225–236.

Uprichard, S., Kupshik, G., Pine, K., & Fletcher, B. (2009). Dynamic assessment of learning ability improves outcome prediction following acquired brain injury. *Brain Injury, 23,* 278–290. http://dx.doi.org/10.1080/02699050902788444

Vaughan, L., & Giovanello, K. (2010). Executive function in daily life: Age-related influences of executive processes on instrumental activities of daily living. *Psychology and Aging, 25,* 343–355. http://dx.doi.org/10.1037/a0017729

Voelbel, G. T., Goverover, Y., Gaudino, E. A., Moore, N. B., Chiaravalloti, N., & DeLuca, J. (2011). The relationship between neurocognitive behavior of executive functions and the EFPT in individuals with multiple sclerosis. *OTJR: Occupation, Participation and Health, 31,* S30–S37. http://dx.doi.org/10.3928/15394492-20101108-06

Von Ah, D., Russell, K. M., Storniolo, A. M., & Carpenter, J. S. (2009). Cognitive dysfunction and its relationship to quality of life in breast cancer survivors. *Oncology Nursing Forum, 36,* 326–336. http://dx.doi.org/10.1188/09.ONF.326-334

Weiner, N. W., Toglia, J., & Berg, C. (2012). Weekly calendar planning activity (WCPA): A performance-based assessment of executive function piloted with at-risk adolescents. *American Journal of Occupational Therapy, 66,* 699–708. http://dx.doi.org/10.5014/ajot.2012.004754

Weingartz, S., Wiedl, K. H., & Watzke, S. (2008). Dynamic assessment of executive functioning: (How) can we measure change? *Journal of Cognitive Education and Psychology, 7,* 368–387. http://dx.doi.org/10.1891/194589508787724088

Wiedl, K. H., Schottke, H., Green, M. F., & Nuechterlein, K. H. (2004). Dynamic testing in schizophrenia: Does training change the construct validity of a test? *Schizophrenia Bulletin, 30,* 703–711.

Wiedl, K. H., Wienobst, J., Schottke, H. H., Green, M. F., & Nuechterlein, K. H. (2001). Attentional characteristics of schizophrenia patients differing in learning proficiency on the Wisconsin Card Sorting Test. *Schizophrenia Bulletin, 27,* 687–695.

Wolf, T., & Baum, C. (2011). Impact of mild cognitive impairments on participation: Importance of early identification of cognitive loss. In N. Katz (Ed.), *Cognition, occupation, and participation across the lifespan: Neuroscience, neurorehabilitation, and models of intervention in occupational therapy* (3rd ed., pp. 41–50). Bethesda, MD: AOTA Press.

Yaffe, K., Kurella-Tamura, M., Ackerson, L., Hoang, T. D., Anderson, A. H., Duckworth, M., . . . Townsend, R. R. (2014). Higher levels of cystatin C are associated with worse cognitive function in older adults with chronic kidney disease: The Chronic Renal Insufficiency Cohort Cognitive Study. *Journal of the American Geriatrics Society, 62,* 1623–1629. http://dx.doi.org/10.1111/jgs.12986

Yeates, K. O., Swift, E., Taylor, H. G., Wade, S. L., Drotar, D., Stancin, T., & Minich, N. (2004). Short- and long-term social outcomes following pediatric traumatic brain injury. *Journal of the International Neuropsychological Society, 10,* 412–426.

Yilmaz, N., Mollahasanoglu, A., Gurvit, H., Can, M., Tuncer, N., Inanc, N., & Yavuz, S. (2012). Dysexecutive syndrome: A specific pattern of cognitive impairment in systemic sclerosis. *Cognitive and Behavioral Neurology, 25,* 57–62. http://dx.doi.org/10.1097/WNN.0b013e3182593c75

Zelazo, P. D., & Carlson, S. M. (2012). Hot and cool executive function in childhood and adolescence: Development and plasticity. *Child Development Perspectives, 6,* 354–360. http://dx.doi.org/10.1016/j.actpsy.2003.12.005

Zelazo, P. D., & Müller, U. (2011). Executive function in typical and atypical development. In U. Goswami (Ed.), *The Wiley-Blackwell handbook of childhood cognitive development* (2nd ed., pp. 574–603). Malden, MA: Blackwell. http://dx.doi.org/10.1111/b.9781405191166.2011.00026

Subject Index

Note. Page numbers in *italic* refer to exhibits, figures, and tables.

Citation Index

Note. Page numbers in *italic* indicate tables.